THEORY OF TEACHER TRAINING

THEORY OF TEACHER TRAINING

Edited by

S.P. NAIK

ANMOL PUBLICATIONS PVT. LTD.
NEW DELHI - 110 002 (INDIA)

ANMOL PUBLICATIONS PVT. LTD
4374/4B, Ansari Road, Daryaganj
New Delhi - 110 002
Ph.: 23261597, 23278000
Visit us at: www.anmolpublications.com

Theory of Teacher Training

ISBN 81-261-0163-6

PRINTED IN INDIA

Published by J.L. Kumar for Anmol Publications Pvt. Ltd., New Delhi - 110 002 and Printed at Mehra Offset Press, Delhi.

Contents

Preface

Theory of teacher education, Planning for effective teaching, Learning essentials, schema for teacher education; Teaching to learn; Teacher leadership etc. like topics are elaborately discussed in this book.

This book is intended to serve as an authoritative reference work to the scholars and teacher in the field of teacher training.

I am thankful to all the scholars and authors whose writings are cited or substantially made use of in this book. I am also grateful to Mr. J. L. Kumar for agreeing to publish this book.

—Editor

1

Theory of Teacher Education

A unifying theory of teacher education should rest upon clearly stated assumptions about the meaning and purpose of education, the role of the school as an institution, the limitations of the school's responsibility, the role of the teacher within the school, the nature of the learning process, and the content of the curriculum.

If present programs for the education of teachers reflect any such theories, they are implied rather than stated, and the observer can only guess at the assumptions held by those who planned them. The theories underlying the Ph.D. program for college teachers have almost nothing in common with those that provide the basis for educating elementary teachers; programs for secondary teachers represent an uneasy compromise between the two extremes. Some of the differences among these programs reflect the real differences that exist between teaching small children and teaching adolescents or adults, but this cannot account for all of them. It seems reasonable to ask whether there ought to be as much difference as there is between the preparation of those who teach high school seniors and the preparation of those who will teach the same students as college freshmen a few months later.

Most of our present-day programs for educating elementary teachers reflect a set of assumptions that first came into prominence in the early nineteenth century, dominated the normal schools of that period, was transferred, in a somewhat revised form, to the teachers colleges of the first half of the twentieth century, and still plays an important part in determining policy in university schools of education. This tradition also is dominant among those groups that determine certification requirements and those who set the standards for accreditation in teacher education.

In this tradition the primary emphasis is upon process—the processes of teaching. of learning, of growth and development. School programs based upon it are not subject centered but child centered. Teacher education programs stemming from it stress the teacher's responsibility for understanding the child, for motivating him, guiding his growth, and supervising his learning. A teacher is expected to be something more than a scholar, and perhaps something less, but at any rate something different.

The normal school movement originated in Europe and was brought to New England in the 1830s from where it spread rapidly across the nation. It reflected the educational theories of such divergent writers as Rousseau, Froebel, Pestalozzi, and Herbart and, much later, was influenced by the views of Dewey and Thorndike, but the emphasis continued to be on process and on understanding the child. Although normal schools now are obsolete, and teachers colleges are rapidly being replaced by general purpose state colleges, the normal school point of view continues to dominate the professional education of elementary teachers. Although the normal schools of the nineteenth century stressed the process of teaching, and the brevity of the program and the low entrance standards made it impossible for them to require academic work on the college level even if they had wanted to, it was assumed that the elementary teacher should be thoroughly familiar with the subjects taught in the elementary school and should be skilled in reading, writing, and computation. Some of the leaders, particularly the Herbartians, stressed the importance of well organized content and of sequential presentation of subject matter. The teachers colleges that evolved out of the normal schools after 1900 increased the amount of academic content in the curriculum and raised its level, but they also increased the number and variety of professional courses. It was possible to increase both at the same time because the program required for teachers was being increased from a few months to a year or two and then to a four-year college course following four years of high school. But those most thoroughly steeped in the normal school-teachers college tradition are convinced that the prospective teacher should begin working closely with children and should begin taking professional courses during the freshman year of college.

The normal school tradition was based upon a clear assumption that the beginning teacher should have been taught *how* to teach—that he cannot be counted upon to learn the necessary skills and understandings on the job. When normal schools were first established, this view represented a sharp break with the past, for, prior to that time, it seems to have been assumed that almost any literate adult could teach children the three R's. Even today it differs drastically from the view of those responsible for the preparation of college teachers whose preparation rarely includes any introduction to the process of teaching. The two views have almost nothing in common.

Since the founding of Johns Hopkins University in 1867, the great majority of American college teachers have been prepared in programs leading in the direction of the Ph.D. degree. Although fewer than half of all college teachers hold this degree, most of them have at some time worked toward it. The assumption behind this program is that the college teacher should be a research scholar who is both willing and able to advance the frontiers of knowledge; and the better scholar he is the better teacher he is likely to be. Or perhaps the assumption is that teaching is so much less important than research that there is no need to prepare for it.

The Ph.D. tradition was imported from Germany where the structure of secondary and higher education was different from that found in America. In the German university of the nineteenth century a professor was a distinguished individual who held a chair, and normally, there was only one professor in a department. Although the professor gave occasional lectures, much of the teaching was left to private docents who were not professors and who were not, strictly speaking, members of the faculty. It was logical that each professor should be expected to be a productive scholar.

In American colleges there are no private docents. The teaching is done by professors of the various ranks or by instructors who hope soon to become professors.

There are good reasons to doubt that a program designed to prepare professors for German universities (where there are no liberal arts colleges) is really the best possible program for preparing teachers for American undergraduate colleges. Yet the sporadic efforts in a few places to design new programs have met with little acceptance. College faculty members want the Ph. D., and their employers want them to have it. College students want better teachers but are not in position to do much about it. In any case, there is little agreement as to just what form a proper program for college teachers should take¾about the only thing that college professors and deans agree about is that they do not want a program that stresses the process of teaching at the expense of content. The absence of a sound theory of teacher education is probably the greatest barrier to the development of new programs for college teachers.

Even if it were agreed that programs based upon the normal school-teachers college tradition represent sound preparation for elementary teachers, and that the Ph.D. program is sound for college teachers, the question of how best to prepare high school teachers would still be in doubt. Adolescents are neither children nor adults. Unlike the elementary teacher in a self-contained classroom, the secondary school teacher usually teaches only a single subject or a selection of closely related subjects—in this respect his work is more like that of a college teacher. But the teacher in a contemporary high school can no longer escape the problem of teaching the slow learner by rejecting him—a solution still available to the college teacher.

The public high school did not become an important part of the American scene until several decades after the normal school movement had reached the United States, and it was not until the twentieth century that the normal school tradition had any important influence on the preparation of high school teachers. Throughout the nineteenth century and even into the twentieth, high school teachers, like the teachers in private academies and preparatory schools, were prepared in liberal arts colleges without professional courses or practice teaching.

Three developments in secondary education forced a change in this procedure: the introduction of new high school courses of a kind not offered in the liberal arts colleges and which the graduate with an A.B. was totally unprepared to teach, compulsory attendance laws which made it necessary for the high school to retain many slow learners who previously would have been dropped, and the emergence of the junior high school.

The expanded program of the high school made it necessary for these institutions to look to new sources for high school teachers. It was possible to find liberal arts graduates to teach English, foreign languages, history, mathematics, and science, but these graduates were not prepared to teach agriculture, home economics, or the wide variety of other vocational courses that came into the curriculum of the comprehensive high school.

Universities responded to the new demand by establishing separate schools or colleges of education at the undergraduate level. Prospective elementary teachers, as well as those planning to teach the non-academic subjects in high school, flocked to these new institutions, but the majority of those preparing to teach the academic subjects at the secondary level preferred to remain in the liberal arts colleges and to take only such professional courses as were required for certification. The result was that the university schools of education became more distinguished for the variety of their professional and non-academic offerings than for their academic excellence. A few psychologists, historians, and philosophers, who had become professors of education, strove to maintain a high intellectual tone in the schools of education, but they were outnumbered by those who were more concerned with the new additions to the curriculum, the practical problems of school teaching, and the "whole child."

The establishment of certification requirements for secondary school teachers made it necessary for liberal arts colleges to introduce professional courses for teachers. Because these requirements were imposed from outside the college, they were accepted reluctantly, and the new professors of education brought in to teach them found their role a difficult one. Certification laws did not lead to a well planned curriculum for teachers. A few courses in educational history, psychology and philosophy, and a brief period of practice teaching were patched on to the conventional liberal arts course, and, unfortunately, this came at a time when the program leading to the A.B. degree in most American colleges gave little assurance of a liberal education. The elective systems had swept through our colleges, and it was not at all unusual for a college graduate majoring in literature to know nothing of science and for a science major to know little of literature. Even in his own specialized field, the knowledge possessed by a college graduate often was more appropriate as a preparation for advanced scholarship than for teaching at the high school level.

Many professional educators had long been convinced that some of the procedures developed in the normal schools for the preparation of elementary teachers ought to be extended to secondary teacher education. So long as the normal school was a two-year institution it offered no real competition to the four-year college, but when it extended its program to four years, began granting degrees, and became a teachers college, efforts were made to add the preparation of high school teachers to its responsibilities. The demands became pressing during the twenties when sixty-nine normal schools became four-year teachers' colleges within a decade. Liberal arts colleges and universities vigorously opposed this move, partly because they doubted that the teachers' colleges were prepared for their new task, and partly because they feared competition for students from the tuition-free state colleges.

It was the emergence of the junior high that provided the opening wedge. Neither the normal schools, legally authorized to prepare elementary teachers, nor the colleges, authorized to prepare secondary teachers, prepared teachers for an educational unit that encompassed grades 7—9 *and* 9. The colleges contended that the junior high was a secondary school and that its teachers should be liberal arts graduates with a strong academic major. Those institutions with experience in preparing elementary teachers maintained that the junior high was a new kind of institution, and that its teachers should have the kind of preparation long required of elementary teachers, with a strong emphasis on the process of teaching, plus, perhaps, some additional preparation in a speciality that need not necessarily be an academic subject.

In a number of states a compromise was reached that made it possible for *both* liberal arts colleges and normal schools to prepare junior high teachers, and the result was that many of these new schools were staffed with people from both sources. The teacher from the liberal arts colleges had stronger academic majors, but less preparation for teaching children of junior high age, while the normal school graduate teaching next door probably knew less about his subject but more about the children with whom he worked. Naturally, they disagreed about the form the junior high school should take.

It was the normal school graduates who placed the greater emphasis on homerooms, core curricula, and activity programs; while the college graduates were more likely to prefer to teach a single subject much as it was taught in senior high. The first group won out, partly because they remained in the junior high and worked to mould it to their views, while the majority of liberal arts graduates moved into the senior high schools as soon as openings appeared.

Having won their battle to prepare junior high teachers, the normal schools were ready to move on to the preparation of teachers for the senior or the four-year high school, and in the process they ceased to be normal schools and became institutions of a new kind, while retaining a considerable amount of the normal school philosophy.

Today the normal schools are obsolete, and, in the majority of states, the teachers colleges which grew out of them have become general state colleges which prepare public school teachers for all levels but also offer a wide variety of other courses.

Unfortunately, the teacher education programs found in these colleges today are not based upon a clear and consistent theory. When the normal school became a teachers' college and began preparing secondary teachers, it did so without first asking whether the theories underlying its programs for elementary teachers were equally appropriate for the education of secondary teachers. The faculty members who were holdovers from normal school days often seemed to assume that what was good for an elementary teacher was equally good for a teacher of adolescents, and that the high school teacher, too, should take courses in child growth and development, methods of teaching, and the conventional period of practice teaching.

But the new faculty members brought in to teach the expanding list of academic subjects came from a different tradition—many of them held Ph.D.'s from university graduate schools in fields other than education. They had little sympathy for the normal school tradition, which they regarded as soft, sentimental, anti-intellectual, and totally inappropriate for high school teachers. Many of them were not greatly interested in teacher education at any level except insofar as it meant scholarship in their own fields. They set out immediately to transform their colleges into general state colleges or universities, and in the majority of states they have succeeded.

The new academic emphasis was essential to the sound preparation of secondary teachers, but the programs for teachers now found in the state colleges represent, not a unifying theory of teacher education, but a compromise between the liberal arts view and that of the normal school.

The Master of Arts in Teaching can probably be said to be the first program for high school teachers that rests upon some clear cut assumptions about high school teaching as distinct from both elementary and college teaching. Those who designed the program rejected the college-teacher theory that academic scholarship is the only essential for teachers. They also rejected the teachers-college view that a program for secondary teachers should be similar to that for elementary teachers, but with a little more emphasis on the major.

The MAT program implies that the teacher ought to be a liberally educated person with a scholarly knowledge of a subject *before* he begins his professional studies. (This contrasts sharply with the teachers-college view that all prospective teachers should begin working with children and should begin taking professional courses in education as early as possible.) Those who set the requirements for these programs are somewhat vague about the content of the undergraduate curriculum—they seem to accept the notion that an A.B. degree from a "good" (i.e., prestigious) college is sufficient evidence of a liberal education— but they all require four years of some kind of liberal studies, with a strong academic major, plus a fifth year consisting in part of professional courses or seminars and an internship and in part of academic specialization at the graduate level. In some of these programs courses or seminars in educational psychology and educational philosophy are available during the junior or senior years but these are taught as liberal subjects.

Roles of the Teacher

The education appropriate for a professional group depends upon the responsibilities assigned to members of that profession. A physician is responsible for keeping his patients alive and healthy as long as possible, and his education must prepare him to discharge this responsibility well. A civil engineer is responsible for building bridges and roads that will support the traffic. The teacher's responsibilities are both more broad and less clearly defined, and this is why we are uncertain about how to educate him.

Throughout history, people called teachers have played many different roles and they continue to do so today. An examination of these possible roles may help us to decide what should be the responsibility of the teacher in our society.

The Teacher as Demonstrator

If a boy works for several years alongside a skilled carpenter the probability is high that the boy will become a reasonably competent carpenter. He learns to hammer nails, to saw boards, and to frame rafters by doing these things, and he corrects his early errors by observing the work of the master. If the master carpenter explains how and why he performs his various operations the boy will learn more rapidly, but even if the master is mute, the boy will learn a great deal about carpentry if only he is willing to observe and to practice what he observes.

The demonstration of observable skills provides the basis for the apprenticeship system that has been an important educational device for centuries. It is useful not only in the skilled trades but can be adapted to the teaching of such varied pursuits as football, auto driving, and brain surgery. Under the apprenticeship programs for teachers, it is used by the master teacher in showing beginners how to teach; but when the activities are on a professional level, the demonstration of the skill normally comes after a considerable amount of instruction of other kinds.

The Teacher as a Dispenser of Information

As the subject matter of education shifts from physical skills to intellectual activities, the teacher must make increasing use of symbols, either verbal or mathematical, as a larger part of the teacher's work consists of imparting information. The pupil cannot determine for himself, or observe directly, the speed of light, the population of a city, the land area of a continent, or the events of history. He can be told about these things, and although telling does not always result in learning, the pupil is not likely to learn such things unless he is told. The result is that ever since man has had language at his disposal teachers have been expected to be repositories of knowledge and to pass this knowledge on to their pupils.

Since the invention of movable type the need for teachers who can dispense knowledge orally has declined sharply. The facts and figures to be found in books are frequently incorrect; but, if the books are carefully selected, the facts in them are likely to be considerably more reliable than those dispensed by a teacher who relies on his memory.

Even today, however, teachers of all levels and particularly college teachers have continued to give a considerable portion of their time to the passing of information to their students. They justify this by pointing out that some learners give closer attention to a lecturer than to a book; and that the teacher, particularly the graduate school professor, sometimes possesses information not yet available in books; but often the real reason is that the teacher likes to hear himself talk or does not know what else to do with his classroom time.

The Teacher as Taskmaster

If a visitor from another planet were to observe the work of a large and well selected sample of teachers throughout the world he would probably conclude that the role of the teacher is that of taskmaster. The work of the great majority of teachers in many nations and cultures consists of assigning tasks, listening to recitations, asking questions, correcting answers, and, in many cases, assigning marks or grades based upon the pupil's success in completing the assigned tasks. The assumption is that if the pupil completes these tasks to the satisfaction of the teacher he has learned the things that the teacher considers it necessary for him to know. The assignment may take any of many forms depending on the subject taught and the maturity of the pupil. It may consist of writing a theme, computing a sum, analyzing a poem, performing a laboratory experiment, painting a picture, or constructing a piece of furniture; but in each case, the teacher assigns the task and the pupil does the work.

Many educational theorists, particularly in Western Europe and the United States, have been highly critical of this view of the teacher's role but the fact remains that it is one that is extremely difficult for the teacher to avoid, and most teachers continue to play it to a greater or lesser degree.

The Teacher as Disciplinarian

Since the doctrine of original sin has fallen into disfavor, there are few who hold that the teacher's primary role is that of punishing indolence and wrongdoing. Many still believe, however, that the teacher must accept a considerable amount of responsibility for curbing mischievous behavior and for seeing that the child sticks to his assigned tasks even when the teacher has found no way of making them interesting. It seems a safe guess that even in the early 1960s more elementary and junior high school teachers are discharged for their inability to maintain order in the classroom than for any other single reason.

The Teacher as a Model

If there is any truth to the commonly held belief that children learn more from example than from precept, it follows that the teacher should provide a model for children to follow. That teacher, like the scoutmaster, the parent, or the minister, is expected to set a good example for the young. Many of the normal schools of the past refused to graduate students who were known to violate the moral codes of the communities in which they planned to teach, and in many cases these codes prohibited the use of profanity, cigarettes, alcoholic beverages, and any deviation from standard forms of dress. Such restrictions made teaching an unattractive profession to many bright young men and women, and, happily, they have been relaxed greatly in recent years.

It is no doubt true, however, that many children do imitate their teachers, particularly those teachers they like best and admire most. Any theory of teacher selection and education must include some assumptions about the extent to which the teacher should represent a model of behavior. This is probably more important in the case of the elementary school teacher in a self-contained classroom than in the case of the teacher in a higher institution in which each pupil has many teachers, but even the university professor provides a model for some of his students.

The Teacher as a Surrogate Parent

The "whole child" concept, which transformed American education during the first half of the present century, resulted in an enormous change in the role of the teacher. If the teacher is held to be responsible for the child's health, social adjustment, recreation, emotional health, and character development, as well as for his intellectual development, it seems obvious that teacher education must include preparation for all these roles. Leaders in the field of teacher education accepted this responsibility, and the result was that the teachers college of the 1920s and 1930s broadened their scope enormously, often at the expense of the rigorous intellectual development of the teacher. Many of the employers of teachers came to believe that the responsibility for the child's intellectual development was only one of the teachers many responsibilities and one no more important than any of the others. There appears now to be some evidence of a reversal of this trend, but the elementary school teacher at least still carries a very broad range of responsibilities and is expected by many parents as well as supervisors to exhibit competence in all of them.

The Teacher as Therapist

The widespread concern over mental illness and the emotional maladjustments of "normal" people has led some educators, as well as psychiatrists and clinical psychologists interested in education, to the view that schools and teachers must accept a large measure of responsibility for mental health. The widespread acceptance of psychoanalytic doctrine has led many to the conviction that mental health cannot be achieved through conscious processes alone.

If these views are accepted, it follows that the teacher should accept some measure of responsibility for unconscious and preconscious processes. It follows, too, that the teacher's preparation should consist in large part of psychological or psychiatric training.

Carried to its logical extreme, the result of acceptance of such a point of view would be that subject-matter teaching would disappear and the role of the guidance offic—who would be psychoanalytically trained and whose work presumably would be supervised by a psychiatrist—would be enormously enlarged. In the extreme form this view carries with it an implied denial that problems can be solved or decisions reached through conscious intellectual processes alone. It represents the most drastic alteration of the teacher's role that has ever been suggested, but a considerable amount of educational theorizing seems to be moving in this direction.

The Teacher as Midwife

The Socratic View of the teacher's role rests upon the conviction that the aim of education is neither an accumulation of empirical knowledge nor the ability to perform physical acts. The aim is wisdom and the road to wisdom is rational thought. The teacher is the guide to this thought and the teacher's primary role is that of the questioner who guides the pupil's thought processes by asking him the questions that will lead him, eventually, to come to wise conclusions. It is assumed that the pupil does not need to be told the answers, and, indeed, that he can achieve wisdom only by doing his own thinking and arriving at his own conclusions.

The Socratic method of teaching works most effectively with problems regarding which the pupil already has some background of experience and the answers to which are dependent upon logical thought stemming from that experience. If the question is: What is wisdom? What is the best form of government? or What is the nature of tragedy? or almost any question of values, the method is highly effective when employed in its highest form. It is not an effective method of arriving at an answer to such questions as "How rapidly is the population of the United States growing?" but it can be used in seeking an answer to the question "Is the population growing *too* rapidly?" once the *facts* of population growth are available.

If this method is to be used effectively, the teacher must be wise (even though Socrates himself insisted that he was not). In the hands of a poor teacher, or when used in search of answers for the wrong kinds of questions, it can quickly deteriorate into a sharing of ignorance or at best a form of group dynamics.

The Teacher as Evangelist, Persuader, or Propagandist

The world's great religious leaders—Christ, Mohammed, Buddha, Confucius—are often referred to as "great teachers". By this we mean that they demonstrated remarkable skill in persuading others to accept their views. Since their views differed it cannot be assumed that they were equally successful in leading their followers to the truth, unless it is assumed that truth itself is highly flexible.

Every teacher finds it necessary, at times, to try to persuade his charges to live virtuous lives—not to lie, steal, attack their classmates, or cheat on examinations. So long as the virtues taught are consistent with the mores of the community, no one doubts that the teacher is discharging one of his proper responsibilities when he teaches them. If teachers had been successful in discharging this responsibility, there would be no crime today except among those who failed to attend school.

Teachers also work vigorously to persuade their students to prefer Shakespeare to Mickey Spillane and Bach to rock-and-roll music. They do this with different degrees of subtlety and varying degrees of success, but most of them try. Even at the college level professors of literature, music, and the arts often are eager to have their pupils accept their own judgments of which poems, symphonies, or paintings are masterpieces and which are worthless. Professors of psychology try to pass on to their students their own views of the relative merits of behaviorism and psychoanalysis, and historians are equally eager to pass on their own views about the merits or demerits of the economic interpretation of history. Professors of education are particularly prone to propagandize for a point of view, and whether a graduate student in education learns to accept or reject an ideology such as progressive education depends in large part on what university he attends and in what decade.

The distinction between teaching and propaganda is often difficult to maintain. Ideally, the teacher wants his pupils to follow the truth wherever it may lead—the propagandist wants them to accept a pre-established point of view. The difficulty is that the teacher who is really a propagandist often is so confident of his own version of truth that he is unable to see that his teaching is propaganda. We can easily see that the teacher has become a propagandist when he tries to teach his students to accept fascism, the advantages of a life of crime, or some religions other than our own. It is more difficult to see the distinction when the teacher is eager to promulgate democracy, Christianity (if we are Christians), or other views that we accept as virtuous.

The Teacher as a Stimulator of Inquiry

Since earliest times some teachers have been aware that the student who makes his own discoveries is more likely to learn, to remember, and to understand than is the student who is told the answers. Socrates understood this as have many educational philosophers of recent centuries. John Dewey stressed this fact in several of his earlier works, including *How We Think*, and the principle was an important one—and one of the soundest—of the theories at the heart of the progressive education movement.

Unfortunately the principle is not easy to apply in the classroom and when misinterpreted and misused it can lead to aimless activity on the part of the pupil while the teacher sits back and waits for the child to "discover" or "inquire". Unless the child's inquiry is skillfully guided the curriculum loses all form and pattern, but if the guidance is excessive or less than adroit the child loses his sense of freedom and excitement, and often his interest.

The Socratic dialogue is one form of inquiry, but only one of many. If a child is eager to know the answer to some question of a factual nature, an empirical approach is more appropriate than a rational dialogue. Once his curiosity is aroused he can observe for himself how levers and gears work, how seeds develop into plants, and how a bird builds a nest. He can measure directly the effect of heat on the length of a metal bar or the pressure of air against a vacuum. He cannot measure directly the distance of the sun from the earth, but he can inquire into the methods used by those who have made the measurement. He cannot, in most cases, observe historical events, but he can inquire into the methods used by historians in reporting and interpreting these events. In many kinds of academic learning the best inquiry takes the form of selective reading with a definite aim in mind—the child reads because he wants to find the answer to a question that is troubling him—but even in academic learning inquiry may take any of many forms.

Since the student himself must conduct the inquiry, the teacher's role in this method of learning is not entirely clear—it depends in large part upon the age and maturity of the student, the range of his previous knowledge, and the extent to which he is already motivated to learn. In some cases, the teacher's role will consist of helping the learner to formulate his questions so that inquiry may be fruitful. In others, it will include guidance in the process itself and helping the child decide what kind of an approach to a problem—rational or empirical—seems most likely to yield reliable results. If the learner's motivation is vague or diffuse, he may need the teacher's help in bringing it into focus. In some cases, when the student is highly motivated, intellectually curious, and has the necessary tools at hand, it may be best for the teacher to get out of his way, but in most situations the teacher can help by setting the stage and by asking the right questions at the right time.

IMPLICATIONS OF THE VARIOUS ROLES FOR TEACHER EDUCATION

Each of these roles has important implications for anyone designing a program of teacher education. If the apprenticeship system is to be used exclusively, and the teacher's role is to be that of demonstrator, the teacher clearly must be a master of his craft. Probably it will help if he receives some instruction in how to demonstrate most effectively and how to explain what he is doing, but it is doubtful that very much professional teacher education is necessary—the apprenticeship system has always been self-perpetuating.

Insofar as the teacher is a dispenser of information, it is essential that he possess a great deal of pertinent information about a subject and know how to organize it and to present it effectively. He should be able to discriminate between the important and the trivial. He will also need to know what kinds of information to present to children of various levels of maturity, and how to capture and hold their attention while it is being presented.

The great majority of teachers continue to be taskmasters, but, because educational theorists have been prone to denigrate this kind of teaching, the present generation of teachers is not well prepared for this role.

Anyone can assign tasks but if they are badly chosen, and not properly related to the goals of the schools and the capabilities of students, the result is mere busywork. A considerable amount of "homework" probably falls into this category. Many teachers continue to be taskmasters because they have discovered no other way of teaching that keeps the children busy and results in some reasonable degree of learning. This is unfortunate because the assignment of tasks is not teaching in its best and highest form; but the fact remains that if the task is properly selected, assigned, and supervised, and if its accomplishment is properly reinforced or rewarded, learning will result. Since teachers are going to play this role for at least a part of the time, they may as well be prepared to do it well.

The role of disciplinarian is another for which teachers are not well prepared—and again the reason is that educators have rejected this role. In their professional education, teachers are given some help in understanding the reasons for aggressive behavior, but they are not taught what to do when the understood child continues to disrupt classroom activities.

If a child persists in attacking or threatening his classmates, understanding, diagnosis, and therapy are indicated, but these are long-range solutions and the teacher's immediate task is to see that the other children are protected. Psychological therapy can be an important adjunct to discipline, but it does not replace it, and it would be optimistic to suppose that it can completely obviate the need for it.

Educators have placed great emphasis on *self*-discipline as an educational aim. As an ultimate goal it is sound, but it is important for teachers to understand that it is a goal rather than an achievement. Even civilized adults cannot be counted on to drive their automobiles wisely without traffic laws and policemen to enforce them, and no school in the world, with the possible exception of Summerhill, exists without some degree of adult control. The teacher in a public school cannot escape his responsibility for discipline and he ought to be prepared to discharge it wisely.

Insofar as the teacher is expected to be a model for behavior, teacher selection is probably more important than teacher education. Teacher education can, however, help the teacher to develop a code of professional ethics.

The notion that the teacher should be a surrogate parent, playing all the roles of the parent, rests upon an exaggerated idea of the responsibilities and potentialities of formal education. Perhaps a boarding school, in which the teachers are responsible for their charges for twenty-four hours a day and the major part of the year, requires teachers and other staff members who can assume all the responsibilities normally accepted by parents. But the American public school is a day school. The whole child comes to school, but in the middle of the afternoon the whole child goes home, and the majority of parents do not wish to delegate their responsibilities to teachers. The teacher's education should help him to distinguish between the responsibilities of parents and those of teachers—it should not lead him to believe that he could or should replace the parent.

The teacher's role as therapist has been encouraged by the authors of textbooks used in courses in educational psychology, mental hygiene, child growth and development, and guidance. This emphasis is an outcome of the expansion of the field of clinical psychology and has been greatly influenced by psychoanalytic theory. It is related to the expanded public interest in mental health.

It is not always easy to distinguish between education and therapy, but it is important to try. Education makes it possible for the child to reach his fullest possible development by learning new responses—therapy is the treatment of disorders or malfunctionings. In therapy there is always the assumption that something has gone wrong and must be corrected, in education there is no such assumption. Guidance lies somewhere between the two. As viewed by James B. Conant, it is a part of education; as viewed by many guidance specialists, it involves a great deal of therapy of one kind or another.

The distinction is made more difficult by the fact that psychological therapy requires a considerable amount of learning or re-learning, while much that is called education also requires a correction of faulty habits or responses. But education and therapy become identical only if we assume that *all* learning is a correction of something previously learned—an assumption that cannot possibly be supported.

A knowledge of the basic principles of psychology should be a part of the preparation of the teacher, and, although the emphasis should be upon learning theory, individual differences, and the psychology of the normal child, this preparation should include at least an introduction to the problems of psychological mal-adjustment. This is necessary to enable the teacher to avoid making those mistakes that contribute to maladjustments on the part of his pupils. The teacher should also be able to recognize some of the gross symptoms of psychological disturbance in order that children in need of psychological diagnosis and treatment may be referred to the proper specialists, either in or out of the school. But, if the school is to remain primarily an educational rather than a therapeutic institution, it cannot be expected that the teacher will be prepared himself to conduct therapy or that he will have the time for it.

If the teacher is expected to be an evangelist or persuader it will no doubt be best to select teachers who are convinced of the rightness of the causes being espoused and then to teach them the hortatory skills. It seems unlikely that many educators today will wish to stress this kind of education for treachers, but there are many groups within our population who believe that the schools should accept greater responsibility for teaching patriotism, civic virtue, and morality. Whether these virtues can adequately be inculcated through a rational approach alone will continue to be a subject for debate.

The use of the Socratic method does not require that we have a Socrates in every classroom, but the leader or questioner should understand the method and try to emulate Socrates in his approach. How such teachers or questioners should be prepared is a difficult question. Presumably they should have undergone the kind of liberal education that holds wisdom as its goal. Perhaps they should be skilled in logic and rational thought. Certainly they should be highly intelligent, for this method makes heavier intellectual demands upon the teacher than most of the other methods we have discussed.

When the method of education by inquiry is extended to include empirical as well as rational approaches to truth, even Socrates would not be fully qualified to be the teacher. The *ideal* teacher would combine the intellectual traits of Socrates, Aristotle, Bacon, and Locke. With a lesser teacher the method can still yield good results, but as a minimum the teacher must possess a high degree of curiosity, intellectual flexibility, a broad range of information, and skill in planning the kind of learning situation in which inquiry can take place. He must know when to lead and when to let the learner follow his own bent, when to organize and when to permit confusion, when to lend encouragement and when to allow the pupil to accept the natural consequences of his failures. This is teaching in its best and highest form and this is why it is so rarely seen.

Teacher education for such a role must be selective —if, in order to get enough good teachers for our classrooms, it is necessary to accept many of limited intelligence and intellectual curiosity, it may be better to prepare them to be good taskmasters than to be poor leaders of the process of inquiry. Many of the failures of the progressive schools of a generation ago may be attributed to inadequate use of a sound method by teachers who were not qualified to use it intelligently.

Toward a Unifying Theory

Although it is to be hoped that a continuing effort will be made to establish and maintain educational priorities, it seems probable that teachers will continue to be expected to discharge, in varying degrees, many of the responsibilities I have discussed. It does not follow that any one teacher must be expected to discharge them all, and it is obviously impossible to find teachers for all our million and a half classrooms who can do so well.

The only feasible solution is to organize the staff of the school in such a way that the various responsibilities may be allocated on the basis of the ability of each teacher, or other staff member, to discharge them. "Team teaching" is probably as good as any term available to describe the kind of organization needed, but it can be misleading because the teaching, at any given moment, is done by an individual rather than by a team. Perhaps "team planning" would be better.

Once the idea of the team is accepted it follows that different members will require different kinds and amounts of education. But the major task of anyone attempting to propose a unifying theory of teacher education is to provide a theory appropriate for the education of those professional career teachers who aspire to become master teachers or team leaders. Perhaps only these should be dignified by the title "teacher" and other terms such as "instructor," "assistant," or "aide" should be applied to the others who assist in the educational process but do not make a career of teaching.

What, then, is the unifying theory that lies behind the kinds of teacher education here discussed? Probably the only completely honest answer is that we do not yet have one—certainly no one contributor to this volume can yet state a theory of teacher education that will be completely acceptable to all the others.

It appears, however, that we are approaching a consensus. A theory is emerging and it appears to this writer that it rests upon these assumptions:

1. The ultimate goal of education—as distinguished from training—is to prepare each individual to make wise, independent decisions, choices, and judgments, based upon rational thought and a wide variety of empirical evidence.

2. Although some individuals have achieved this goal with little or no formal schooling, the goal is much more likely to be achieved in a formal institution called a school in which professional teachers accept responsibility for the guidance and direction of the learning process.

3. The schools of free men in a free society must make such education available, not to a limited few, but to each boy and girl to the upper limits of his individual capacity.

4. The teacher's primary responsibility is for the motivation, guidance, and direction of the learning process. Other responsibilities are supplementary and secondary.

5. Although the learning process may take many different forms, the most important is the processof inquiry in which the pupil is motivated to ask this own questions and seeks his own answers.When this process is properly guided the learner accumulates a wide variety of accurate information, learns to evaluate it, to think logically and critically about it, to make decisions based upon it and, at times, to take creative steps that go beyond it.

6. The teachers and other staff members within a school may properly play a wide variety of roles, but it is neither feasible nor desirable that any one teacher be required to play them all. Some responsibilities should be divided among different teachers and others are best delegated to specialists, assistants, or aides, who are not professional career teachers.

7. The overall direction of the learning process should be the responsibility of a professional teacher who may be called a "master' teacher" or "team leader" or perhaps simply a "teacher." It is the education of these professional teachers, and those apprentices who aspire to such a role, that is our primary concern here.

8. The child's educational experience, from the time he enters school until he completes his formal schooling, should be planned as a unit rather than as discrete segments. this will require that teachers for all levels be familiar with what

comes before and after their own period of teaching, and that teachers for the elementary, secondary, and higher institutions have *some* professional preparation in common.

9. Because the quality of education depends in large part upon the competence of the teacher, the education of teachers is of greatest importance to the welfare and progress of society. For the professional, career, teacher this should consist of four inter-related but distinguish able parts:

a. Liberal education

b. Sufficient specialized study of a subject or field to provide a scholarly grasp of some discipline taught in the schools

c. Systematic study of such knowledge from the sciences, humanities, and particularly the behavioral sciences as is particularly relevant to the work of the teacher

d. Practice in the application of a, b and c in a classroom situation under competent supervision. (In order to keep the emphasis where it belongs it seems best to call this period "teaching" or "supervised teaching" rather than to apply some euphemism such as "field experience" or "professional laboratory experience" that seems to put other activities on a par with teaching.)

The development of a unifying theory will, of course, require more than the listing of a set of assumptions. The next step will require that we add to them, enlarge upon them, clarify them, and organize them into a logical pattern. The step has not yet been taken but we are nearly ready for it, and the coherent theory should emerge within the near future.

2

The Study and Practice of Teaching

A basic assumption in the education of teachers is that the systematic study of a subject called *education* will improve teaching ability. To be sure, practice under the supervision of an experienced teacher and the experience of teaching itself are also regarded as effective means of learning how to teach. However, we shall be concerned here with the study of education and particularly its relation to the practice of teaching.

Because *education* is a subject that is both systematic and related to the practice of teaching, the prospective teacher and his teacher are compelled to deal with two kinds of questions: those about the factual accuracy and the theoretical consistency of the subject matter; and those about appropriate courses of action in hypothetical situations or in real situations. The relationship between the two kinds of questions and of each to the actual practice of teaching is a complicated one. Generally, it assumes that systematic study will provide valid empirical information, methods of inquiry, and perspective that will enable the teacher to know why he does certain things. This approach to teaching is respectfully referred to as the rational or intellectual approach as opposed to the intuitive, common-sense, rule-of-thumb, or bag-of-tricks approach. The intellectual approach is often more enthusiastically accepted by teachers of education than by prospective teachers or by practitioners, who are likely to object: "It may be all right in theory, but it has little value for practice." However hackneyed this criticism of courses in education, it apparently makes sense to many scholars;

though actual practice, with or without supervision, as a means of learning how to teach apparently escapes this criticism.

Such differences in attitude toward systematic study are not peculiar to the teaching profession. The businessman is likely to exhibit the same attitudes toward academic economics or toward the study of business administration. The practical politician is likely to react in the same way to political science or the sciences of human behavior, even when courses in these subjects are designed to be practical. In the arts we observe what appears to be a similar posture; the artist does not rely on the aesthetician and may, in fact, take a scornful stance. Those of us who have lived on a farm well remember the contempt in which the book farmer was held by the experienced practical farmer.

However, if we look to scientific pursuits—and particularly to medicine, our favorite analogue in education—the circumstances appear to be different. Much of the academic study of medicine yields principles that are valuable for practice; and in this respect the engineering sciences are similar to medicine. Nevertheless, some discontinuity between study and practice remains. The practitioner in medicine must adapt the information and the general principles to individual and public cases, and he must assume responsibility for the results. Also, despite its highly scientific nature, the practice of medicine still includes highly intuitive methods of diagnosis, inimitable bedside manners, and skeptical attitudes toward new methods of therapy. In engineering, too, the practical engineer must rely on experience and individual judgment in applying his scientific knowledge.

This interval between systematic study and practice has been accounted for in various ways. One explanation tends to ignore the universality of the phenomenon and to emphasize the comparatively close relationship between systematic study and practice in medicine, engineering, and other scientific pursuits. The assumption is made that the sciences of medicine and engineering, and the sciences on which they are based, have developed to the point where they are extremely and immediately valuable to the practitioner in performing, controlling, and predicting under the conditions of practice. The further assumption is implicit that we may expect the study of education, along with the other social sciences, to have a comparable relevance for practice when it becomes truly scientific. These assumptions arise out of an epistemological monism that characterizes the age of faith in science.

The history of scientific progress strongly suggests a development of this kind. Any number of illustrations may be cited. For example, during the last decade of the sixteenth century, the judicious Hooker wrote:

> Education and instruction are the means, the one by use, the other by precept, to make our natural faculty of reason both the better and the sooner able to judge rightly between truth and error, good and evil. But at what time a man may be said to have attained so far forth the use of reason, as sufficeth to make him capable of those Laws, whereby he is then bound to guide his actions; this is a great deal more easy for common sense to discern, than for any man by skill and learning to determine; even as it is not in philosophers, who best know the nature both of fire and gold, to teach what degree of the one will serve to purify the other, so well as the artisan who doth this by fire discerneth by sense when the fire hath that degree of heat which sufficeth for his purpose.

Today, the scientific metallurgist has a great deal more to say to the artisan than the philosopher who knew the nature of gold and fire; and while practical experience and common sense still have their place, science can "teach what degree of the one will serve to purify the other." From many examples of this kind, the inference can be made that the theoretical and empirical success of science is responsible for the close relationship between systematic study and practice in many of the arts that once relied largely on experience and intuition. If this explanation is correct, we must await the development of the sciences of human behavior, education, and aesthetics to the point where they have as much practical value for business, politics, teaching, painting, and composing as metallurgy has for the goldsmith or the medical sciences for the physician. According to this notion the present gap between systematic study and practice may be due to the complexity of the phenomena involved, the lack of scientific progress, or the inhibiting influences of complacent practice. In any event, it is assumed that to attain a close and congenial relationship between study and practice we must advance the social sciences as sciences.

The difficulty with this explanation is that it not only fails to consider the inevitable gap between systematic study and practice in all fields, but it also fails to account for all instances of a comparatively close and congenial relationship. It we look at one phase of the legal profession, the judiciary, we observe that study and practice are closely allied. Although jurisprudence is not an empirical science, the practicing jurist relies heavily on legal theory, learned vocabulary, and case law. There are many exceptions, and common sense is certainly an important element in making legal decisions. However, legal theory has generally enjoyed more respect from the practicing jurist than academic economics has from the businessman or educational theory from the teacher. To explain this difference by saying that law is a learned profession, business is not, and teaching is attempting to become one is highly tautological. If we compare law and teaching, it may be possible to view the teacher's dependence on the systematic study of his subject as analogous to the jurist's respect for study of the law. But, regardless of these complications, it is apparent that the hypothesis that is invoked to account for the friendly relationship between the sciences and the scientific professions fails to explain similar relationships in some of the non-scientific professions.

Another explanation for the discrepancy between systematic study and practice recognizes that this condition is general and assumes that there is a fundamental difference between the two. This difference is explained as the difference between thought and action. The explanation takes various forms. Sometimes it is applied *ad hominess,* and with apparent success; there are obviously men of thought and reflection and men of action. Thus, Tonio Kröger contrasts Hans Hansen and himself: "You are always spending your time with some right and proper occupation. When you have done your prep you take your riding-lesson, or make things with a fret-saw; even in the holidays, at the seashore, you row and sail and swim all the time, while I wander off somewhere and lie down in the sand and stare at the strange and mysterious changes that whisk over the face of the sea." Sometimes the explanation is applied to contrasts in kinds of knowledge; there is knowledge for action, and there is knowledge for the sake of further knowledge; and there is intention to act, decision to act, and criticism and reflection of the act. However valid the distinction based on the differences between thought and action may be in various contexts, the distinction is hardly coterminuous with that between systematic study and practice. First, the language in which the distinction is expressed presents problems for the behaviorist, unless the word *action* is modified by some adjective like *overt*. Second, systematic study includes action that is not unlike practice. For example, experimental studies in education involve decisions and expectations of the same kind, if not for the same purpose, as the practice of teaching. It may be argued that experimental studies fit into a theoretical framework, whereas the practice of teaching fits into a practical framework; and that consequently the former is restricted by logic, while the latter is bound by the exigencies of concrete experience. But practice involves both intention, which is framed by standard expectations, and reflection, which views the consequences of the decisions in the light of those expectations. Therefore, there seems to be no clear, hard and fast distinction between the kinds of mental activities that are designed to organize and to test knowledge, and activities that are designed for practical consequences.

We shall now attempt to account for the interval between systematic study and practice, for its universality, and for the varying width of the interval in various crafts and professions. The universality we account for by the differences in the conditions under which study and practice occur. These differences appear to be of three kinds: differences in the control of complexity, differences in the imperatives of time, and differences in the kinds of consequences.

I shall discuss, first, the differences in the control of complexity. The student of education can make his problems as simple or as complex as he chooses, and he can select them to fit the tools, or methods of study, that are available. The teacher has some control over the complexity of the problems he has to solve, but generally he is at the mercy of the practical situation. For example, a student of learning may construct a theory of enormous complexity and reduce the conditions of testing to the simplest possible, or he may construct an extremely simple theory and test it over a wide range of conditions. He may abstract from the appearance of chaos and disorder those elements that appear to be orderly or recurring, or he may select the simplest reflex for intensive study. He is under no mandate to deal with the whole complex phenomenon at one time, and he may make a contribution to knowledge by limiting himself to one simple aspect of education. But the teacher in the classroom is forced to make decisions about a great number of complicated situations that involve many aspects of learning and the conditions that influence it. He must deal with forces over which he has no control—heredity, for example. He must deal with forces about which he knows little¾perception, for example. And he must deal with forces that he can control¾—the spacing of practice, for example. He must make decisions about matters that are too complicated for research to handle whole. The conditions of practice set the problems, not the available information or the precision of the methods available.

In a general way the effectiveness of teaching has been responsible for the kinds of tasks the schools have traditionally undertaken (although there is some question as to whether formal teaching is an effective method for dealing with some of the responsibilities assumed by the modern school). However, it is important to remember that the measurement of the effectiveness of teaching has been a gross, practical measurement, not a precise, controlled one. We should mention also that the student of education is likely to find his greatest satisfactions in adding order to, and reducing complexity in, what appear to be extremely complex problems; to establish a reputation in scholarship he must deal with what appear to be complicated and esoteric matters. He may, therefore, create complexity for the purpose of bringing new order into things. However, the distinction remains; the student of education has more control over the complexity of the problems he selects to solve than the practitioner in education.

To some extent this difference between systematic study and practice seems to hold when we view the fields of medicine, business, or politics. The physician may be called on to treat a complicated illness for which he has only crude and ineffective methods of therapy. To be sure, the responsible researcher in medicine will in all likelihood also feel an obligation to find out more about this malady; but he can select aspects of it for investigation that appear promising for research. Also, an entirely different kind of problem presents a similar difference. A practicing physician may have to make a decision about whether to be frank with a patient who has an incurable disease. He must consider the effect on the patient, the general morality of the action, and such questions as: Is it better for one patient to know the truth and lose hope than for many people who go to physicians with alarming symptoms to wonder whether physicians tell the truth when they reassure them? The student of medicine does not have to deal with these complicated matters at all unless he wants to.

In business and politics, the differences between study and practice are similar to those in medicine. The fluctuations and exigencies of public opinion and preference, the rapid swirl of events, with innumerable and unpredictable forces interacting, present complicated problems for which the best systematic knowledge offers only clues. Lacking adequate, precise knowledge, the man of action must rely on his judgment, his intuition, his practical sagacity, and "a feeling in his bones." Students of economics and politics concern themselves with the same problems and often with more complicated phenomena than the practitioners in these fields, but the students are permitted by the conditions under which they work to separate the various components of the problem and to select those that promise to be amenable to the techniques of investigation.

At first glance, the arts appear to be exceptional. The practicing artist, composer, or performer seems to have as much control over the complexity of his tasks as the critic or the aesthetician. But, if the artist, actor, or musician commits himself to a career, he subjects himself to certain irreducible complexities in the works of art as entities, to the tastes and whims of the public, to the complications of travel and performance, and to the hazards of juries, lighting, and excessive patriotism. The student of the arts at least has an opportunity to reduce the work of art to its components for study and analysis.

The second difference in the conditions under which study and practice occur lies in the control of time. Decisions on theoretical matters can, and should, be made at leisure; in practice, decisions are forced by circumstances. This is one fundamental difference between theory and practice: It is not that the theoretical man does not make decisions but that he can delay them, while the practical man cannot. The teacher must give a grade by the end of the month; the student of testing may ponder the validity of tests at length. The teacher may have to make a decision about a behavior problem before the class is disrupted; the student of adolescent behavior can postpone his decision about the effectiveness of punishment indefinitely. The teacher must teach some lesson in physics tomorrow; the Physical Science Study Committee may wait a year or two before deciding what aspects of physics should be taught in the secondary schools.

In the study and practice of other activities, this same difference in the control of time occurs. The politician must electioneer before the election; the student of voting behavior can wait until after the election to decide on the efficacy of techniques. The businessman must buy before his stock is exhausted; the economist can wait to observe the fluctuation on prices. The artist must paint before the light changes; the aesthetician can take his theoretical work into the evening. The physician must diagnose in emergencies; the medical researcher can postpone his judgment. Even the experimental scientist may have to meet the imperatives of time, while the philosopher of science may be oblivious of them.

The third difference in the conditions under which study and practice occur lies in the kinds of consequences of each kind of action. The consequences of writing this chapter are of a different kind from those of hiring a teacher. Writing this chapter does have consequences, often remotely practical, but frequently immediately related to further speculation. The clichi—speculation for speculation's sake, or knowledge for knowledge's sake—has little meaning, but it makes a great deal of sense to say that speculation is carried on for the sake of more speculation or that knowledge is acquired for the sake of more knowledge. A student of education may spend two years in formulating and testing a theory of teaching reading. His theory stands all the tests of logic. From this theory he rigorously deduces testable hypotheses, which, when tested empirically, indicate conclusively that his theory does not correspond to reality or to a publicly verifiable experience of reality. Consequently, the theory is re-examined and revised or discarded. But even if the theory is discarded, it is no disaster, and there are significant results. The experiment may become a part of the literature on education; it may add support for an alternate theory; and it may provide new insights into the problem. If the theory is accepted for a considerable length of time before it is discarded, it may still remain historically interesting, and the author may occupy a respected place in the history of education. However, if a teacher acted according to this theory for two years and failed to teach his pupils to read, he would, in all likelihood, be fired.

We find an analogous situation in other fields. The economist who has made a study faces consequences that are different from the consequences faced by a trust officer who invests a widow's legacy. The physician, the artist, the engineer, and the jet pilot face less lenient consequences for making incorrect assumptions than the medical scientist, the aesthetician, or the physicist. We can multiply examples. A good illustration is provided by the fact that a psychologist may be forced to use rats or statistics from past performances to test his theories rather than experimentation on people. The latter is fraught with the kinds of consequences that the practitioner must face if the situation demands that he work with people.

These differences in the conditions under which study and practice occur appear to be desirable. One of the worst things that could happen to study, research, and investigation would be to exact the same kind of penalties for failure that are incurred in practice. The implausible hypothesis has a poor chance statistically of being correct; but occasionally it is correct, and when it is, it gives a new direction to the course of human understanding. If the penalties for being wrong in research were as immediate and irrevocable as they often are in practice, the number of unlikely ideas that would be tested would be diminished. In study and research, it is necessary to provide an environment in which the penalties for being wrong in one's guesses are not so drastic and irrevocable as they are under the conditions of practice in professions.

While these differences in the conditions under which study and practice occur may account for the general gap between the two, they fail to explain why in some fields the gap is much wider than in others. Even the most cursory observation reveals that teaching resembles the other social sciences in the width of the gap. Politics, business, and social practice rely to a great extent on proverbs and generalizations that are the result of unsystematic study and experience, and on theoretical knowledge that is so ancient that it has become common sense. Our cliches about government, business, and human relations are theoretical formulations that have become folklore. For example, "The government that governs least governs best." "The law of supply and demand is responsible for increases in prices." "Not every teacher who knows his subject is capable of imparting it." This knowledge may be expressed in imperatives that are clearly or obscurely related to generalizations. For example, "Sell when you can make a profit." "Work through channels; do not go over the head of your immediate superior." "Take your case to the people." Imperatives of this kind are extremely common in teacher education. In a recent article on classroom control, the beginning teacher is advised "to be business-like," "to be prepared," "to keep your lesson and presentation interesting," "to know when to overlook," "to be consistent." In the social sciences there is an obvious conservatism about accepting in practice recent results of systematic study. In education the same lag is often deplored.

Now let us compare the relationship between study and practice in other fields. In medicine this relationship is comparatively close; as a matter of fact the practitioner in medicine may be premature in the application of the results of systematic study, and he is constantly looking to the medical sciences for help. To account for this situation by saying that medicine is a scientific profession is to offer a tautological explanation, for this close relationship between systematic study and practice is one of the meanings given to the word *science*.Furthermore, the explanation fails to account for the close relation between the study of jurisprudence and the action of jurists. If we examine art and literature, we observe what appears to be a reversed relationship. The study of literature and aesthetics identifies, organizes, and explains the results of practice, but practitioners in the arts expect little help from either the methodology or the results of systematic study.

Apparently the great desideratum for professors of education is that the practice of teaching resemble medicine in the relationship between systematic study and practice. Medicine is regarded as successful, not only in respect to its prestige and its ethics, but also in its effectiveness. However, professors in disciplines other than education prefer to think of teaching as a common-sense activity or an art or both. But professors of education admit that teaching is not a scientific profession and that the relation between the study of education and the practice of teaching is often a strained one. The reasons frequently given as to why education has not developed to the point where it is an exact science include the episodic nature of teaching, the complexity of the phenomena with which it deals, the unpredictable nature of human nature, and the lack of rigorous study. We propose another hypothesis to account for the width of the gap between systematic study and teaching: The more important the precise results of practice are, the more seriously will the phenomena involved bye studied systematically, and the closer and more congenial will be the relationship between such study and practice. It is possible to pursue this line of inquiry only briefly in this chapter, but we shall attempt to marshal some cogent reasons and illustrations.

The first of the sciences to develop was astronomy, allegedly because the phenomena of the firmament are startling, observable, comparatively regular, and recurring. But these reasons may be indirect, at best; for a long time the stars were regarded as having a direct influence on the lives of men. There is no reason to believe that they were regarded as influencing the lives of men simply because they were regular and observable, although this fact may have had something to do with astronomy's becoming a science. All kinds of mythical beings, unseen forces, and curious natural phenomena were also regarded as influential and were consequently the subject of systematic study by medicine men, augurs, and soothsayers. The study of astrology was not left to common-sense or general experience, and the relationship between a sophisticated study of the stars and the practice of astrology must have been intimate indeed. When astrology became astronomy, the relationship between study and practice continued to be close, for a knowledge of astronomy continued to have important results for small differences in practice.

In jurisprudence, we find another example of a close relationship between practice and systematic study that is not scientific. Both the logic and the traditions of the law are closely related to practice. In the minds of most people, it is highly important that justice be administered under a close alliance with a highly organized body of theory and fact and with great dependence on ritual acts that have standard meanings. We conclude that this close relationship between systematic study and practice is due to the importance of small differences in the administration of justice. It is expected that the study of precedents and the application of rigorous reasoning will lead to great precision in the administration of justice. But the results of the administration of justice are difficult to measure with precision. Hence, we find an emphasis on ritual, on the appropriateness of the procedures, and on method. Thus we have come to the third proposition in our series: Whenever the small differences in results of practice are important and at the same time the precision of an empirical science is lacking, we find a strong emphasis on the appropriateness of the methods and the development of rituals and conventions, although these are rarely entirely lacking in the most scientific of the professions.

Our theory of the relationship between systematic study and practice can now be stated as follows:

1. There will always be an interval or a gap between systematic study and practice because of the different conditions under which each occurs.

2. The more important the precise results of practice are, the more seriously the phenomena involved will be studied and the closer and more congenial the relationship between systematic study and practice. We shall try to reduce chance results by the controls derived from systematic study.

3. Since the conditions of practice often do not permit the same precise control over the results as systematic study and research, the efforts to control will often shift from the results to the appropriateness of the procedures in their own right.

Let us now return to the social sciences, where we have classified education. Generally, in these activities we have been reasonably well satisfied with the results of common-sense practice. To be sure, the social sciences have been studied systematically, and there has been a tenuous relationship between systematic study and practice. In economics, perhaps, we find the most highly developed discipline; and with the establishment of schools of business administration, we find a closer relationship between academic study and practice than in the other social sciences. The question may arise: Why, according to this theory, has business not become an exact science or a highly ritualistic enterprise, since for most of us small differences in the results of economic practice are important? Those aspects of economics in which we demand accuracy, such as accounting, have a highly systematic number system. In those aspects of economics that depend on physical events, such as weather, we have a highly developed meteorological system. In the other aspects, either we have been reasonably well satisfied with the results of common-sense judgment or we have actually enjoyed the unpredictability and the surprises that result from our lack of scientific knowledge. However, during the great depression of the 1930s when the surprises of common-sense economic behavior were exaggerated and could not be accounted for by a breakdown in the number system or by natural or supernatural causes, the relation between academic and practical economics became more intimate, if not more congenial.

If we look again at the arts, it is obvious that we do not want scientific precision or logical consistency. We want surprises, paradoxes, and new patterns. For this condition, we are filling to pay the price of unpredictability, inefficiency, and blighted expectations. Therefore, there is a tenuous relation between the study of aeshetics and the act of painting.

In teaching we have been reasonably well satisfied with the results of practice based on common-sense and ancient adages. Most children learn to read because some kind of teaching goes on; it is not, or at least has not been, a matter of crucial difference if they learn to read six months later than they would have if we knew a better method of teaching, or if they read two hundred and fifty words a minute rather than three hundred and fifty words a minute. Crucial differences in results are gross. Furthermore, teaching does not depend intimately on a critical and precise logic or ritual. Generally, we have been satisfied with teaching and its results as it is carried out by common sense and generally acceptable behavior.

The situation in education may be changing. If the current interest in the educational enterprise as a whole creates a demand for more precise results, we may expect the systematic study of teaching to increase and a closer relation between such study and the practice of teaching to develop. The systematic study is likely to include both the normative and the empirical aspects of education; and teaching, therefore, is likely to become both more scientific and more ritualistic than it is now.

3

Planning for Effective Teaching

New and powerful developments are changing our schools. Perhaps the most visible is the enrollment explosion. We are not yet over the hump at the elementary and secondary levels, where the problems of drop-outs, retardation, and the salvaging of talent are putting new demands on the schools.

The rising student population is only one of the growing pains in American education. Another is the explosion of knowledge. The specialists turned out by colleges and universities continue to create new knowledge that affects the courses of study. Education thus stirs up a propitious circle of expanding knowledge.

A third demand on our educational system springs from the new role that education has assumed in our pattern of national survival and advancement. This was recognized when Congress passed, and recently revised, the National Defense Education Act.

A fourth factor that is altering the role of the schools is the development of new tools of teaching and learning. In the last fifteen years, new means of communication have become available that can stimulate students to learn. These new devices have the capacity to revolutionize education. But, just as we cannot fully exploit the advantages of major technological achievements like automation in industry without altering the structure within which they operate, so we cannot reap the full advantages for education of television, electronic tapes, and programmed learning, unless we are willing to break the rigid conventional patterns of our schools and introduce flexible class size, team teaching, and other organizational rearrangements.

Faced with these new challenges we seem to have reached two basic decisions. First, we realize that our need is not merely for *more* education, but for education of higher quality. Robert Ulich pinpointed the truth that emerged from the reappraisal of our educational goals that characterized the decade of the fifties: "Prolongation of school age is in itself not a blessing, but may even be a curse to civilization unless there goes together with the prolongation a revolutionary rethinking of the total program and a restructuring of the total education system from the secondary school upwards."

The second decision which seems to have emerged from the Great Debate is that money alone will not solve the critical educational problems. Our schools need more money, but they also need *more than* money. More money to enable the schools to do more of what they are already doing will mitigate but not solve the educational crisis. Our educational system must perforce change under the impact of rising enrollments, the accelerating growth of knowledge, education's new role in our struggle for national survival, the availability of new means of communication, and the demand for higher levels of quality and efficiency in our instructional programs. The question is not whether to make changes; the question is whether the inevitable changes that are coming will be merely suffered by the teaching profession, or welcomed, planned for, guided, and turned to the advantage of pupils and teachers. As Francis Bacon wrote: "He that will not apply new remedies must expect new evils; for time is the greatest innovator." The challenge facing American education today is to match the unprecedented innovations of our time with educational innovations bold enough to turn the new forces to maximum advantage.

The chief efforts of teachers to upgrade their profession have thus far been devoted mainly to improving the *conditions* under which they perform their traditional functions. They have sought mainly higher pay and better working conditions. In their more enlightened efforts they have striven to formulate codes of professional behavior and to build and advance professional associations. But rarely have they tried to improve the profession through changes in the intrinsic *structure or content* of the teacher's job. They have, in fact, adhered to a rigid pattern-one teacher with a fixed number of pupils in a self-contained classroom-despite the fact that fifty years of educational research have failed to establish its validity.

This reluctance to accept changes in the actual role of the teacher has had two unfortunate consequences. First, it has limited students' learning by the range of competencies of the few teachers with whom each student comes into contact, and by the limitations of the printed and spoken word. Second, by their reluctance to try new tools teachers have put a ceiling on the status and rewards provided for teachers. The teaching profession has been left behind in the revolution that has transformed practically every sector of the American economy in the past half century. Other professions have changed their old ways of operating in order to make the individual practitioner more productive and thereby raise his professional status and his standard of living. Teachers, unable to demonstrate that they are doing a better and more efficient job than they did in the past, have been unable to claim their rightful share of this professional upgrading. The challenge faced by teachers was recognized three centuries ago by Comenius, the author of one of the first systematic treatises on education: "Surely shame should compel us," he implored teachers, "to emulate the inventive spirit of other professions and find a remedy for the difficulties with which schools have hitherto struggled."?

Professional training alone will not produce professional teachers. Teachers can only function professionally to the extent that their role is professionalized. As sociologist Everett Hughes says: "The professional group will go through a process of self-consciously studying its work and deciding what functions are really professional and what can be delegated to non-professional or less-than-professional people." Or, we might add, delegated to mechanical or technical devices. "The simple truth," argues B.F. Skinner, pioneer in programmed learning, "is that as a mere reinforcing mechanism the teacher is out of date." Clearly, any teacher or organization that blindly opposes the development of mechanical aids to learning is not defending the teaching profession, but blocking its true development into a modern profession. What needs defense and promotion is the truly professional core of the teacher's role, the guiding of learning, not the peripheral tasks of drilling, conveying information, etc. There are only two courses for a teaching profession faced with new and powerful means of communication and learning: upgrading or down—grading. Teachers will become more than they are, or less. As has truly been said, any teacher who can be replaced by a machine, should be.

If teaching can only become truly professionalized through changes in the role and function of the teacher, then exactly what changes would contribute toward increasing their effectiveness and efficiency—that is toward truly professional functions?

To function as a professional, the teacher must first of all have the opportunity to spend most of his time teaching. Yet job analyses reveal that teachers spend from 20 to 70 per cent of their working time on housekeeping chores like keeping records, collecting lunch money, and preparing classroom equipment. By using teacher aides to perform these non-educational tasks, teachers can be free to do what they are trained to do: teach the children. Such a plan, launched in Bay City, Michigan, ten years ago, has since proved its effectiveness in communities in Utah, Colorado, Iowa, Minnesota, Connecticut, Massachusetts, and throughout Michigan, and it has worked in big cities like New York, Chicago, and Detroit.

Lay readers are a special type of teacher aide. They are college educated housewives assisting English teachers in over one hundred high schools by correcting and grading student compositions. This makes it possible for students to get at least twice as much writing practice as they can when the professional teachers must do all the paperwork.

A second requirement of professionalization of the teacher's work is that he have the opportunity for career advancement based on recognition and reward for individual abilities and for professional growth. Such a career pattern is provided by the adoption of team teaching, an outgrowth of the teacher aide plans. Team teaching organizes teachers into instructional groups that take advantage of individual talents, specialized training, and variations in personality. By letting each teacher do what he can do best, the plan offers both inspiration and leadership, and provides a much broader experience for students than they could get from teachers working with small groups. By becoming team leaders outstanding teachers can qualify for higher pay. Under present regulations, the only future for teachers seeking advancement is moving out of the classroom and into administration. Along with team teaching come other devices associated with professional status in various professions: differential assignments, and a system of pay according to degree of professional responsibility involved in each job.

A third route to genuinely professional teaching is mastery of the new tools of communication. In no area has greater progress been made in the last fifty years than in communication¾which, of course, is basic to the transmittal of culture from one generation to the next. Through the inventions now at our disposal the best teachers can reach an ever-widening audience. There is no longer any reason why a child in a rural or slum school should have instruction inferior to that of a child in the most favored suburban school. Among these newer tools are radio, motion pictures and television, records, teaching machines, electronic desks, and audio tapes which are now being used in language laboratories in more than one hundred colleges and universities across the country.

The fourth and fifth requirements of thoroughly professionalized teaching involve changes in the attitudes of teachers. These changes can best be described through a comparison of teaching with other occupations in contemporary America.

America's productive development stands as a marvel of the ages; for at present, with only about 6 per cent of the world's population and land area, the United States produces over one-third of the world's goods and services.

In industry and agriculture the average American worker today produces five times what he did in 1870. In a single generation output per person has doubled, and industrial efficiency has risen about 3 per cent each year. Nearly half of our jobs did not even exist in their present forms a generation ago.

By contrast, the professions and service occupations have lagged behind agriculture and industry. Here the problem is complicated by the rapidly growing demand for well-educated persons in all fields. According to Professor Harold Clark, in the early years of our history only twelve occupations needed high caliber manpower. Now there are about 2,200, with ten to twenty new ones added to the list each year. Shifting educated people from one profession to another cannot meet a demand of this magnitude. The only possible answer is to increase the efficiency of each person by extending his effectiveness in new ways.

Medicine offers an outstanding example of how the quality of professional service can be raised through imaginative use of skilled manpower. In 1900, three out of five professional health workers were doctors, while in 1950 only one out of five was a doctor. But in spite of the fact that the number of physicians has not grown at nearly the rate of the general population in the past fifty years, medical services have been improved and expanded.

How has this been done? The modern doctor has become the leader of a team of assistants and technicians drawn from more than two hundred medical sub-professions. Their existence makes the doctor many times more productive than if he had to carry out all their duties singlehanded, and enables him to devote all his time to using his special skills most effectively.

How has the United States achieved this position? Other countries certainly had human and material resources equivalent to ours in the 1700s. Why is it that they did not develop as we did?

Obviously, the genius of our country lies in the combination of its inventiveness and its resources. Our social, economic, and political institutions created a climate that tended to foster individual growth. Opportunities for education, free choice of government, work, power, and wealth have been offered to more citizens without respect to social class, heritage, or origins than in any other of the world's nations. Resources alone were not enough, however; for without the driving force of great concepts, grand ideals, we would have lacked the impetus to develop them. Our goals were clear and meaningful, our problem was how to achieve them, and our ingenuity went to work to devise effective ways.

The ways in which this ingenuity saved manpower are intimately related to our steady growth; for without more efficient farming methods, we would not have had the labor force needed for industrial development. Without more efficient methods in industry and agriculture, we would not have had the manpower needed for the professions. Leisure would not have existed for education, and educated persons would not have been available for the research on which so much of our progress depends. In essence, we have advanced because we devised ways of doing more with fewer people and, conversely, extending the effectiveness of our highly skilled by labor-saving devices of many sorts. For reasons not readily apparent, we failed in education to apply this inventiveness to extend the effectiveness of our best teachers, relying instead upon traditional practices.

Thus the two changes in attitude required of the educational profession are; first, adoption of a favorable attitude toward change, which has transformed American society; and second, full acceptance of professional responsibility to improve through ingenuity and innovation in the practice of teaching.

Because teachers as an occupational group have not yet cultivated these attitudes, the profession of teaching is the only profession in American life that has been untouched by the revolution that during the past fifty years has affected agriculture, the ministry, industry, health services, and other professions. Only in teaching do we continue to place an arbitrary limit on the number of people a professional worker can serve. In all other professions, the worker is rewarded in prestige and economic return through the number of people he serves. In medicine and dentistry, for example, society judges the success of the professional worker by the number of patients he can treat. Similarly, in law, engineering, and other professions, the hierarchy of success is built upon the number of clients served. New possibilities can and must be developed in the teaching profession to extend the utilization of the best teachers and to reward them accordingly. The problem of recruiting good teachers would be drastically affected, for example, if it were common practice to recognize and to pay teachers according to the competencies required to carry on their duties and the number of students they can teach effectively. Competent and experienced teachers might become the directors of learning for 150 to 200 pupils where they would supervise the work of less able or less experienced teachers, of interns, and of aides. Under the direction of these supervisors, regular teachers, assisted by apprentice teachers and aides, might be in charge of groups of fifty or more students. The "team" might also include specialists in various areas of the curriculum, such as reading.

The total personnel required under such arrangements would presumably be just as large as under our present system, but the proportion of professionally trained teachers could be substantially smaller. More importantly, the professionally trained teachers might look forward to increased responsibilities and larger scope of activities as they worked with more students. They would also command correspondingly higher salaries as their experience and competence gained official recognition.

Three basic principles that have been applied to other professions over the last half century to bring about a "professional revolution" have not been applied to teaching: (1) the division of labor whereby the professionally trained person concentrates upon professional functions, other tasks being handled by less skilled persons; (2) the use of capital equipment and advanced technology as a means of raising the productivity of human beings; and (3) a system of incentives under which the able person entering the field may expect recognition in greater opportunities, higher status, and larger salary for meritorious performance. Teaching is alone among the professions in having been "frozen" into a fixed pattern of manpower use, and in lacking a system of incentives whereby rewards are adjusted to ability and performance.

In summary, as outlined above, these are the changes that must be made in the occupational role of the teacher if there is to be real professional functioning in the school. The instructional evolution now in progress is a search for ways to make the most efficient and economical use of the time, talent, and skills of our teachers, with the ultimate aim of improving the quality of education for all the nation's youth. Through full dedication in these tasks, the teaching profession can render its noblest service.

4

The Learning Essentials

The purpose of this chapter is to identify some of the appropriate tasks of the school in the hope that their importance and difficulty of attainment will serve to highlight the need of prospective teachers for some specialized skill, knowledge, and training in dealing adequately with them. There are many things which students will learn without schools, but there is little assurance that the tasks to be cited will represent the kinds of learning likely to be achieved without the intelligent direction of teachers who are competent to plan, conduct, and evaluate this instruction.

To identify the tasks that are peculiarly the responsibility of the school is to suggest the kinds of learning that the school, by the nature of its purpose, structure, and development, is best qualified to perform. By the same token, this identification is likely to reveal the tasks which other agencies, like the home and the church, are either not disposed to perform or are presumed to be less well equipped to do.

The important demands to be cited are all complex in their fulfilment. Their interpretation may vary from community to community, from school to school, and even from student to student, but basically they appear to represent the root tasks that the school can best do. Their importance to society (and to the individual) gives urgency, therefore, to the question: Does their doing require of prospective teachers any special knowledge, or skill, or training not normally an expected outcome of liberal education or knowledge of the subject to be taught?

If the point can be made that many of the current demands upon the school are injudicious, ill-considered and harmful to their main purpose; that schools ought reasonably to do what no other institutions can do; things that will not be done well unless schools do them; then a certain priority of tasks for the school can be established. It will then be possible to place proper emphasis on the type of training that teachers will need to accomplish these ends. Should society continue, without providing either sufficient funds or facilities, to heap upon the schools demands that outrace the capacity of teachers to serve students, then an obvious dilution of the quality of service to students and the training of teachers is certainly indicated.

With increasing demands being made on the schools, it is important to center attention on the root tasks of the school, emphasizing them in contrast to obligations which may more appropriately be assumed by mass media, youth agencies, the home, the church, or the general community and to raise questions about the possibility of bringing about the performance of those tasks in the schools more competently than heretofore.

The things the school can best do—a list expanded beyond five learning essentials originally suggested by Ralph Tyler—are likely to be found in one or more of the following classes:

1. Learning which is directed to the mastery of the tools of learning.
2. Learning which involves complex and difficult things that require the organization of experience and distribution of practice over an extended period of time.
3. Learning which requires knowledge and skill on the part of teachers in developing in students an under standing of principles and concepts.
4. Learning in which the teacher has the opportunity to add new dimensions, since the experience of the learner is not direct.

5. Learning which, if not provided by the school, would deny to students opportunities to come in contact with the best in literature, art, music, etc.
6. Learning which examines and interprets experience
7. Learning which is derived from the interplay of people and ideas.
8. Learning which requires of students critical and logical exposition of ideas.
9. Learning which comes from evaluation.

Before an attempt to describe each of these essentials briefly it may be worthwhile to consider some assumptions about the role of the school:

1. The school cannot teach everything.
2. The school cannot teach some things at all.
3. The schools cannot teach some things without the cooperation of other agencies.
4. The school cannot teach some things to all students.
5. The school cannot teach anything to all students in such a way as to insure for all the same degree of learning.
6. The school cannot guarantee learning for anyone; it can only provide some of the conditions for learning.
7. The school cannot teach all there is to be known about anything, since it cannot set up controls to exclude incidental or supplemental learning on the part of students.
8. The school cannot (or should not) assume responsibility for teaching things which seriously interfere with its teaching the essentials.
9. The school cannot (or should not) teach things which are inimical to its purpose.
10. The schools cannot (or should not) attempt to teach things which lie considerably beyond the known capacities of learners.
11. The school cannot (or should not) attempt to teach things which lie beyond the known capacities of teachers.

12. The school cannot (or should not) take the position that the essential values are not for all students, even though come may require more help in attaining them.

13. The school cannot (or should not) leave to the individual teacher the decision to teach or not teach these learning essentials, but should give him wide latitude in determining ways in which his teaching may help make them attainable.

The problem of the school is to make these tasks central in its program. The problem of the teacher is threefold: to comprehend their nature and importance in the light of the requirements of the disciplines whose content will be employed; to interpret them in the light of the experiences that can be given students to bring about their attainment; and to take into account the nature of the learner in his individual approach to these imperatives.

As a social institution the school defines the desirable knowledge and skills to be expected of students. The role of the teacher is to organize instruction that will lead to the realization of these expectations. Since the relationship of teacher to student is never a single, fixed, isolated person-to-person kind of relationship, but one which takes place in a social context that varies from school to school, from group to group, and from moment to moment, there is no possibility of laying down any neat, well-defined rules for the close control of learning by individuals. The informal organization of a particular school may modify greatly both the teacher's institutionalized role of providing instruction and the student's institutionalized role of participating in and profiting from it. The prospective beginning teacher should have at least a minimum awareness of some of the significant factors which may condition learning in a rather wide variety of situations. A teacher who is at least aware of some of the forces which may be at work in his classroom would appear to be in a better position to modify his instruction than one who sees his role in all its institutionalized aspects as fixed, complete, and unchanging in all contexts.

The task of the teacher is a complex one, involving continuous decisions growing out of his understanding and appreciation of the role of the school as well as changing social values, social needs, and social problems. The instruction he provides students within this context takes place through some content or subject matter that he must employ—whether taught as content itself or as a means of promoting other desired changes in individuals. To use this content sensibly he has to cut through conglomerate detail and determine the precise materials out of which he hopes to uncover or develop the concepts, the intellectual processes, and the emotional ingredients which will contribute to the appropriate tasks. Yet it would be unwise on his part to fail to consider the problems of the learner in any decisions he would make.

Though society may make imperative certain learning essentials for the school, it does not follow that the learner will do likewise. Developing the ability to read may be one of the tasks society imposes on the school. Society may ask that this skill be learned with a maximum of meaning, yet society cannot dictate this learning for the individual student. A decisive factor in the situation is the learner himself. Since any meaning for him is likely to come from individual experience, any effort to place a learning essential on the continuum of meaningfulness has to stand against the effort of the learner himself. He may place it higher or lower.

While the assumption is often made that one of the easiest tasks facting the teacher is the determination of content, this is likely to prove the most baffling. Many of the real shortcomings in teaching grow out of the selection of content, including activities and experiences, which bear little if any relation to the realization of the goals of either teacher or learner. The increased efforts at differentiation in schools today have greatly magnified the enormity and extent of these crimes. The unimaginative plodding of countless students through textbook pages in search of bodies of facts to be learned testifies to the inability of many teachers to organize really significant instruction related to the tasks appropriate for the school.

In developing plans for his daily instruction the teacher is confronted with questions that relate both to choice of content from the point of view of its importance to the subject being taught and its usefulness in achieving an appropriate task. Among such questions: Is the problem to be considered of importance? What makes it important? Is it of value to students in relation to the appropriate task? Is it within the range of the maturity and experience of students? In what ways is it likely to insure further growth? Are there sufficient and various sources to which students may turn? Are the problems the best that can be provided in a given situation?

Among the resources available to the teacher in this decision making will be, of course, his understanding and appreciation of the role of the school; his specialized knowledge of the subject he is teaching; his awareness of significant research to help in his assessment of the nature of individuals and their learning; his ability at analysis of his own goals in relation to the goals of his particular school and of individual students; and the fruits of his experience in analyzing the learning process in his own classroom.

The problem facing the teacher is to know as far as he is able the precise kinds of knowledge to be taught. This requires the selection of curriculum content and the activities which, as they are experienced by individuals, help them to acquire this knowledge. The lesson, under the direction of the teacher, must be so organized as to produce the interactions likely to cause growth in this knowledge. If the growth is wanting, the teacher must be skillful enough to analyze the teaching situation—testing his objectives, his materials, his methods, the reactions of students, and even his own evaluation of the process. Not all teachers possess this required analytical skill, and one way to help them develop it is to insure opportunity in their preparation for considerable practice in learning how to analyze, criticize, and modify their structuring and conduct of specific teaching situations under the direction of more experienced teachers. Unless prospective teachers are given some opportunity to carry on this kind of analysis of their own beginning efforts to teach and to attempt to analyze under supervision teaching situations in which they participate as neophytes, there is always the possibility that their later efforts to improve their teaching may result in patching, tinkering, and dosing, which seldom will make any significant difference to learning.

It has been suggested that common sense will be sufficient to lead intelligent persons who want to teach to bring about modifications of this nature, but the low rate of the teaching of science in the secondary schools indicates that common sense has not been particularly effective in guiding many teachers to develop instructional programs that will meet the tests which have been suggested.

"The constructive role of science," as Ralph Tyler has pointed out, "is not to have the student memorize a number of dead facts about plants, animals, physical phenomena, and so on. The purpose of science is to help give the student a way of understanding the phenomena and a way of solving problems relating to the physical and biological environment. In place of being dead matter to be remembered, the subject matter becomes ways of thinking, feeling, and acting that students can use to help make their own lives more meaningful and effective."

Such a point of view suggests an urgent revision of the aims, the content, and the methods of conventional courses in science, especially in the secondary school. No longer can the notion of coverage, of conveying the current knowledge of a field, suffice. Authoritative possession of a body of knowledge about physics, for instance, no longer will be sufficient to qualify a person as a science teacher. His preparation for teaching will necessarily involve something more than the inculcation of conclusions and training in the ways and means of passing them on. The old meanings, embalmed in the older statements of science, are no longer adequate. The lecture, the textbook, the conventional "cookbook" laboratory manual are inappropriate to develop the ability of students to conduct scientific inquiry. These are some of the conclusions of the Physical Sciences Study Group as it goes about the task of getting students to deal with science as inquiry and encouraging teachers to become adept in aiding students to deal with phenomena in such a way as to achieve understanding and insight. Relegated to the past is the conventional method in which the laboratory serves as the place where generalizations already learned are demonstrated and perception is restricted within the framework of terms and concepts already introduced in the classroom in some fixed and formalized fashion.

There will be the temptation to say that the prospective teacher's own understanding of the nine learning essentials derives from his liberal education and his professional preparation; that his knowledge of how to achieve these comes directly from his specialized knowledge and professional preparation; and that his commitment to their extension and development grows out of all three: liberal education, specialization, and professional education. It is obvious that the development of these learning essentials requires that the teacher be much more than technician; for these experiences give a primacy to the stimulation of intellectual growth and development, including imagination and creative power, as well as critical judgment and reasoning on the part of students. They lay upon the teacher obligations that are indeed worthy of his greatest talents. Except for the rare teacher, it is not likely that a high order of skill in dealing with these learning essentials will come without some organized, critical consideration of the various components that underlie the act of teaching in a wide variety of classroom situations, and the encouraged application to his own teaching of whatever methods or emphases appear warranted on the basis of empirical research, experience, prudence, or common sense. Whether this critical consideration for the prospective teacher is to come wholly out of practice, or out of formal study to be followed by practice, is a question that need not be answered now, but this much is likely: Its benefits can scarcely be realized unless his training for teaching, formal or otherwise, somewhere, somehow embraces this experience under the tutelage of an experienced mentor.

The learning essentials considered most appropriate for the school follow:

1. *Learning which is directed to the mastery of the tools of learning.* If the school fails to assist students to achieve mastery of the fundamentals of reading, writing, and arithmetic, it fails in its effort to attain other learning essentials which require students to make optimum use of these tools. While neither research nor accumulated testimony suggests one right way to teach reading, both have much to say about some of the conditions that facilitate growth in this ability. The teaching of reading involves many

problems. Among them will be decision-making regarding the kinds of behavior in reading that are deemed important and attainable, the selection of curriculum content and the activities which, as they are experienced by students, move them toward attainment of the desired standards of behavior; the organization of instruction to facilitate this learning; and the evaluating of process as a basis for revising the learning experiences.

The focus of the teacher here—as with all learning essentials—is not on the end product, but on the process as it develops meanings and understandings that modify individual behavior. The focus is on what is happening to the student—what he is learning and whether he is learning with efficiency and economy. This requires the teacher to know a great deal more than the mechanics of reading and the use of reading aids.

Using the work of authorities cited in Strang, *Reading in General Education,* it should be possible to bring to the attention of prospective teachers the kinds of reading difficulties inherent in content and raise questions relative to ways of helping students to deal with these more effectively than at present.

Many questions with respect to the preparation of teachers need answering. Why, for instance, is it assumed that teachers of elementary school pupils, where initial skill in reading is developed, generally require formal training to teach this subject; but that teachers in secondary schools, where pupils have still not learned to read, do not? Why, for instance, has it been assumed that secondary-school teachers of the content subjects do not consistently have special problems of reading with which to contend in teaching these subjects? And that no training is required?

The revolution that appears to be taking place in the field of mathematics, in which it is now being suggested that some of the basic notions such as set theory be introduced to students at an early age in place of the present over-concern with computation, suggests the need for some training in teaching arithmetic which may not grow out of specialized study of mathematics.

2. *Learning which involves the organization of difficult*

and complex materials over an extended period of time. Agencies other than the school can teach things which will be quickly or casually learned, but more complex forms of learning represent an appropriate task of the school. A student, for instance, may pick up words and phrases in a given foreign language; but his growth in ability to speak and to write that language, to appreciate its nuisances and understand its structure as a basis for more learning is likely to be the result of an organized approach for which the school is uniquely equipped. When such learning must be carried on over an extended period of time, when its attainment rests firmly on an organization of sequential experiences and distribution of practice, it is to the school that society looks for this kind of teaching. This kind of learning essential is further illustrated by the choice of the school as the appropriate agency for developing, say, an understanding and appreciating of literature, mathematics, or the natural sciences—all tasks that demand knowledge and skill in decisions affecting content, method, and evaluation. The prospective teacher needs more than common sense in making the decisions.

A new development in the teaching and learning of a second language is the hearing-speaking approach in which, at least at the beginning of this learning, one learns to use the language without reading, without writing, and without translating by dint of listening to the teacher speaking and responding to what he says. Far from being easy, teaching in this way requires considerable skill. Since the teacher (and not the book) is conducting the lesson, the teacher is required to bring to the task something more than knowledge of the subject. With the language laboratory increasingly being employed to facilitate this direct method, the teacher becomes the director of a situation in which the learners listen to master teachers; in addition, they listen and respond to one another. This forces the teacher to take the language the student has, build upon it, extend it, enrich it, and gradually introduce correctness while all the while preserving spontaneity and confidence. It is likely that success in developing this method of learning will require of the teacher far more than a knowledge of the language he teaches. Implied is specific training in achieving this kind of classroom learning.

The changes in curriculum and teaching being promoted by the National Science Foundation seemingly give the lie to the notion that "the way to teach is the way you are taught"; for in biology, mathematics, chemistry, and physics it is being discovered that what is in the secondary school curriculum now is so outmoded as to require both new content and new ways of teaching. The Physical Sciences Study Committee, for example, found in its recent survey of high school courses of study in physics that almost without change the basic structure in physics being taught in 1956 was the physics of 1900 and that none of the revolutionary developments in this field since the turn of the century were even included. This study group has reduced the number of basic concepts to forty and asked for a whole new teaching approach. Teachers now in the schools without these insights are working without the advantage of the best scholarship in the field. Indicated are new instructional content, the redistribution of student time, and newer techniques of teaching that will have implications for all who prepare to enter the field as well as for those who are presently engaged in teaching it.

3. *Learning which requires knowledge and skill on the part of teachers in developing in students an understanding of principles and concepts.* Because concepts are never simple but usually abstractions with many dimensions whose unity must be perceived in many unlike situations before meaning is acquired, teachers must take this into account in arranging learning experiences. Unfortunately, for some teachers this accounting has resulted in nothing more meaningful to the student than a word, an arbitrary association with which to identify—if seldom to understand—a given concept. If teaching a concept consisted only in defining a term, giving an apt illustration or two to pin it down, and then requiring students to repeat the definition and use the term appropriately, the problem for teachers would be simple; but this is completely remote from conceptual learning.

The kind of learning that will build concepts requires knowledge and skill on the part of the teacher, for in this type of learning the central factors are not obvious to students observing the phenomenon; the basic principles and meanings must be brought to the attention of the learner. As Ralph Tyler suggests, just by working with plants over a long period of time, for instance, will not bring to one who cares for these plants an understanding of the nature of the concepts of cell structure and genetics. Conceptual learning is likely to come about in those situations that include activities that have been purposely organized to guide students to conceptual learning; it invariably must be supported by many opportunities for the student to sense the concept in differing situations. The role of the teacher is to guide the learner in this experience, toward eliciting the meaning of the experience, and aiding the student to crystallize tentative generalizations to be tested in alternate situations. The task is to have the conceptualizing begin with the particular go, on to theory in the widest sense, and conclude again in a heightened sense of the particular. If the experience does not begin with the particular, it is not likely to be significant to the student. If it does not go on to a general explanation then it will not promote the grasp of a principle. If it does not bring about increased power over the particular, it will inevitably lose significance for the student. The task of designing the experiences requires of the teacher a high level of skill.

4. *Learning in which the teacher has the opportunity to add new dimensions, since the experience of the learner is not direct.* A simple example will suffice to show that this is a task quite appropriate for the school. Students through their day-by-day experience are not likely to acquire in offhand fashion an understanding of Asia or an appreciation of the Roman Empire. This experience needs to be re-created, and the teacher must play a central role in this re-creation. fortunately he has wide latitude in guiding learning and in the opportunity to develop imaginative teaching materials. Technological aids may come to help students to acquire more readily the backgrounds so that teachers may assist them to carry on inquiry either individually or in small groups in a much more efficient way than has been formerly true; but the obligation of the school to highlight the past continues, and the training which the teacher receives ought to equip him in ways of preserving and perpetuating the past against insistent demands for glorification of the ephemeral present.

Language is a powerful factor in aiding students to acquire understanding about lands they are unable to visit and about events which happened a long time ago; yet language is an ever-present threat to both teacher and learner. A number of studies of the vocabulary burden and leading difficulty of some textbooks, especially in the social studies, emphasize the inability of learners to gain meaning from their efforts in this direction. Efforts to get students to recite well, to get and give correct answers, to pass objective tests, to follow prescribed methods, to meet minimum standards—all encourage verbal memorizing and defeat efforts to encourage inquiry. The more unlikely the opportunity the learner has to experience the learning directly the more critical the importance of language as a vehicle in insuring his understanding. This is an area in which much study is warranted; it is an area in which the teacher needs help.

5. *Learning which is not provided by the school should deny to students opportunities to come in contact with the best in literature, and art, and music.* As the school has been forced to undertake increasing responsibilities in learning, it has been challenged with the need to be selective in the things it is prepared to teach. The need for choosing the most essential content has grown increasingly strong as the range of things that might be taught has become greater. In this selective process some primacy ought to be given to learning which requires experiences of higher quality than are commonly found in the student's environment. To develop interests in music through experiences commonly had with radio and joke boxes is to miss the opportunity to develop interest in music of greater variety and higher quality. The school cannot forgo the latter, any more than it can afford not to develop appreciation and understanding of esthetic principles in art and literature. Again, this is a problem centered on the development of instruction as it should be related to widely varying student interests and abilities.

6. *Learning which examines and interprets experience.* This task is central to the role of the school, for it is the means by which the school sets the learner free by equipping him with the

ability to insure his own learning. It helps him to become familiar with the kinds of questions that illuminate the problems he faces. It gives him insights into the ways in which observation, invention, datum, and concept help form the fabric of knowledge. The school's obligation here is to see that the student not only has experiences, but that there is opportunity for reflection upon and examination of these experiences and an effort to interpret them so that they hold meaning.

7. *Learning which is derived from the interplay of people and ideas.* Life outside the school allows considerable opportunity for the student to exchange and probe ideas and experiences, but the school is peculiarly fitted to make provision for these interchanges on some sort of systematic base useful to his intellectual growth. Discussion is one of the useful ways to bring this about, since the school to some extent can control and motivate the opportunities for the interplay of students and ideas in such a way as to advance understanding. Discussion is valuable in learning, since it allows for the sharing of information, the challenging of concepts and viewpoints, the clarification of ideas. While effective discussion probably requires reasonable background or preparation on the part of students and interest in a problem of real concern, it invariably demands skillful guidance on the part of the teacher. This guidance is reflected in the success with which the desired interplay of students and words rises above the mere exposition of ideas and involves grappling with ideas, so that there is a careful weighing of the facts and ideas presented.

8. *Learning which requires of the student critical and logical exposition of ideas.* One of the recurring criticisms of schools is that they fail to turn out students capable of offering critical and logical expositions of ideas. If ability to think holds a high place in the abilities which schools should endeavor to develop in students, it follows that the ability to express ideas cogently is also an imperative. In the book *College Freshmen Speak Out,*[1] Agatha Townsend makes the point that the writing of a paper of some length that forces him to explain an idea is the thorniest problem faced by the average college freshman. Problems of

organization, emphasis, coherence, clarity, prove plaguing in even the simplest development of ideas. As between teaching that gives students an understanding of the knowledge they have acquired but leaves them helpless as to its application, and teaching that gives students experience in its application but leaves them without an understanding of it, there is perhaps little to choose; but students who are handicapped in either respect are quite incapable of the critical and logical expression of ideas that must rest on both.

9. *Learning which comes from evaluation.* A persistent and perhaps valid criticism of schools is that they fail to equip students to evaluate their own learning. The basis of evaluation can be only what a student knows and understands and his ability to use this knowledge functionally in a wide range of situations, but always in terms of either his or the school's goals, or both. This view appears to make teaching, learning, and evaluation inseparable and imposes on the teacher obligations that relate to both goal-defining and evaluation. If the quality of thought and action of students as they meet varied situations is a test of learning, then evaluation which takes into account the behavior of students in actual situations is demanded. This will require skill on the part of the teacher in direct observation. Anecdotal records in which situations and behavior responses are written from time to time by the student himself may be a way of getting a student to perceive his own behavior. Written also by his peers as they observe him in the situation, these records provide a basis for comparing interpretations and for raising questions to which some systematic attention can be given. It is possible that more useful practice in evaluation will be developed by cues that may be coming out of research in the behavioral sciences.

If the nine learning essentials described do represent prime and valid obligations of the school, their importance and difficulty would appear to warrant on the part of prospective teachers specialized knowledge, skill, and training in making their fulfilment possible.

5

College Teaching

There is a lot of cheap talk about college teaching. Everyone has an opinion, probably because everyone at some point has experienced very "good" and very "bad" teaching.

It is a favorite pastime of students to discuss their professors; and it is instructive, if you ever get the chance, to listen. Much of the discussion is personal. They don't like someone's ugly ties or oxford shoes. So and so twitches and blinks. Prof. X puts you to sleep and Prof. Y shouts too much. Dr. Jones is never prepared. Dr. Smith never allows time for questions and Ms. Barker always gets off the subject. The philosophers always answer your questions with questions, the English profs. expect too much, and the Chem. profs. always smell bad. Nobody takes a personal interest. But the very worst is the guy who puts you down for asking a dumb question. That's inexcusable.

So it goes ... a lot of glib opinions without much depth. But then, why should we expect more? Sitting in classrooms for 12 to 16 years¾especially classrooms where the teaching has been less than outstanding¾hardly qualifies one to be an expert on teaching. Should we really expect students to have reflected deeply on what the teaching-learning process is all about? We should attend to their comments (e.g., it *isn't*, in fact, productive to "put people down"), but we can hardly anticipate that our students will come up with full-blown theories about effective teaching.

The talk in the faculty lounge isn't much better. Most faculty members want smaller classes, lighter teaching loads, and fewer committee assignments. "If we just had these...and better students! We must do something about admission standards. The students here just aren't motivated. They can't read; they can't write; they can't *think.*" There is a pause in the discussion. A neophyte instructor suggests that the students could be reached if they had better instruction. A brief discussion follows but is ended abruptly when the most senior member of the geriatric oligarchy pontificates, "It's always been my opinion that great teachers are born not made." A conversation-stopper, indeed!

But most college teachers grow dissatisfied with the glib talk about teaching. We know in our hearts, or at least we suspect, that teaching is a much more complicated task than it appears on the surface, and we begin to search for a more solid basis for our opinions. Being academically inclined, i.e., scientific, we feel a need to look at the evidence. Sooner or later the questions arise: What do we know about college teaching? Are there research studies? What do the studies show?

Research on College Teaching

There are, indeed, research studies; it seems sometimes that there is no end to them. The following sampling of journal article titles illustrates the nature and scope of these studies:

> "The Effects of a Programmed Textbook on Achievement Under Three Techniques of Instruction"
>
> "The Effect of Intelligence and Social Atmosphere on Group Problem Solving Behavior" "
>
> The Effect of Class Size on Achievement and Attitudes"
>
> "An Experimental Study of the Use of Lectures to Large Groups of Students in Teaching the Fundamentals of Speech"
>
> "The Relative Merits of Lecture and Recitation in Teaching College Physics"
>
> "A Comparison between Lecture and Conference Methods of Teaching Psychology"
>
> "Reading Improvement as a Function of Student Personality and Teaching Method"

"Comparison of Directed Self-study Versus Lecture in Teaching General Psychology"

What do the studies conclude? That is a difficult question. Some studies make significant conclusions about a particular teaching method, but one does not need to search far for other, seemingly similar, studies which contradict those conclusions. Unfortunately, most of the studies produce the researcher's anathema: "No significant differences." It is important, therefore, to examine a collection of studies, not simply individual studies, to see if there are any overall trends in this growing body of research literature. Fortunately, such reviews have been completed by some very competent scholars.

One of these reviews was done by Wilbert McKeachie for a chapter in the first volume of a reference work entitled *Handbook of Research on Teaching,* edited by N.L. Gage (McKeachie, 1963). While the *Hand-book* includes chapters which review many aspects of teaching at all levels, McKeachie's chapter focuses on studies of teaching at the college and university level. McKeachie reviews studies which examine lecturing, discussion, laboratory methods, independent study, and automated teaching methods. He finds the usual contraditions and studies with "no significant differences," but he formulates some tentative conclusions. Lecturing seems to be an effective way of communicating information, but other methods seem to be more important in achieving higher cognitive and attitudinal objectives. Discussions prove helpful in achieving certain objectives, but vary in their effectiveness according to the manner in which the discussion is conducted, the size of the group, and the degree of "student-centeredness." Laboratory methods develop problem-solving abilities, provided that the emphasis in the laboratory is on solving problems. While independent study seems to increase motivation, it may be less effective in bringing about other desirable educational outcomes. Automated techniques vary in their effectiveness according to the quality of the materials used and the objectives pursued.

McKeachie's earlier survey has been brought up to date with a more recent review published as an ERIC Clearing-house Report

(McKeachie, 1970). In that report McKeachie is much more cognizant of the methodological problems involved in doing research on college teaching, but he still finds in the studies he reviews certain trends and tendencies. He concludes that small classes seem to be better for basic retention, problem solving, and attitude differentiation. Discussion method seems best for increasing problem-solving ability and for dealing with attitudes and motivation. Large lectures coupled with small discussion sections seem to be generally more effective than lecture sections of unwieldy size. Student-centered discussions seem more favorable for the more complex educational outcomes. Students may not learn more with automated devices, but they may learn more efficiently or like it better. Although McKeachie makes no direct attack on the methodology of the studies he reviews, he is cautious in drawing conclusions. The overall theme is that different methods seem to be effective for different objectives.

A more recent collection of research can be found in Ohmer Milton's *Alternatives to the Traditional* (1972). Milton makes the case that the effectiveness of traditional methods of instruction at the college level has never been proven. Traditional methods are vigorously supported, yet there seems to be little concrete evidence to warrant such enthusiasm for conventional teaching and learning arrangements. In developing this argument, Milton discusses a wide variety of studies done on different aspects of college teaching. He notes, for example, that the tremendous assumption about transfer of training, which underlies much of the teaching that takes place at the college level, has been generally disproven; that there is little evidence that the four-year lockstep is the only, or necessarily best, format for a college education; and that there is some evidence that students do not require nearly the surveillance in the learning process that their professors think they need. Milton cites studies that cast doubt on the traditional grading and evaluation systems employed at the college level, studies that suggest that grades are unrelated to job performance and that most tests penalize bright students. The studies Milton has drawn together demonstrate that the current research on college teaching fails to lend much support for continuing to use traditional teaching methods. Unfortunately, there is not much evidence that alternative methods are much better. Milton admits the lack of evidence, but concludes by asking. "What do I have to lose?"

The American Educational Research Association recently has published a *Second Handbook of Research on Teaching,* an expanded and up-to-date version of the earlier volume edited by Gage. It contains a current summary of research on teaching in higher education, in particular, a summary of research on "Teaching Technology and Methods" (Cohen, Rose, and Trent, 1973) in which it is reported that students experience higher tension, poorer achievement, and less satisfaction in competitive as opposed to cooperative class discussions. One study demonstrates a high interaction among instructional methods, learner characteristics, and subject matters in a pattern that may be designated "learning style." Another study suggests that students with high creativity and high social needs perform best in small discussion groups. Several studies of class size were inconclusive. One noted that large group lectures combined with small group discussion were no more or less effective than conventional classes of 50 or 60 students.

The conclusions of another review are much more systematic but also much more pessimistic. In 1968 a controversial monograph was published entitled *The Teaching-Learning Paradox: A Comparative Analysis of College Teaching Methods* (Dubin and Taveggia, 1968). Its authors undertook a systematic analysis of the research on college teaching. Their analysis involved some complicated procedures, but in essence they set about to tally the results of the studies on a balance sheet. They analyzed the studies which showed no significant differences, but they also balanced those studies favoring one method with those favoring another. The end result was that one trend cancelled out another. Their conclusions are summarized in the following statements: "In the foregoing paragraphs we have reported the results of a reanalysis of the data from 91 comparative studies of college teaching technologies conducted between 1924 and 1965. These data demonstrate clearly and unequivocally that there is no measurable difference among truly distinctive teaching methods of college instruction when evaluated by student performance on final examinations" (p. 35).

Does Anything Make Any Difference?

What are we to conclude? If there seem to be no differences between teaching methods, does anything make any difference? Is one method as good as any other? Is there any reason to hold workshops on teaching or to institute faculty-development programs? Should this endless discussion of teaching methods cease? Is one teacher's opinion as good as another's in the faculty lounge discussions? Even worse, are teachers perhaps born and not made?

It is tempting to conclude, when faced with an unresolved problem, that there are no answers and that what one does makes no difference, since there is no factual basis for a decision. It may be, however, that the answer remains elusive not because there is no answer, but because the problem is more complex than was anticipated. Perhaps the answer remains obscured because the question has been put in the wrong way. Perhaps the methodology is insufficient for analyzing the complexity of the phenomena.

It was exactly that conclusion which Dubin and Taveggia drew from their studies. They were astounded to find that competent scholars would persist in repeating studies using methods which had already yielded inconclusive results. The need is not for replication, they argued, but for a new research design. Several pages of their monograph are devoted to an attack on the conventional design for undertaking research on college teaching

A New Research Design

Most research on college teaching follows a rather simple design. Teaching Method A, let us say, using the lecture method, is compared with Teaching Method B, using the discussion method. Student performance on final or standardized exams is used to measure and compare the teaching effectiveness of Teaching Method A and Teaching Method B. As even the neophyte can guess, there is something wrong with that design. Teaching is more complicated than that. There seems to be a far greater range of variables which enter into the teaching-learning process than are represented by the labels "lecture" and "discussion" method. What about the materials used? What about the objectives? What about the teaching strategy? And what about the students themselves? Will they all respond in the same way? Will the learning outcomes for one student be different from those of another? Will the student evaluate his learning by standards which might be quite different from those used by the teacher?

While Dubin and Taveggia were attacking the conventional model for doing research on college teaching, another set of scholars was engaged in a systematic analysis of the problem and the development of a new model. In a provocative but almost unnoticed journal article, Laurence and Lila Siegel set forth guidelines which are sending inquiries about the effectiveness of college teaching techniques in a new direction (Siegel and Siegel, 1967). Siegel and Siegel point out that comparisons between two or more instructional procedures can be made only if the procedures are independent and homogeneous. By independent, they mean that the procedure (lecturing, for example) must be sufficiently isolated from other factors to be considered a distinct and separate influence on the process. Lecturing must be sufficiently differentiated from providing information through a textbook to be regarded as a separate and distinct entity. If what takes place in a lecture is not sufficiently different from what takes place when a student reads a text, it is not surprising that those students in the control section (Method B—discussion), who also read the text, do as well on the final exam as those who hear lectures. Before one can make comparisons between teaching methods, one must first be sure that the methods are distinct and different.

The procedures must also be homogeneous. By this the authors mean that the method must involve only one variable. The method to be examined cannot be a general method which is in fact several methods subsumed under one label. Behind the generic label "discussion method," one must make inquiries into the nature of the verbal interaction taking place, the role and personality of the teacher, the objectives of the discussion, the nature of the inquiry process, the atmosphere of acceptance, and other factors. "Discussion method," therefore, is probably not a homogeneous procedure; it is a collection of variable, not a single variables. In comparing teaching procedures, one must isolate single variables for comparison.

Furthermore, the authors contend, final examinations are probably inadequate criterion measures. Student performance on final exams (the dependent variable in conventional research designs) can be motivated by factors which range far beyond the classroom methodology and may include such familiar influences as another student's carefully taken lecture notes or the desire to avoid the aversive stimulus of catching the devil from home. Most final exams test a narrow range of cognitive skills and probably are not adequate measures of teaching effectiveness.

What is needed, the authors argue, is a multivariate research paradigm which is sufficiently broad to include the full multiplicity and patterning of factors entering the teaching-learning configuration. Siegel and Siegel suggest that further research on college teaching ought to include an examination of independent and homogeneous variables in the following categories: learning environments, instructor variables, learner variables, and course variables. The criteria ought to include a full range of learning outcomes and achievements. The research design probably should employ the statistical techniques of factor analysis and multivariate analysis.

What structure would emerge from such a design? What results could be anticipated? One might identify certain key variables to examine and manipulate, holding constant, to the extent that it is possible, all other variables. Thus, one might vary and examine class size, attendance requirements, personal contact between teacher and student, students' previous knowledge of the subject and general academic aptitude, and teaching strategies. One teaching strategy might involve discussion using an inquiry approach, and the other might involve a lecture with a daily end-of-period test and immediate feedback of results. The criterion measures might test for ability to retain information, to solve problems, and to state a position. In other words, one would select what seem to be the most important learning environment variables, instructor variables, learner variables, and course variables and gather data on each of them.

The results of such research might reveal, for example, that students who had high academic aptitude and some previous knowledge of the subject were best at factual recall if taught in large classes with minimal contact with the instructor under a lecture teaching strategy evolving sophisticated awareness of information processing techniques. In other words, certain variables would tend to interact with other variables and would tend to suggest a pattern of instruction which will produce certain results for certain kinds of students. The underlying research question for such a model might be phrased as follows: Under what conditions do what kinds of students learn what things?

Everything Matters

Most readers of this volume probably will not engag e in systematic research on college teaching. The statistical methods are available, the theory is in hand, and the need for such studies is great. It is more likely, however, that the typical college teacher will need to attend to more immediate and pressing practical concerns. Thinking through the problems involved in doing research on college teaching is a helpful exercise, however, for defining what is at stake in the teaching-learning process. For the classroom teacher, the practical question is more likely to be phrased: What do I need to pay attention to if I am to become a more effective college teacher? What are the important variables over which I might have some control? In other words: Does anything make any difference? Contrary to the original inclination to respond by saying "Nothing matters," it seems more likely now that the answer will be, "Yes, everything matters!"

Everything matters! The class size may make a difference. The entering behavior and motivation of the students may matter. The intellectual climate and even the geography of the institution may matter. The nature and pacing of rewards for learning may matter. The way information is received, processed, and remembered may matter. The process by which inquiry is carried on may matter. The quality of interpersonal relationships between teacher and student may matter. The ways students are examined and evaluated may matter. Different students will probably respond to instruction in different ways. And the learning outcomes for some will be different from the achievements of others. Everything matters.

Furthermore, most of the variables are related in important

ways to other variables; no variable functions in simple isolation from the rest. The ecologist's model serves as a helpful way of understanding the teaching environment. Everything matters and every important factor in the process is related to all the other factors. Our tendency in thinking about teaching, as in thinking about the environment, is to reduce complex interactions to simple cause-effect relationships, to examine the properties of isolated parts of the process at the expense of developing a comprehensive overview of the total system. If we are to improve our teaching we must examine the total ecological web of the learning environment.

But it is rather overwhelming, even frightening, to know that everything matters, especially when we know that as college teachers we can't control all the variables. This is often why the most dedicated efforts to effect learning sometimes end in great frustration. But if we cannot control all the variables-and we need to come to terms with that fact—we can at least control some of—the variables. We can control to a large extent one of the key variables: teaching behavior. We can reflect deeply upon our role as teachers in the teaching-learning process and devise teaching strategies which are based on theory, are consistent, and are carried out with single-minded dedication.

Teaching Strategy: A Definition

The *Random House Dictionary of the English Language* defines strategy as "a plan, method, or series of maneuvers or stratagems for obtaining a specific goal or result." Applied to college teaching, the term strategy refers to a plan, method, or series of activities designed to achieve a particular educational goal. Sound teaching strategies are based upon clear understandings of how people learn. Different strategies involve differing conceptions of what learning is and how it takes place. The debate about such issues is not easily resolved, nor should it be. The important point, for our purposes, is that the effective college teacher must employ *some* strategy.

This is precisely the point at which most talk about college teaching falters, whether the superficial criticism of students, the aimless discussions in the faculty lounge, or the sophisticated-sounding reports of research on college teaching. Almost none of the talk about teaching gets down to examining whether or not the teacher has a strategy for achieving goals.

Most teaching at the college level has followed a convention known as the "talking tradition." For some reason it is assumed that a college professor, well prepared in a discipline, can walk into a classroom, start talking, and as day follows night, something educational will just happen. It is the thesis of this book that effective teaching doesn't just happen; to the contrary, effective teaching depends in large part upon the instructor's having a clear set of goals and a sufficient strategy for reaching those goals. My hunch is that most professors can greatly improve their teaching by persistently applying one or more of the teaching strategies described in the chapters which follow.

References

Cohen, Arthur, Clare Rose, and James W. Trent. "Teaching Technology and Methods." In Robert M.W. Travers, ed., *Second Handbook of Research on Teaching,* pp. 1023-1035. Chicago: Rand McNally Co., 1973.

Dubin, Robert, and Thomas G. Taveggia. *The Teaching-Learning Paradox: A Comparative Analysis of College Teaching Methods*. Eugene, Ore.: Center for the Advanced Study of Educational Administration, 1968.

McKeachie, Wilbert J. "Research on College Teaching: A Review." Report 6, ERIC Clearinghouse on Higher Education, Washington, 1970.

McKeachie, Wilbert J. "Research on Teaching at the College and University Level." In N.L. Gage, ed., *Handbook of Research on Teaching,* pp. 1118-1172. Chicago: Rand McNally Co., 1963.

Milton, Ohmer, *Alternatives to the Traditional*. San Francisco: Jossey-Bass, 1972.

Siegel, Laurence, and Lila C. Siegel. "A Multivariate Paradigm for Educational Research." *Psychological Bulletin,* 68 (1967): 306-326.

6

Specialized Knowledge

An important ingredient in the preparation of a teacher—important çertainly for the secondary school and college teacher and perhaps less so for the elementary school teacher¾is the knowledge he must possess of the subject or field which he is teaching. the importance of such knowledge to the teacher will be determined to some extent by the level at which he teaches. The fourth grade teacher will have considerably more need for breadth than depth, but this will not be true of a teacher in the secondary school who must have knowledge of his subject that goes well beyond that which he gains as part of his general or liberal education. Teachers in secondary schools require a first-rate and solid knowledge of the subjects they are teaching, gained in part from their liberal education, but always supplemented and continued into the graduate years of preparation and hopefully thereafter.

The prospective teacher should find in his major two things: a command in some depth of his subject and a link between his liberal education and his purely professional work. The mastery of the subject well beyond the limits that can reasonably be expected of the better students in his class is an essential minimum, for he should be expected to have reserves of learning that outreach anything that is to be directly demanded of him in his classroom. Hopefully, his major should give him the beginning ability to work in his field at a somewhat advanced level, not only teaching him to think in terms of the methods called for by the materials of the major, but, equally important, stimulating him literally to think in these terms as part of the whole pattern of his living. If there is to be a difference between the biologist and the high school teacher of biology let it not be in commitment to the worth of the discipline.

Unless the prospective teacher has a fairly sturdy grasp of the main body of knowledge—its substance and its methods—from which he is to derive subject matter for his secondary school classroom, he runs the risk of violating the very nature of the discipline itself—losing a sense of its ordering, its coherence, its sense of relationships—in attempting to work out derivations of this knowledge in organizing instruction for his students. The many odd ways in which the study of history is made subsidiary to goals other than its primary one—insights into change and the generalizations regarding the activities which induce this change and illuminate the meaning of objects and events—in certain social studies courses must serve as a firm warning of this danger.

As Morton White says: "Courses in general methodology don't teach people to be scientists. At best, the course in methodology of science gives the interested student an introduction to the spirit of science, but surely nothing which makes him a scientist. He may come to feel something of what the scientific life is like, but if he has not had serious contact with some one science and lived in it for even a short time, no amount of methodological tourism will make him a scientist or scientifically minded."

The increasing need for more adequate instruction in the subjects they are teaching is well illustrated by the situation in which many experienced secondary-school teachers of science now find themselves. The rapid changes that have occurred in a number of sciences in the last few years, changes often complex, require more intensive study on the part of teachers to insure their own comprehension of these developments. New emphases by the colleges on demonstrated proficiency in subject matter areas rather than on the accumulation of high school credits are forcing teachers to prepare their students with greater depth of understanding. A growing concern for the gifted at all grades and the development of programs of college entrance with advanced standing tend to indicate that a higher level of preparation in their subject-matter field is likely to be demanded of many teachers in science as in other fields.

But increased knowledge in their subject on the part of prospective teachers will be scarcely adequate to prepare them for the improvement of instruction now being demanded of the secondary schools unless their preparation makes provision for some form of systematic inquiry into the problems which relate to the selection and application of content in the development of appropriate instruction for secondary school grades. In short, there is increasing need for knowledge that is specialized.

A glance at the secondary-school curriculum will indicate the nature of the problem faced by the prospective teacher as he deals with the derivatives of his knowledge in the formulation of instruction at this level. In English there may be experiences to plan and organize in composition, literature, speech, developmental and remedial reading, grammar and usage, discussion, debate, dramatics, library and study skills, etc. In mathematics, in addition to the conventional offerings in algebra, plane and solid geometry, trigonometry, and sometimes calculus, there will be derivations from these in the form of courses labelled applied mathematics, general mathematics, shop mathematics, non-college mathematics, functional mathematics, and mathematics for nurses. In science beyond biology and physics and chemistry there is the possibility of courses in general science, earth science, physical science, and similar generalized approaches. In social science there will be in addition to American and world history and geography, and sometimes government, courses in civics, problems of democracy, state history, economics, sociology, local history, and many more. Derived courses will occur, naturally, in other subject-matter areas. Nearly three hundred different subjects are now listed as being taught in the nation's secondary schools. In any one school differentiation may have progressed to the point where as many as a dozen curricula are open to a student; the average is about five.

The courses which the prospective teacher has taken in his major in many cases bear small specific reference or application to this highly differentiated program at the secondary level. They offer small help, therefore, in determining objectives and appropriate content for the rather extensive array of specialized courses which are normally offered in secondary schools to meet the widely varying purposes and abilities of students.

Several other conditions militate against the prospective teacher's readiness and ability to organize instruction at the secondary-school level out of his extended knowledge of a subject. In addition to gaps in this knowledge required for with school courses quite unlike any he has himself ever taken, he has had little if any opportunity to become personally acquainted with the diverse learning problems that are customarily faced by secondary-school students, especially those with low levels of capacity and achievement, nor has he had a chance to review systematically the materials and methods conventionally employed to serve this group of students. The knowledge of a subject he is likely to possess as the result of his concentrated study is at an advanced stage, so advanced in fact that he finds difficulty in retracing even the steps he has taken in its acquirement as the basis for organizing similar forms of instruction. Even when a beginning teacher is able to retrace his steps the resultant instruction may bear little relation to the demands of his classes, especially if the latter are of the "non-college" variety.

One thing is certain: The prospective teacher cannot content himself with offering his secondary-school students a thin and truncated copy of the college courses he has taken. many things suggest the lack of wisdom of this approach, for the conditions under which he acquired the knowledge are quite dissimilar to those under which his students must acquire it. As Judson Shaplin points out, the prospective teacher in his college courses acquired his knowledge in a situation "where the conditions of voluntary studentship, a selected student body, assumed self-motivation, older and more mature students, and the intrinsic interest of the subject are all very different" from conditions to be found in the secondary school in which he is to teach. The prospective teacher's dilemma may be illustrated by his efforts to teach a poem by Browning in which he is faced with the problem either of sacrificing Browning's poem to the demands of his students or sacrificing his students to the demands of Browning's poem.

Any attempt to chop off segments of his own learning for subsequent absorption by his students may or may not succeed. On any day in which he is to teach, he will be required to decide what it is that he will have his students learn and why. This will inevitably require an understanding of the general purposes of the course he is teaching and of the subject curriculum of which it is a part. Implied in this is a broad understanding of the manner in which this curriculum reflects the persistent or current issues in the field and the extent to which his own purpose and the goals of the students relate to these in his day-to-day instruction.

As a social institution the school defines the directions of desirable behavior, i.e., the knowledge, skills, appreciations, to be expected of students, reserving pretty much to the individual teacher the task of organizing the day-to-day experiences in his subject that will lead to the realization of these expectations. This embraces setting objectives, arranging the conditions of learning, selecting usable content, employing specialized techniques, measuring the results of instruction.

In this task the teacher is forced to take into account the organization of the particular school in which he teaches, and the conditions of learning there that may tend to modify his objectives, affect his choice of materials, alter his techniques, and dictate certain ways of measuring learning.

High native ability, common sense, and zeal to succeed will help the prospective teacher in this process. Every effort should be made to attract into teaching persons who possess those attributes, but beyond this, their preparation for teaching should be such as to move them from simple, intuitive practice to a somewhat more systematic, disciplined way of analyzing, criticising, and modifying their structuring of specific lessons.

Even if it were wise to do so, the prospective teacher could not hope to rely on elementary and condensed reproductions of content from his study of the subject as a research discipline in order to provide appropriate instruction for his secondary-school students. For most teachers this knowledge is likely to be fragmentary and compartmentalized. Consider, for instance, the prospective teacher of English with a major in this subject. The chances are good that he has had no work in linguistics. He will perhaps have attended a college in which he is allowed to pass off by examination the only required course in composition, thus completing his major in belles-lettres without further work in writing.

Upon arrival at the secondary school, however, he finds that he is expected to teach, and to get results, in such areas as literature, composition, speech, remedial reading, grammar and usage, discussion, debate, dramatics, library and study skills, etc. In addition, he is likely to find that he will be required to assist in, if not direct, one or more of such extracurricular activities as the drama club, the school paper, the school annual, the high school assembly program, or other peripheral tasks which extend his responsibility as an English teacher sometimes beyond warranted limits. The principal concern of his study of literature in college is likely to have been with literary classics and literary history with a probably large emphasis on phases of culture other than our own contemporary culture. In the secondary school in which he is to teach, however, he finds that there is a probable principal concern with contemporary literature, a preference for American rather than British works, a push toward a sociological interpretation of literature, an effort to offer insight into sociology, economics, and current events through "literature." As a matter of fact, a continuing dilemma of the teacher of English at the secondary-school level is whether he is principally a teacher of reading or a teacher of literature.

Reporting in 1960 on the inadequacy of teachers without preparation in this field, the State Board of Education of North Carolina in its *Progress Reprt: Curriculum Study* said:

The selection of English teachers in the high school should be based on a sound appraisal of the college preparation of such teachers. In many instances, the teaching of high school English has fallen into the hands of out-of-field teachers and amateurs—

housewives who teach as an avocation, ministers who wish to supplement their income or to render additional community service, and others who merely like to think that they enjoy teaching English. Such conditions have been in the main deleterious to the effective preparation of students.

The way a teacher learns to use knowledge in his graduate study ought to bear some relation to his use of knowledge in training. Training in research for the purpose of teaching others how to obtain and use evidence is important to some extent for all teachers, but crucially so for the college teacher who tends to see himself first as productive scholar, whose main function is to advance the frontiers of knowledge, and secondarily as teacher. His research training is, therefore, of tremendous importance to him. It should be steadily nourished.

But the secondary-school teacher—while he cannot be a good teacher unless he continues, of course, to study and learn and reflect—does not require in depth the research training imperative for the scholar. what he does appear to need in equal measure, however, is some form of training in his graduate study, that will be just as useful to him in his role of teacher as the research training is useful to the college teacher in the latter's role as scholar.

Since the primary role of the secondary-school teacher is to teach, his training would appear to warrant systematic study which develops and extends his ability to look at the nature of the problems that confront him in organizing instruction. He will need skill in deriving content, in organizing class activities, and in employing a wide variety of methods to ensure learning by his students.

Unless the prospective teacher has training that aids him to restudy his major in the light of the demands of the discipline and those of the school; unless he learns to deal systematically with the problems of content and methods in organizing instruction; unless he is made aware of the conditions of learning that are likely to be operative in his school and in his classroom there is always the possibility of his becoming, like Gradgrind in Dickens, "a kind of cannon loaded to the muzzle with facts and prepared to blow the boys and girls clean out of the regions of childhood at one discharge."

The argument is sometimes offered that a college graduate with good preparation in his major is capable of teaching without any formal study of the problems to be met in deriving content and organizing instruction.

It is worthy of note, however, that when the Physical Sciences Study Committee set out several years ago to reorganize instruction in physics in the secondary schools it required of *experienced* teachers this formalized kind of study. The program developed by PSSC included these features:

1. institutes for teachers which emphasized both substance and *method*,
2. the development of apparatus useful in teaching certain concepts,
3. textbooks containing a body of knowledge to be taught, and
4. *a manual of methods.*

Apparently, the Committee did not feel that the kind of improvement in instruction in physics that it sought could be brought about exclusively by adding to the amount of the teacher's knowledge of physics, but that this needed to be reinforced by a formal consideration of the methods to be employed in translating this specialized knowledge into practice. If this approach is deemed necessary for a selected group of experienced teachers, how much more imperative it becomes for neophytes.

In the development of the curriculum of the modern school in the last two or three decades there have been a half dozen or so movements with which the prospective teachers needs to be acquainted: (1) the aims and objectives state, (2) survey movement, (3) the development of the unit technique, (4) system-wide curriculum revision, (5) the core curriculum, and (6) the new curricula being developed by such groups as the American Chemical Society, the Physical Science Study Committee, and the American Institute of Biological Sciences. Knowledge of these is useful to the teacher in comprehending his role as curriculum builder.

The prospective teacher needs to see the setting of objectives as the basic framework of his instruction, sensing his responsibilities in the setting of societal, institutional, and instructional goals. Skill in the setting of instructional objectives will grow out of his understanding of the aims of education, of the demands of his subject, of the precise requirements of the appropriate task, of the requirements of the learner, and of the essential conditions of learning. There is small guarantee that a prospective teacher's liberal education and specialized knowledge of his major will be sufficient to develop this skill.

Since all teaching consists of an attempt on the part of the teacher to bring about desirable changes in the behavior of students, determining what changes will be sought is a difficult task. Once general directions of behavior change are determined, there remains the task of making clear to students the nature of the desired changes; material must be chosen to bring these about; certain methods must be employed.

As Robert Bush has pointed out "the manner in which a teacher states his aim, how he communicates it to his pupils, the way in which he entices the pupil to accept the aim so that the pupil will be highly motivated to learn, how content is selected, arranged, and presented to the pupil so that intended changes in behavior may be achieved, and how the teachers assesses whether the desired changes have taken place" constitute the teaching act.

The purpose of training is to afford the prospective teacher the highest possible skill in analyzing the teaching act with a view to his developing these sub-skills: ways of looking at the setting of instructional goals; ways of determining significant concepts and knowledges; ways of identifying appropriate tasks in his subject; ways of organizing materials¾derivatives of knowledge; ways of looking at the teaching process; ways of modifying methods, ways of looking at individual and group behavior in the teaching process; ways of measuring growth.

It is on this basis that the prospective teacher has something to learn about teaching, for little in his experience in liberal education or his specialized subject matter has brought him close to these problems although mastery of his subject does represent one useful way in making these problems meaningful to him.

In summary, the beginning teacher requires an adequate mastery of his field of specialization as an academic discipline, with a firm understanding that the knowledge that guarantees his entrance to teaching is to be considered definitely minimal. This scholarship should be extended as part of his continuing training as a teacher so that increasingly what he knows about his subject or field of specialization is marked by a depth of understanding, search for new knowledge, and the appropriate use of these gains clearly reflected in his own teaching.

One learns to teach partly by being well taught. Because of this there may be some merit to the proposal that even teachers in elementary schools stand to gain from concentrated study in a major in an academic discipline. Scholarship in depth in a discipline not only contributes to personal growth, but may develop in the teacher a way of learning that has significant overtones for all of his teaching. Lack of time is the chief block to the attainment of this desirable goal, however.

While the prospective elementary school teacher may appear to have need for more breadth than depth in his preparation, the point should not be lost that current efforts to reorganize instruction in the elementary school may actually force certain teachers to have greater depth and advanced knowledge in a single field. If the FLES program—the Foreign Language program in the Elementary School, sponsored by the Modern Language Association—is ever to be successful, teachers will need much more than a minimum proficiency in languages.

It is possible that the developing use of teachers with specialized knowledge in other fields—mathematics is a prime example—may point the way to desirable new directions in organizing instruction in the early grades. The lack of success of many core programs, in high schools and especially in the junior high schools, tends to suggest that perhaps specialization will no longer continue to be so rudely sacrificed in order to give prospective teachers a spurious breadth of preparation in certain unrelated fields—fields in which they sometimes have little talent, interest, or capacity.

There is a methodology of teaching inherent in any discipline—its order, its essential relationships, its mode of conceptualizing, and the subtle ways in which its body of knowledge is increased—which any beginning teacher must understand and appreciate before there are any attempts on his part to organize derivatives of this knowledge for teaching purposes. Without this, he is incompetent to teach, for he is a threat not only to the discipline but to his own students—basing his instruction in ignorance rather than on knowledge.

Given a good liberal education and a firm footing in the subject he proposes to teach, the prospective teacher has need of both pre-service and in-service *study, observation,* and *experience* (or *practice)* in the organization and direction of learning. The purpose of pre-service courses or seminars or directed practice is to provide an admixture of direct and abstract experience to give point to generalizations and principles. Specifically such preparation should focus attention on the factors which tend to influence his understanding of the following:

1. The setting of objectives
2. The selection of content
3. The choice of methods
4. The conditons of learning
5. Analysis of the proces of teaching
6. The measurement of learning.

What is proposed is no tedious formal consideration of the minutiae of teaching techniques typical of many courses. Instead, each beginning teacher should engage in an extended inquiry, or intellectual analysis, into what a teacher actually does in seeking to bring about changes of behavior in his students. This inquiry should be under the direction of a professor who knows both the content of the field and the applicability of learning principles. He should, of course, be a competent scholar.

The purpose of the extended inquiry—a link between academic and professional education—should be the equipping of the prospective teacher with a means of asking searching questions about his specialized knowledge and of enabling him to take advantage of available research and accumulated testimony in setting objectives, selecting materials and methods, and evaluating instruction in his subject field. This inquiry is likely to be more meaningful when it is interlaced with practice which raises problems requiring this kind of intellectual analysis. The precise form this inquiry should take—a formal course, seminar, or directed practice— should be determined by the institution developing a program of teacher education in the light of the overall purposes of the preparation which it provides its students.

As Samuel Bower Sinclair quoted in another memorandum— says in *The Possibility of a Science of Education.*

If a course of training has nothing to offer but a number of shibboleths and cut-and-dried methods of doing things, based on no other authority than that someone says they have worked fairly well in the past, it will be of little benefit to the student. On the other hand, if during a professional training course the teacher gains an insight which will enable him to originate his own methods, to reconstruct his own experience at every step so as to react in the best possible way, and also at the same time gains an impulse for further development, such training will be valuable.

If somehow there is to be a discipline of education distinctive in its content, its concepts, its laws, and its methods of inquiry and practice, universities might well experiment, as some now are, in the development of a systematic, disciplined way of analyzing the teaching act, bringing to the study of the teaching process the same kind of intellectual integrity and ability that characterizes study carried on in the sciences and in the humanities. The challenge which this holds is sufficient to bring eventually into professional education an increasing number of students and professors of the highest integrity and intellectual ability. When prospective teachers are able to command instruction from such persons who have a scholarly background in the basic discipline involved and who at the same time have specialized knowledge of educational theory and practice, then there will be some hope that the pursuit of excellence in the schools will be something more than a fond hope, and that well-trained teachers will be available to help make this a reality.

7

Educational Decision-making

The character of education at any place and moment is the result of many decisions, some of them made at times and places far removed from the present point of observation. These decisions are sometimes interrelated, frequently conflicting, and commonly irrational. The decisions and the processes that go into their making are complex, significant human phenomena. Few thoughtful persons deny their appropriateness for rigorous, scholarly inquiry. And yet, few college graduates can (or even care to) confess casual, let alone systematic, exposure to the methods and products of such inquiry, unless they be candidates for certification to teach in elementary and secondary schools.

Educational decisions and decision-making may be classified at several levels of remoteness from learning processes, the end product. Like all such schemes, the following has untidy edges but nonetheless provides a brief ordering of educational subject-matter:

1. At the societal level, there are decisions regarding who shall be educated and for how long, regarding sources of authority in controlling public education, regarding what schools are for, and so on. This level of educational decision-making provides a mighty forum for the ideas of political and military leaders, philosophers, subject-matter specialists, philanthropists, and many others, each with his own special plank to sand. The decisions made at any given time and place do not necessarily reflect the best ideas, whether "best" be seen as the views of most people, the knowledge most

generally agreed upon by subject specialists, or the values of most ancient and renowned ancestry. The decisions tend to reflect, rather, interests and expectations of those individuals and groups who have been most successful in using the political structure (conceived in the broadest sense) to serve their ends. To be understood, educational decisions and decision-making at the societal level must be viewed from many vantage points: philosophical, anthropological, sociological, to name only a few.

2. At the institutional level, there are decisions regarding the formulation of specific educational objectives, selection of fields of study, placement of content, selection of materials, deployment of resources, evaluation of students and programs, and so on. This level of educational decision-making is commonly regarded as the responsibility of selected local lay leaders in conjunction with professional school administrators, supervisors, and teachers. Decision-making here, however, is significantly influenced by prominent national figures, federal and state policies on education, subject matter study groups, special interest groups, and certainly by the interplay of local politics. Imbedded kaleidoscopically in the decisions themselves are the prejudices of strong-willed board members, the expectations of powerful community figures who choose often not to seek the limelight, the desires of special pressure groups and vocal persons who have managed to "get through" to the superintendent, values prevailing at earlier epochs in educational history, the results of scientific and pseudo-scientific studies into subject-matter sequences and human learning, and the passing whims of school personnel. Many of these decisions are highly complex, demanding insights from many fields for their understanding, knowledge of appropriate data-sources, and technical skills of many kinds for their making. Such concepts, methods of inquiry, and specialized skills are not commonly found in the generally educated person.

3. At the instructional level, there are decisions regarding the selection of immediate goals, diagnosis of student learning and accomplishments, grouping of pupils, timing and pacing of learning, utilization of space and equipment, remediation, and so on. This level of decision-making embraces the recognized "home ground" of

the teacher. But it is not sacred ground. Virtually everyone who has been through one educational institution thinks he knows a good deal about what should be taught and how. Furthermore, the ground is seldom ploughed systematically or rationally. Teachers, like other people, are influenced by those who "get to them." They are gotten to by persons seen as influential in determining teacher welfare, by persons successful in using the political structure to serve their ends, and by sundry others who have children to be educated, textbooks to sell, or advice to peddle. All of these influences contribute to the values teachers bring with them into decision-making processes. One way to improve the decisions made is to educate teachers in the understandings and skills pertinent to their making; in effect, to professionalize the decision-making processes.

A basic assumption here is that the general education curricula of higher education currently make little provision for studying the educational phenomena outlined above. A prospective teacher inquires into them in only the most casual fashion in his general studies or specialized study of the field he plans to teach. The central question of this chapter, however, is whether the study of educational decisions and decision-making, their significance fully recognized, is of fundamental importance in the education of a teacher.

An Analysis of Some Specific Educational Decisions

Education as a field of study has been emerging as higher education's answer to the need to inquire into educational decisions and decision-making. But schools and sometimes departments of education have emerged simultaneously to assume higher education's custodial responsibility for teacher education. Consequently, the study of education and the education of teachers have tended to become equated or at least inadequately differentiated. As a result, a common answer to the question "What should teacher preparation include beyond knowledge of the subject taught?" is "that which is taught in schools and departments of education." This is an irresponsible, misleading answer.

A more rational answer is likely to emerge by proceeding somewhat as follows:

1. Identify significant educational decisions and decision making processes.
2. Identify the data sources appropriate to understanding the nature of these decisions and to participating intelligently in their making.
3. Identify the roles demanded of the teacher in the understanding and effecting of educational decisions.
4. Project a curriculum designed to develop in teachers the behavior deemed essential to the fulfillment of such roles.

A process of systematically comparing this projected curriculum with existing curricula of general and specialized studies should then reveal the gaps between the two. The nature of these gaps, in turn, suggests something of the kind, quality, and quantity of studies over and above preparation in a teaching field deemed essential to the teacher. These studies become the professional portion of the teacher's total education.

The purposes of this conference, time, personal interests, and the allocation of responsibilities among conferees suggest the need for and several ways of delimiting the extensive analytical process outlined above. One member of the group (Walton) has developed a substantial justification for including in the education of a teacher certain understandings pertaining to the societal level of educational decision-making. Another (Shaplin) has focused on systematic practice in the teacher education curriculum as a means of developing certain instructional skills and insights. Others have cut across the schema presented here in seeking to justify a wide range of learnings believed by them to be essential to the teacher but not included in his subject-field preparation.

Manageable boundaries for the analysis attempted here are set by selecting only a single decision-making task at both institutional and instructional levels. At the institutional level, the task is that of setting up a program of studies in a field (French or geography or perhaps physics) already chosen for the curriculum of an identifiable institution (elementary, secondary, higher) and specified students (children, adolescents, adults). At the instructional level, the task is that of selecting specific opportunities for student learning (field trip, mock trial, choral reading, etc.) for small groups (of thirty-first graders perhaps) or individuals (such as a gifted chemistry student) within the institution and field of study identified.

It is apparent that there is a dependent relationship between decisions to establish an institutional program and decisions to effect classroom learning. These decisions, in turn, are dependent upon decisions being made and continuously re-made at the societal level regarding what schools are for. To comprehend such relationships is to lay a foundation for identifying rationality and irrationality in educational decision-making. Such comprehensions may very well lay the basis, too, for more rational participation in educational decision making. To the extent that teachers participate in such decisions, this comprehension is a goal to work for in their education.

In pages that follow there is developed a way of viewing the problem of developing an institutional plan of studies and an illustration of specific procedures in elementary, secondary, and higher education. This is followed by an attempt to apply a comparable scheme of analysis, again using examples, at the instructional level. Only two of many types of decisions are identified here. It is important to remember, further, that only a sketchy treatment of what is involved in making these two types of decisions is attempted. Obviously, then, the development of competence in understanding, let alone making, educational decisions calls for rigorous study. If a teacher is called upon to participate in any way in this process, the education of that teacher becomes demanding and complex.

Developing an Institutional Plan of Studies

An institutional plan of studies emerges in answer to some usually vague and loosely stated aims of society for education: to inculcate the central values of a democracy, to teach fundamental learning skills, to prepare dentists, to develop the potentialities of the individual. Such aims call for further analysis. What are the central values of a democracy? Which are the most fundamental learning skills for what? What does a dentist need to know and be able to do? What potentialities do individuals have and which of these should be developed?

The determination of responsibility for such decisions often dictates the values that prevail in the decisions themselves. Thus, the professional body of dentists largely determines what a dentist is to learn. There is much disagreement, but it is disagreement within the family. Dental school faculties are able to move rather quickly away from general questions of aim to the delineation of rather precise behavioral objectives. With public elementary and secondary education, the problem is different unless education is under control of a dictator. Responsibilities are not clear; lines of communication are complex. School people hear a clamor of disagreeing voices. The agreements they think they hear are in turn distorted as they pass through educator's perceptual nets.

The first major decision, then, in developing an institutional plan of studies is to determine in at least a general way what the institution is for. To the extent that this can be done precisely, a rational link between societal and institutional levels of decision-making is established. Further refinement processes are intended to make clear the kinds of outcomes anticipated in the students, the attainability of ends in relation to time and other factors, the consistency and comprehensiveness of these ends, and so on. It is essential that those engaging in these processes recognize when logical in contrast to empirical operations are involved. The development of such insight is the intent of courses in curriculum theory and practice.

Development of a plan of studies calls for delineation of the fields and kinds of inquiries that will contribute to institutional ends. If quantitative inquiry is one of the ends, the importance of mathematics quickly becomes apparent. But what mathematics? Certainly, the maturity, past experiences, and expectations of the students to be enrolled in the institution effect this decision. If, however, development of individual potential is one of the ends, means are not immediately apparent. And, if the development of quantitative competence be identified as an aspect of individual potential, what level of competence would be developed by what time in the individual's life?

This second major educational decision, that of selecting appropriate means for the attainment of educational ends, sometimes involves primary consideration of learner circumstances and sometimes involves primary consideration of subject-matter rigor. It always involves both to some degree. The emphasis upon one or the other stems from educational intent which, in turn, stems from considering such factors as maturity of the learners, new advances in a field, and the critical nature of societal circumstances. Thus, if the intent is to teach ten-year-olds some understanding of how man is affected by where and when he lives, variability in time and place may be the most important subject-matter criterion to apply in selecting countries for study. There is no need for a course of studies prescribing topics "to be covered." Teachers should be left largely free to apply the old generalization, "use the problems and interests of the learners." But if the intent is to prepare a group of government agents for service in Communist-infiltrated countries, commonality of interest and problems must be assumed in focusing attention immediately upon the Communist techniques to be understood and countered.

Specialized knowledge is available to assist in asking and answering the several curriculum questions involved. There are generalizations and methods of inquiry arising out of the field to be studied. Sometimes these arbitrarily determine the principles of sequence to be applied in selecting content, the amount and kinds of student variability that can be readily encompassed within an instructional group, and the amount of learning failure or lag that can be carried over into new instructional realms. These kinds of considerations are rarely dealt with in the course sequence of a college major in any field. Similarly, there is knowledge pertaining to learner readiness, concept development, forgetting, individual differences, and much more that can be used to temper decisions that might be made inopportunely on the basis of subject-field knowledge alone. Understanding of what is involved in cognitive, psycho-motor, and affective learning also conditions the selection of topics to be included in any plan of studies.

Study of questions of sequence, scope, principles of organization, and criteria for choosing learning opportunities is not now the recognized business of any conventional field within the college curriculum. The nature of these questions and of the data-sources for dealing with them is, however, the very subject-matter of curriculum courses offered in departments of education. Curriculum as a field of study raises certain questions pertaining to the nature of knowledge in given fields, the limits of human behavior, and the best conditions for learning that can be answered only by other fields and which must be dealt with in developing institutional plans of study. These inquiries must be brought within the comprehension of those who make curriculum decisions if the decision making processes are to become, hopefully, more rational.

The foregoing pages have presented the briefest sketch of what in involved in curriculum decision-making at the institutional level. A substantial body of literature provides rationales, principles, case studies, and some empirical findings that are useful in understanding these processes. The next several pages provide brief samples of applying knowledge selected from several sources to a small part of program planning first in elementary and then in higher education.

Some Elementary-School Decisions

Individual potentiality for learning anything varies widely among children beginning school and makes itself glaringly apparent soon after instruction begins. By the intermediate and upper grade levels of the elementary school, the overall range in average achievement is as much as the grade-level classification: three years in the third grade, four in the fourth, five in the fifth, and so on. In the field of reading the overall range often is as much as twice these figures. Furthermore, only 10 to 15 per cent of the children in any of these grades is at grade level in all subjects by the middle of the year; the remainder range several years above or below the grade-level designation. It is of interest to note that teachers of these grades, when called upon to estimate, place this figure at about 50 per cent. Obviously, they have not made analyses appropriate for acquiring information pertinent to decisions they must make, as we shall see below:

One appropriate approach to dealing with these realities educationally is to reduce their presence in the educational environment. Presently, there are a number of proposals for grouping students and moving them through the school that have a certain common-sense face validity for so ordering the school environment. These include, for example, grouping pupils according to similarity in ability upon entry, or soon after entry into the school, and retaining slow-learners until they master grade-level requirements. Both proposals deny certain research findings and practical realities present in most elementary schools. Youngsters grouped on a general criterion of ability soon become very unlike each other in specific areas of attainment; non-promoted slow-learners tend to do somewhat less well than their promoted counterparts. More penetrating approaches that take into account refined analysis of individual differences in both children and subject-matter are called for. Far more pure and applied research is available for such analysis than is currently known and used by teachers, let alone by the lay citizens who so glibly propound answers. Anyone who is to participate in such decisions must assume responsibility for learning the level of sophistication in available research and tested know-how, Anyone who is to prepare persons to make such decisions must become an avid student consumer, if not producer, of such lore.

The general lack of sophistication in these realms among present practitioners is nowhere more glaring than in the selection and distribution of materials for reading. Books in a reading series, for example, are distributed on a group-per-class-per-year basis, the spread in materials thus made readily accessible to pupils and teachers being little more than a year. The vast majority of teachers utter "common-sense" generalizations about individual differences while ignoring the six- or eight-year spread in reading accomplishment in their use of materials spreading over only a small fraction of these differences. The comprehending teacher, on the other hand, in trying to act on the basis of what he knows, becomes a nuisance, his pleas for appropriate materials upsetting the systematic grade-level scheme of distribution currently in operation. In effect, to become professional that is, to come to act on the basis of best available evidence—is to upset long-standing practices perhaps appropriately established on the basis of "common sense," but stupidly and often stubbornly maintained in the face of contradictory scientific evidence. The remediation and prevention of oft-repeated circumstances such as these must become recognized as central to education for intelligent participation in these decision-making processes.

Ends and Means in Higher Education

College instructors vigorously defend their right to plan the college curriculum. Meddling such as that occurring at elementary and secondary levels of education would quickly bring the cry of violation of academic freedom from the college group. Most college instructors engage in one fashion or another in planning general as well as specialized curricula. Students in their classes are preparing for professional pursuits, advanced study in a subject field of specialization, or for no particular end. The only one of these three major student ends for which their instructors are specially prepared to contribute is that of majoring in a subject-field. It may very well be that their lack of preparation for contributing to the others is a major reason why so many able students drop out during the first year or two of college and why relatively few existing programs of general education appear in the literature of higher education as examples of what is good.

Two assumptions being put forth here, then, are: (1) that college personnel are not specially prepared for certain important educational decisions they insist on making; and (2) that certain unfortunate consequences result from their lack of special preparation. An earlier section of this chapter suggested that the institutional curricular decisions to be made and the data sources pertinent to making them have to some extent been classified. These classifications are available to college personnel. The task now is to show the pertinence of such knowledge to the decisions college faculty members insist on making.

Few college instructors would admit to being concerned only with the inculcation of information in their students. We want our students to be able to apply, to make value judgments, to think, they say. Yet, studies by university examiners indicate that the evaluative procedures used by college instructors assess only a small portion of the student behavior they claim to be concerned with developing. A large proportion of their examination questions sample only the possession of information, a low-level cognitive behavior. They leave almost untouched the measurement of depth of understanding, extrapolation, synthesis, and other higher cognitive processes. It may be that their teaching and student learning probe deeply into these other behaviors. However, are these other ends unplanned for and thus left to chance, only sporadically developed? There is some evidence, too, to suggest that students come to direct their studies toward those ends they know are to be evaluated.

A considerable body of information is developing that would be useful, first, in opening the eyes of college personnel to the importance of clarifying the kinds of learning sought, and, second, in planning a range of learning and evaluative situations appropriate to these ends: the taxonomy of educational objectives developed by Bloom and others, case studies of institutions that have sought systematically to apply rationales of general education, analyses of the relationship between given ends and means, files of test items designed to measure specific learning outcomes. The vast majority of college teachers are ignorant of this lore; some, unfortunately, possess a mind-set that is not conducive to their heeding, let alone using, it. These unfortunate circumstances are due partly to perpetuation of the myth that all one needs to know in order to participate intelligently in decisions of the educational market place is one's subject field.

The preceding examples have illustrated something of what is involved in developing institutional plans of studies. Let us now turn to some processes found at the instructional level of decision-making. Focus here is upon those day-to-day and moment-to-moment decisions one is forced to make in inducing individuals or groups of students to learn.

Instructional Decisions

The moment teacher and students come together, a dynamic interplay is set in motion. The quality of the relationship and the learning accompanying it are determined by a multiplicity of factors, many of them elusive. A central teaching task is to arrange for and guide this relationship in the hope that near-optimal learning will occur. The "stuff" of such arranging is people and things. A central thesis developed on succeeding pages is that learning is enhanced as teachers gain insight into the people and things present in the teaching-learning relationship. Such a thesis might very well be stated as an hypothesis and empirically tested.

Theories have been and are being developed to explain learning and instructional phenomena. Research undoubtedly will spring from these theories to provide greater insight into factors that condition teaching and learning and which, according to the above thesis, should be understood. The chapter by Shaplin classified some of the operations and they may be identified, analyzed, and interpreted in practice. The approach attempted here is quite humble. It is assumed simply that there are factors identifiable in and profoundly affecting the learning-teaching relationship whether or not teachers are aware of and account for them. These include teacher and learner personalities, subject-matter brought into consideration, materials, factors of time and place, and so on. Accounted or unaccounted for by teachers, these factors nonetheless affect the quality of learning. The fact that some teachers appear to be almost intuitively aware of them denies neither that they can be learned nor that even good teaching can be improved through teachers coming to understand their nature.

The most significant factor a teacher brings into teaching is *himself*. As yet, we cannot define precisely what a teacher should know about personality structure in order to control the impact of his own personality. Perhaps he should be a student of psycho-analytic inquiry; perhaps he should be required to undergo psycho-analysis. We do not know enough to decide. But he probably should know something about value acquisition and the influence of his own values on instructional decisions. Some psychologists maintain that there is a correlation between the grades teachers award their students and the congruity of their values with those of their students. Knowing this fact will not change the condition the fact describes. But greater awareness of how personal values affect teaching decisions may very well urge some caution in making decisions that so profoundly affect the welfare of students.

A teacher brings into the instructional relationship some *sense of direction.* He is more likely to buttress other learning experiences the learners are receiving if this sense of direction is influenced by understanding of institutional goals. He is more likely to be successful in moving forward if the direction set takes into account the goals brought into the instructional environment by the learners. If his sense of direction calls for more than mere student acquisition of information, it is important for him to see the relevance of questions like, "Why does Brazil produce coffee?" over question like "What are some of the crops grown in Brazil?" The assumptions here, then, are that instructional goal-setting is improvable and that insights are currently available for effecting such improvement.

Learners inevitably are present in learning. The unfortunate, sentimental excesses perpetrated in the name of "teaching the whole child" have tended to obscure the availability and relevance of a growing body of data about learners. The problem of selecting that which is of most worth to teaching from all that is available is a formidable one, but the teacher must select. The study at the college level by Sturgis suggests that for teachers of physics even to possess much personal information about their students is to enhance the achievement of these students on tests of physics.

Knowledge of learners is important to teachers in making decisions that involve *materials.* Sensitive awareness of what a child is trying to do, reflected against understanding of child development in general, guides the teacher to select rough, absorbent paper and viscous paint when he judges it important for the child to control his pictorial representation. The study of value acquisition guides teachers, too, in the identification and analysis of cultural-loading in instructional materials. The content presented may be forthright, inviting analysis, while the questions and study guides which follow may be subtly loaded to promote partiality under the guise of academic objectivity. Again, these conditions will prevail whether or not teachers understand them. It is assumed simply that teachers must come to understand them if they are to rise above servitude to a complex of otherwise mystifying circumstances in the instructional environment. If teachers come to understand the people and things involved in the decisions they must make, there is some likelihood that they will achieve greater mastery over their pedagogic destinies.

It is difficult to conceive of a teacher proceeding without some view of what *learning* is, however primitive, naive, vague and non-functional his view might be. Learners always go through some process in learning, however fumbling, inconsistent, and unproductive this process might be. Psychologists disagree on learning theories and are reluctant to specify the significance of any given theory for teaching. Nonetheless, they are prepared to suggest at least minimal circumstances for the acquisition of certain human behaviors. Theory and research have provided useful insights into concept development, the refinement of motor skills, and the modification of attitudes. After defining the type of goal sought, the teacher takes a step toward rational provision for its attainment when he relates learning circumstances relevant to concept development to cognitive goals, circumstances relevant to value formation to affective goals, and so on. If the learner behaviors sought have already been identified at the institutional level, as recommended in a preceding section of this chapter, the teacher has available to him a thread around which to organize specific learning activities. He then applies specialized, technical competence in probing more deeply into particular aspects of the behavior to determine the next most appropriate instructional decisions. Is this child's failure to move forward in reading the result of visual deficiency or failure to develop word-attack skills? What does this student's response say about his present level of insight into economic principles and his readiness for more complex analyses?

The teacher's view and understanding of *subjec-matter* carried with him into teaching is a prime determinant of what confronts the student. Few students will be exposed to the differential approach to grammar urged by linguistic scientists until their teachers, most of whom use the referential approach, are educated in it. Means for reaching thousands of teachers, future teachers, and teachers of teachers in providing them with more appropriate specialized knowledge to be used professionally is one of the key problems recognized by various national subject-matter committees. (See Chapter 3.) The various concepts, generalizations and methods of inquiry of given fields, like the behaviors specified as appropriate for the learners, become threads to guide the teacher in his day-to-day selection of specific topics and problems for study.

To suggest that knowledgeable blending of data about learners, subject matter, and learning processes bears a one-to-one relationship to the quality of the learning product is to be naive. Nonetheless, if the initial selection of the learning opportunity is based on compatibility of the data drawn from these components of the teaching-learning relationship, the chance of productivity in learning is enhanced. Even the most carefully planned teaching is rudely buffeted by conflicting currents arising in the outside environment and within the classroom. From society come directives to shake and confuse even the sturdiest of professionals: raise standards, develop creativity, prepare for a scientific age, keep away from controversial issues. From the institution come pressures to cover, to conform to administrative directives, to keep away from content prescribed for the next grade. Teaching disadvantaged by ignoring those factors that can be studied and planned for is likely to prove too fragile to withstand exigencies such as these that most assuredly will arise along the way.

In Conclusion

This chapter has outlined a relatively small portion of learnings here deemed essential for anyone who is to participate intelligently in educational decisions, some close to and others remote from institutionalized learning processes. Only one group of these decisions—those dealt with under the "instructional" rubric—can be properly classified as teaching. However, teachers are called upon to participate in and to be intelligent students of societal and institutional decision-making.

The preceding pages focused on educational decisions generally classified as curricular since they are of central importance to teachers. The factors involved in these decisions may be identified and studied systematically within the disciplines of which they are a part; they may be pulled together with a wide assortment of other factors pertaining to educational decisions and studied with that class of subject matter encompassed by the field "education"; or they may be studied as functionally related to what teachers do in a professional curriculum necessarily limited by special circumstances of time and place. When these factors are examined according to this third set of conditions, they constitute what a teacher should learn "beyond knowledge of the subject he teaches."

Other chapters have suggested how these learnings should be organized in the teacher education program. For the present and perhaps for the future, it is desirable that institutions of higher learning approach this problem in many ways, just as they now exercise considerable autonomy in the conduct of other professional curricula. The writer's experiences over the past ten years in developing the Agnes Scott College, Emory University, and University of Chicago teacher-education programs have conditioned his present viewpoint summarized below:

1. Teaching a given subject places certain demands upon that subject that are not usually confronted in general or specialized collegiate inquiry into it. Each field should be subjected to analyses to determine, for example, how its nature (assumptions concerning knowledge, principles of organization, methods of inquiry, and so on) conditions or disciplines the decisions teachers must make. A portion of the teacher education curriculum—preferably jointly planned and conducted by specialists in the field, professors of education, and "master" teachers at the level for which the novices are being prepared—should involve prospective teachers in such

analyses. Until we learn more about how to correlate many learnings in a single stream of curricular activity, it is recommended that such inquiry be conducted in its own right, enriching and supplementing any similar inquiry going on simultaneously in the "practice" part of the teacher education curriculum.

2. Teaching demands team planning for many kinds of institutional endeavor. This planning is now characterized by much fumbling search for productive questions to deal with in resolving vexing curricular issues. Too frequently, the issues are disposed of but not resolved by expediency, by administrative fiat, by recognizing the loudest and most persistent voice, or by the onset of fatigue. We have more know-how in this area of decision-making than we used to. Recommended, therefore, is a seminar directed to consideration of these issues placed at the same priority level as the studies of school role proposed earlier by Walton in Chapter 6. Such a seminar, for the present at least, should exist in its own right, buttressed but not supplanted by any parallel inquiry accompanying practice or into the subject-fields as proposed in Point 1.

3. Careful guided practice should provide the test in action of learning recommended above, together with the uncovering of and inquiry into whatever relevant new issues arise out of teaching itself.

The above suggestions, for the most part, already are incorporated in the Master of Arts in Teaching programs of the University of Chicago and at other universities.

Preceding pages suggest several summarizing statements:

1. A number of complex decisions must be made in planning the programs of studies of educational institutions.

2. Curriculum inquiry has resulted in certain classifications of these decisions and data-sources to consult in making them.

3. In practice at elementary, secondary, and higher levels of education, pressure of circumstances together with the relatively primitive development of the data-source fields have forced what might be called a common-sense approach to curriculum decision-

making. This common-sense or, better, practical "know-how" approach should and undoubtedly will continue. To assume that the day for abandoning it is come would be the height of folly and of ignorance of human behavior. Nonetheless, the persistence of decisions so made in the face of the rapid advance of pertinent knowledge represents a frightening cultural lag that a nation with burgeoning educational demands can ill afford.

4. Filling in the pertinent data-sources is a demanding task for many fields of inquiry and must be approached through the discipline of each of the several fields. Classificatory schemes for identifying and relating the educational decisions and their data-source fields is, however, the business of education as a field of study.

5. Not all that is the business of education as a field of study is of central importance to the teacher. The need to prepare large numbers of teachers as quickly as possible creates a certain urgency for careful selection, just as pressure for numbers and a glut of potential learnings from which to choose create similar urgency in planning curricula for other professions. This chapter has attempted to justify and to illustrate the usefulness of certain learnings in the realm of curriculum and instruction. Needed are more carefully conceived theoretical constructs than we now have designed to guide inquiry, research, and practice in curriculum development. A next step in experimentation is the educational testing of logically organized subject matter with learners of all ages and abilities. As the results of such experimentation become available, we will be able to deal systematically and scientifically with the field of curriculum in seeking to prepare teachers.

8

Learning to Lead

In this chapter we focus on reacher leadership as it is practiced at one elementary school in Gorham, Maine. The Narragansett School, a K-3 elementary school, has been engaged in an ongoing process of reflection and reconstruction for almost five years. Much of its work has been documented previously. Narranganset's restructuring effort is distinguished by its focus on "what children know and how they know it"and by its expectation that teachers who conduct systematic and collaborative inquiry in their classrooms will invent new ways to organize instruction and to assess performance. The school makes an explicit connection between the intellectual engagement of teachers and the engagement of the students they teach. It assumes that when teachers take leadership in matters of instruction and school organization, authentic change happens. Serving over 400 children, Narragansett defines itself as:

> a center of inquiry....serious in purpose, joyous in accomplishment.....where teachers are more than technicians. They are those who instruct, engage in thoughtful reflection, seek out research and conduct their own, and regularly meet with colleagues.

The emergence of teacher leadership at Narragansett School has been both gradual and dramatic. Beginning with formalized roles for team leaders, teacher leadership has come to assume a variety of forms. Some teachers took leadership in developing new instructional arrangements, such as multigraded, team-taught classes. Others designed new assessment tools, concentrated on expanding their teaching strategies, or led staff development seminars for their colleagues in the school. A teacher/scholar position was created a rotating position in which a teacher on leave from the classroom for a year conducts systematic investigations into learning and teaching on behalf of the whole school faculty.

In the pages that follow, the development of teacher leadership at Narragansett School is explored through portraits of four teacher leaders. The purpose of this chapter is to show how teacher leadership emerges, what teacher leaders do, and how teacher leaders think about themselves as they take on new roles. Data for the study were collected through written responses to questions, interviews, observation, and analysis of documents.

PORTRAITS OF PRACTICE

Mary Jo O'Connor: Leadership from Experience

Mary Jo O'Connor is a respected member of the Narragansett School community. She has established herself as an accomplished classroom teacher, a conscientious colleague, and a committed parent. There is nothing flashy about Mary Jo. She goes about her business in a way that neither calls attention to herself nor seeks recognition and approval for her achievements. She is a "teacher's teacher," grounded in classroom practice and comfortable with the daily routine of schools and teaching. A graduate of a small New England college, Mary Jo majored in elementary education before entering teaching; she had accompanied her husband to Japan and took time out to raise her family before she committed herself to a full-time teaching career. She has been at Narragansett School for seven years.

In the fall of 1990, Mary Jo assumed the newly created position of teacher/scholar at Narragansett. She viewed the position as "multi-dimensional in design .... allowing me to be released from the classroom for a year to work intensely on areas identified by myself and other staff." The move from classroom teacher to teacher/scholar was neither abrupt nor dramatic for Mary Jo. She saw her new role as a logical extension of her development over the past few years:

> As a teacher working in a school which not only encouraged—but celebrated reflective practice, I had been making changes in my teaching in small incremental steps over the last four years. Each time I would make changes, I found myself self-correcting along the way, making adjustments based on my own tacit understanding, as well as on current research.

Two years previously, Mary Jo had decided to stay with her first-grade class for another year. Curious about the next step for the children she taught and intrigued by the implications for student learning if expectations and routines were not interrupted, she approached her principal with her plan. The next year, she moved to second grade along with her class. What followed set the stage for Mary Jo's transition to teacher/scholar.

> The next year was a tremendous learning experience not only for me, but for my students as well. During that year I was sure enough with my students' ability levels that I implemented a new approach to reading instruction. Using qualitative research methods I was learning in a graduate course at the university, I was able to get some answers about the ways children liked to be taught reading. The research left many avenues open for further exploration.

As a classroom teacher, Mary Jo had come to incorporate research and inquiry into her practice. When the teacher/scholar position was announced, Mary Jo applied without hesitation. She saw herself as ready for the challenge of the job. She viewed the year away from classroom teaching as an opportunity to explore the issues of early literacy acquisition that had begun to interest her. After being a leader in her classroom, Mary Jo was ready to become a leader in a larger arena:

> I had seen myself as a leader in my own classroom, charting curriculum, making a difference; I now felt ready to assume a new

leadership role, out of the classroom, but still viably connected to teachers in a very unique but important way.

In her role as teacher/scholar, Mary Jo is involved in a variety of activities—some intended and others improvised along the way. She has focused her scholarly inquiry on issues of literacy acquisition in the primary grades. Melding nicely with this work has been an opportunity to design a curriculum notebook for language arts. The notebook reflects the school faculty's current understandings about how children learn to read and write. Also connected to this line of investigation is ongoing work with two other teachers in the area of alternative assessment. As part of this collaborative effort, Mary Jo is helping to articulate an expanded notion of assessment, one that showcases student skills and achievements beyond paper and pencil tests. A model for portfolio-based assessment is being developed and tested.

As Mary Jo's role has developed, she has stimulated teacher dialogues and collaboration. She has had the time and the opportunity to share ideas about teaching and learning with her teaching colleagues. She has become a "sounding board" for teachers, who often drop in to chat with her in the course of the school day. "I don't have all the answers for sure, but I do share a common understanding of children and the dailiness of teaching." As a result of these informal interactions, teachers have invited Mary Jo into their classrooms to do demonstration lessons, to observe, and to work with small groups of students. "I have become an available and willing partner, working with them and for them."

Mary Jo also works closely with a group of teacher assistants. The teacher assistants at Narragansett play an important role in the school's restructuring effort. They perform duties that free teachers from clerical responsibilities and assist them in classroom instruction. Teacher assistants not only collect milk money and run off dittos; they also teach small groups of students, provide tutorial assistance, and collect data about student learning for teachers. As teacher/scholar, Mary Jo serves as the liaison between the assistants and the whole school program. She helps make the connection between what the assistants do and the school's commitment to ongoing inquiry. Mary Jo and the assistants meet once a month in a formal setting where they discuss diverse educational topics, ranging from whole language practices to classroom management. She also meets with the assistants on an informal basis—individually and in small groups.

This simple accounting of Mary Jo's worklife provides some insight into the depth and breadth of her role as teacher/scholar. She notes, "This job has afforded me the opportunity to transcend much of the educational rhetoric and to more closely understand that good education is basic and grounded in common sense." The job has taught her other things as well. As a teacher/scholar, Mary Jo has had the chance to view teaching from a new perspective, as someone looking in. She has discovered, or rather rediscovered, that teaching is complex, intellectual, and challenging work.

> In my early years of survival teaching, I had almost internalized that teaching was a static entity—very few changes in curriculum were made from year to year; my approach remained the same. As I began to have meaty conversations with other teachers, I began to examine my own practices more closely. In this role, I've seen close-up the variety and intricacy of teaching. I know now and appreciate that teaching is complex and certainly not static.

She has incorporated the importance of teaching as learning into her view of teaching. She locates teacher development at the center of school life: "For teachers to be truly effective, they must first see themselves as learners. Teachers don't have all the answers but need to commit themselves to the spirit of reflective practice and ongoing inquiry." Mary Jo not only views teachers as learners; she sees them as leaders as well and makes explicit the connection between learning and leading. "I see teachers as leaders in their classrooms making change in curriculum to meet the needs of their students, inventing assessment pieces, and investigating current theories."

Mary Jo has also come to see teachers as the source and sustenance of meaningful change. Change cannot, to her mind, be mandate from above. It must percolate from below:

Teachers are at certain stages in their own development. When ready, teachers will accept that change is needed, begin to understand it, then eventually become the agents of change themselves. Change cannot be hurried or forced on people if so it will be short-lived.

Finally, Mary Jo has recognized her own abilities and promise. Her sense of efficacy, already strong in her classroom, has expanded to include the whole school—and beyond.

Perhaps what I have learned most is to trust and believe in myself. I am making the most of an exciting opportunity in the position of teacher/scholar. I know that I can organize my time so that I am productive and effective. I'm learning to trust my instincts more, continue to think about things differently, and in this position, build a model for schools which underscores my belief that teachers are the keys to fundamental, lasting school improvement.

Sally Laughlin: Leadership from Knowledge

Sally Laughlin is a relative newcomer to Narragansett and to teaching. Graduated five years ago from a select liberal arts college where she was an honors major in economics and government, she entered the teaching profession through the back door

By the time that I realized that working directly with people and examining how they think was the most energizing type of work for me, I was already a graduate with no teaching classes. When I did obtain enough credits to become certified, I still had no clue as to what teaching was about.

When she was first interviewed for a job are Narragansett School, Sally impressed the principal as someone "who would be outstanding or a complete disaster nothing in between." The principal took a risk and hired Sally, who quickly emerged as a different kind of teacher leader. Her leadership role at Narragansett is neither prescribed nor formalized. She has earned leadership by dint of her intelligence, her driving curiosity, her search for new knowledge, and her power as a classroom teacher.

I focus on children as thinkers. My teaching revolves around the idea that everyone can become smarter if they reflect on their own thinking. I want my students to be advocates for their own learning, to know how they learn best and to examine critically the work they are asked to do.

Sally's growth as a teacher mirrors her growth as a leader. As she moved away from textbooks as the basis for instruction and from traditional tests as the basis for assessment, Sally staked out new territory both for the children she taught and for the colleagues with whom she worked.

When I began to teach, I had a vague notion that teachers took a few years to develop their files and then just kept playing that same old song. In my ignorance, I was quite sure I had an easy job. Good fortune brought me to an environment where people were expected to do their best. I began to realize that each day was mine it's my movie. I'm the writer, director, and star, if I want to be. I am not, as I originally thought, a bit part in someone else's production.

What Sally decided to do with her newly discovered power was to systematically redefine teaching, learning, and assessment as they occurred in her classroom.

She began, characteristically, by seeking new knowledge. She read voraciously and became intrigued by the notions of intelligence proposed by Howard Gardner and the organization of thinking developed by Robert Sternberg. The recent research in cognitive sciences was particularly engaging for her; she acquired an appreciation for work in the area of metacognition.

I have always been fascinated with the mind and its infinite possibilities. I often imagined my students' minds to be full of thoughts that I never get to witness or appreciate. Right now, I'm having a great time experimenting with some very basic variables and I'll bet that years from now I will continue to wonder how the brain works and how to get people to become advocates for their own learning.

Only after spending considerable time expanding her knowledge base did Sally begin to put her new ideas into practice. Her classroom began to take a different turn. She developed heterogeneous reading practices, initiated independent projects with her children, established learning stations in the content areas. She struggled to connect content to process, always raising questions with her students about what they knew and how they knew it. She focused on strategies for learning and on making explicit the purpose of every task and assignment. Her first visible project outside her own classroom was a team-teaching arrangement with a special education teacher. Every afternoon Sally and her special education colleague combined their classes to teach science to a multigraded and diverse group of youngsters. They developed a "science laboratory" where students worked collaboratively on real-life tasks, such as setting up a bird museum. The students and their teachers also formed a tee-shirt design and manufacturing business, where students received fees for their designs.

Sally's emergence as a teacher leader originated with her willingness to think out loud and in public about the knowledge she was acquiring about learning and thinking. She became codirector of the school's staff development program and helped redirect the program from one driven by workshop presentations by experts to one based on systematic, collegial inquiry. She became an informal, and then formal, spokesperson for the school in the area of alternative assessment of student learning. She was one of four teachers who developed a slide presentation on assessment for a national conference. She took leadership in developing new assessment tools for her classes, in sharing them with her colleagues, and in developing a K-8 portfolio system for the entire district.

Sally's leadership in the school in areas of teaching, learning, and assessment is clearly acknowledged and valued by her colleagues. Having no title other than classroom teacher, she has exercised considerable influence on the school and the district. Sally's appraisal of her own leadership is characteristically precise and could as easily be applied to her stance as a teacher.

Leadership is informal, unofficial, offers unobtrusive support, and helps identify opportunities. True leadership enables others to be more powerful; a successful leader assists others to identify their own leadership potential.

For Sally, knowledge is power. And power is to be shared.

I believe that everyone is doing the best they can and that everyone can become an able thinker. My role is not to decide for others what they should do; my role is to guide them so they can be as happy with their decisions as I am with mine.

Wally Ziko: Leading from vision

Wally Ziko has been reinventing himself as a teacher for over fifteen years. He has been teaching in Gorham at the Shaw Junior High School since 1977. He began as an industrial arts teacher, but left that program to develop a technology laboratory for junior high students. Wally has been a dreamer and an entrepreneur all his life. To casual acquaintances he may appear to be preoccupied and he usually is. His personality type has not always been understood or valued in schools.

I was always a misfit in school. I knew that I was different and that I did't fit into the system. As I look back on it, I realize that the system at that time was not tolerant of a wide range of abilities and differences. I really didn't do well until I got to college when people started leaving me alone. The other reason that contributed to my eventual success was that following high school, I spent two years in the seminary; eventually when I did go college, I was more mature. Also, I went to a Jesuit university that was intolerant of intellectual laziness but did tolerate my being an eccentric.

In the six years that he has been operating the technology laboratory in Gorham, Wally has received four grants from the state department of education and three grants from Apple Computer. In addition, he has taught university courses, is a published author, and has been highlighted in trade publications for his innovative use of technology in education. Wally is not a formal member of the Narragansett staff, yet is considered a major player in the school's restructuring efforts. His association with Narragansett began three years ago when the former superintendent saw the connection between restructuring and technology.

Connie Goldman (former superintendent) saw that schools had very little new power or tools to get things done in a system. It was important to use the core of what existed and build on that. She saw that the paraprofessional strand for teachers could be used to free teachers to use their energy to identify needs and make changes. She also appreciated that the computerized portfolio project could drive meaningful change in curriculum and assessment. So, as superintendent with an understanding of the whole system, she literally introduced the right hand to the left hand.

When the Narragansett staff began collaborating with Wally, they were relieved to find him respectful of their own accomplishments and easily accessible as a colleague. An informal working relationship was initiated, leading ultimately to Wally's role as a teacher leader at the school.

The Narragansett staff appreciated Wally's ability to stretch their imagination about what technology could make possible in a school; Wally appreciated the groundwork that the Narragansett staff had done in curriculum and assessment. A major key in sustaining this unique relationship was the availability of time for both Wally and the school staff. The district provided a full-time assistant to Wally, so he could leave the junior high school and work regularly at Narragansett. The teacher assistant program, already in place at Narragansett, was used to provide released time for teachers during the regular school day. What emerged from this frequent interaction between practicing experts in technology and instruction was a project to develop a computerized portfolio for each Gorham elementary student.

The computerized portfolio project was the result of Wally's vision and his ability and willingness to involve others in translating his vision into practice. The vision is quite compelling. It requires that we imagine a new scenario for parent-teacher conferences. The teacher sits in front of a computer and tums it on rather than opening a rank card. With the computer on, the parents see actual artifacts that their child has produced and that were saved via a computer scanner. At the same time, the parents can hear their child read passages of his or her own work or the work of others. This is made possible by a voice recorder that has been connected to the computer. Finally, parents see a project that their child has done and they listen to the child's report of his or her findings. This part of the data has been saved on the computer by a special hook-up and a video camera. Parents, children, and teachers alike are able to see and hear authentic tasks and assess progress over a period of time. In Wally's vision, this collection of data would be available on a yearly basis and could be compiled over a child's entire public school experience. When students graduate from high school, each would have a diploma in one hand and a compact disc portfolio of who he or she is as a learner in the other hand. They could then offer this to trade schools, colleges, or businesses as an accurate representation of what they are capable of doing.

Wally and the teachers at Narragansett are in the process of developing the form and content of the portfolio project. They have developed a sample video-disc and are seeking funding to support the project. Wally's role as a teacher leader is still emerging. He continues to reinvent what he is doing and how he does it.

What do I do? At any one given minute I might be an educational technology curriculum developer and coordinator, an in-service provider, a computer technician, a computer network manager, a computer software trainer, an alternative assessment project coordinator and promoter, a graphic artist and publisher, an educational philosopher and advisor, a writer or a grant writer and administrator. But in the end, I teach. I have a regular classroom position with all its responsibilities, possibilities, and problems.

It is important to note that although Wally is a full-time teacher at the junior high school he has managed to become a teacher leader in another school within the district.

In his role as a teacher leader, Wally has developed powerful insights about schools, the process of change, and the possibilities of leadership.

I work in a profession that cannot escape its nature. Traditional schools remain frantically preoccupied with authority. Schools attempting reform alternate frantically between a preoccupation with authority and a preoccupation with leadership.

He puts his faith in teachers as the legitimate agents of change and as leaders in instruction.

It is clear to me that in times of change in institutions like schools it is better that teachers change faster than schools: the reverse is painful for both the schools and teachers, but much more for the teachers.

And he puts faith in himself as a teacher and as a leader of teachers. "After working in schools for fifteen years, the most wonderful feeling follows on the realization you are middle-aged and were born to reach."

Carolyn Mcgoldrick: Leadership from Respect for Children

Carolyn McGoldrick has been in and out of public school teaching for over twenty years. She began as a fifth-grade teacher in Massachusetts in 1970. After teaching there for three years, she married and relocated in Maine where she taught a second grade in Gorham for five years before leaving to stay home with her children. While out of the classroom, Carolyn kept in touch with former colleagues and what was going on in schools. Through her involvement as a parent, reading to her own children, she developed an affection for children's literature and its power in reaching the whole child. She developed her knowledge and expertise and became a source for recommending book titles to her teacher friends who wanted to address specific issues in their classrooms.

Her return to public schools was mediated by these experiences. At a time when the Narragansett library was without a librarian or an adequate collection of books, Carolyn was hired as a consultant. She developed thematic monthly storytime packets and trained and supported parent volunteers charged with carrying out the program. The packets were designed to address a specific affective need. The program was a success with children, teachers, and parents alike. It had the added benefit of bringing Carolyn back into the system that she had left six years before. This was the first time the school had hired a part-time teacher as a consultant to satisfy a building need. Free of classroom responsibilities, Carolyn explored and implemented aspects of education that, while important, were often overlooked as part of the official curriculum.

When a librarian was finally hired, Carolyn was no longer needed in the role she had created, but she had become a valuable resource to the school. Opportunities surfaced which kept Carolyn involved in the school in new ways. The Gorham school system had committed itself to a new elementary social studies approach that focused on self-understanding and on relationships with others; no one had been designated to design the curriculum. At the same time that the social studies curriculum was being developed, Narragansett School was awarded a state grant for restructuring. The grant application emphasized children's self-awareness and the connections between self-esteem and children's ability to learn about learning. Carolyn immediately saw the link between the new social studies curriculum and Narragansett's restructuring proposal. With the support of the school's principal and teachers, she assumed a new position. Carolyn was hired to write lessons about self-awareness and self-esteem and to help teachers implement them in their classrooms. Since this was a three-year project, Carolyn began her work in the seven classrooms of first graders. Her plan was to move with the children as they progressed to second and third grades. Carolyn spends most of her time in classrooms teaching children. The regular teachers use this time to observe the lessons being taught and to watch their students as learners. Because of Carolyn's knowledge, her belief in the importance of self-esteem, and her skill in working with children, she quickly won the respect of her colleagues.

As they watched Carolyn McGoldrick work with children, teachers often commented on the instant rapport she established with them and her ability to engage them intellectually and affectively. From Carolyn's point of view, this ability stems from her willingness to listen carefully to what children have to say. She sees her classes as being alive with mutual respect productivity.

I have always respected children. I have never adjusted my vocabulary or my faith in their ability because they are young. I treat children the way I want to be treated. As a teacher, I am motivated to reach the whole child. To me education goes deeper than teaching subject-matter—it's working with human beings. I never feel as though I am doing my job unless I pay attention to the whole child.

While Carolyn has always held the belief that to be effective one must pay attention to the whole child, she feels that the structure of schools was not set up to encourage that.

When I first started teaching, I could have been on Mars for all the sense it made. I used to think of myself as a person who was responsible for filling empty holes. It was only intuitive that I attended to the whole child. I wasn't taught that was an important aspect of teaching. The focus was on the program and trying to get each child to fit the program. That process was fraught with frustration on everyone's part.

In her new role, Carolyn is in a position to help teachers change fundamentally the ways that the school structures learning. After three years, she has been instrumental in influencing how children view themselves and how teachers view the learning process. Through her visible and direct work with children, Carolyn has modelled attitudes and behavior that other teachers at Narragansett not only value but also apply to their own teaching. She has taught in every classroom in the school and is welcomed as a colleague, friend, and teacher of teachers.

Carolyn's insights about teacher leadership have developed along with her role. She views reflective practice as a key element.

I have come to understand the importance of reflective practice. Today whenever I am in doubt, I stop and ask myself if what I'm doing makes sense. If not, I make changes until it does make sense. Oftentimes this calls for bravery. We need to develop the courage to speak out against practices that don't make sense for people. We need to question ourselves and we need to encourage our students to do the same.

Carolyn recognizes the strong impact of demonstration and modeling. She has said that when thinking of leadership, a quotation from Emerson comes closest to her feelings: "They're so busy watching you, they can't hear what you say." She honors the sheer power of a good example and she leads by being one.

Learning to Lead: Lessons from the Field

The four accounts of teacher leadership presented here offer insights into the diversity, complexity, and power of new roles as they are developing at Narragansett School. The experiences and reflection of Mary Jo, Sally, Wally, and Carolyn have deeper meaning and value to the extent that they provide a framework for describing and promoting teacher leadership beyond the parameters of one school in Maine. A critical reading of the four portraits leads to some important understandings about teacher leaders.

There are multiple and diverse paths to teacher leadership. Each teacher leader studied followed a unique trajectory toward the role. Each led from a particular strength; each strength has developed over time and was rooted in classroom teaching, the daily life of the school, and the particular dispositions and concerns of the individual. Mary Jo's strength was her experience and reputation as a veteran teacher; Sally led from the power of her knowledge and intelligence; Wally from the force of his vision and invention; and Carolyn from the firmness of her commitment to children.

Teacher-leader roles are improvised, informal, and serendipitous. None of the teacher leaders held a formal leadership role at the school. Narragansett had previously developed a Lead Teacher position at each grade level; yet none of the four leaders held these positions. Rather, their leadership was forged through a coming together of building-level needs and their own particular talents, interests, and readiness levels. Mary Jo's graduate course work promoted her interest in research; Sally's interest in cognitive studies emerged just as the school's interest in learning how children learn was becoming clarified; Wally's knowledge of technology answered the school staff's need for adequate tools for assessment;

and Carolyn's status as volunteer parent and substitute librarian filled a void at the school and ultimately led to the creation of a new position. This is not to say that all teacher leadership is informal and emergent, but rather to emphasize the worthiness of improvisation and invention in the development of teacher-leader roles.

A general ethos in the school, as well as supportive conditions in the district, nurture and sustain teacher leaders. Each of the teacher leaders made reference to both the ethos that had been established at Narragansett School and to the opportunities for leadership that the principal provided. For Mary Jo, the school "celebrated" reflective practice. Sally saw Narragansett as a place where people "were expected to do their best." Wally found in the school a haven for his ideas which had not been embraced by his own school's staff. And Carolyn discovered a match between her deeply held convictions about children and the espoused beliefs and ongoing practices of the school. The role of the principal is key here, both as the clear voice of school. The role of the principal is key here, both as the clear voice of the mission of the school and as the guardian of the vision the staff had developed. As Sally said: "What I said about my own leadership, I learned from watching the principal. That's where it starts."

The teacher leaders also garnered support from the school district, especially from the superintendent. As Wally indicated, the superintendent had "an understanding of the whole system." She linked people to each other and provided the time and the opportunity for meaningful interactions to occur. She supported the creation of the teacher/scholar position, hired paraprofessionals to free teachers from clerical tasks, and promoted dialogue and reflection whenever and wherever possible. When she left the superintendency, she was followed by a man who shared her commitment to teacher leadership and the spirit of inquiry. He continued the policies and practices that she had initiated.

Teaching and leadership are complementary functions; they are woven of the same cloth. All four of the teacher leaders defined themselves primarily as teachers. becoming teachers of adults as well as of children seemed to them a logical extension of their roles. In fact, they all spoke of themselves as having gone through common stages of development. They spoke of themselves as first being novice teachers, ill at ease in the profession and uncertain about their own abilities to adapt. They commented on the growing awareness of the limits and routnization that public schools placed on their colleagues and on themselves, and they identified a moment in time when they began to see teaching in a different light, as having the potential for intellectual work and for professional and personal growth. These transitions from teaching as routine to teaching as active engagement to teaching as leading were both gradual and ongoing.

As teacher leaders, the four carved niches for themselves in a school that was itself in the process of reflection and self-renewal. They became more firm in their commitments as teachers as they became more comfortable in their roles as leaders. They recognized that teachers are key to school improvement and the restructuring of education. They strengthened their faith in themselves and in their colleagues. And they discovered, in their new leadership roles, that, as Wally said, they were "born to teach."

9

A Schema for Teacher Education

Teaching is becoming and eventually will become a distinct profession.

About whom do we speak when we refer to the profession of teaching? Education is a field, the same as, for example, health is a field. The teacher is the basic practitioner in the field of education. He is the person who is presumably qualified both by capacity and preparation to teach in a school and who assumes full responsibility for his action as a teacher. In distinguishing between the profession of teaching and the field of education, I am trying to make clear the fact that all education neither takes place in the school nor is the result of teaching. We often become confused here. Not all of the education that takes place *within* the school is the direct result of teaching. Just as one of the wise teachers in a medical school counseled his students that they should remember that a majority of their patients would get well without or in spite of the treatment that the doctor gives them, we, too, should realize that a pupil may learn what is intended, or something different, without the aid of the teacher or in spite of his efforts to be helpful. Indeed, much of what is learned by any person is learned informally, unconsciously, through imitation, and through an elaborate system of rewards and punishments that accompany everyday living. Many of the cultural imperatives, that is, what society deems essential for youth to learn, have already been imparted by the time a person arrives at kindergarten or first grade. Our concern, then, in the preparation of teachers, is with that part of education that is the responsibility and under the jurisdiction of the school, and especially with that for which a full-time career teacher is responsible in a conscious, formal way in the classroom.

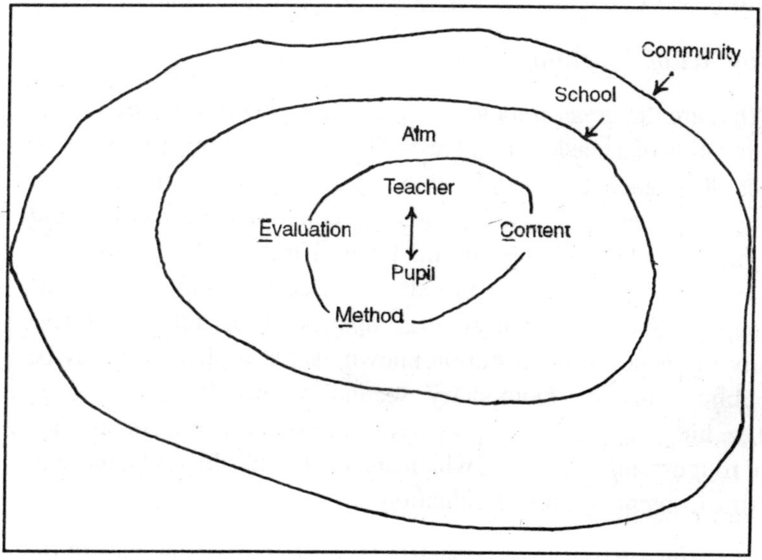

The reason for elaborating this point is to clarify the charge often made that preparation and certification requirements are so elaborate that a distinguished physicist, for example, could not teach in our schools.

Many persons other than the teacher, both within and outside of the school, participate in the processes of education. As new arrangements for education develop, such as team teaching, television, and automated teaching, additional persons, with differing degrees and types of training may be drawn into the process. A more extended use than in the past may be made of talented persons in other professions, such as a Leonard Bernstein, a Pablo Picasso, or a Robert Frost. But they will participate as musician, painter, poet. New arrangements in education will include more persons than at present who can perform clerical, stenographic, and other tasks. They will participate as clerks, and stenographers, not as teachers.

Many different kinds of persons, some with high degrees of skill and training and from different professions as well as others who are less skilled, will participate in schools and in the processes of education. But the teacher will continue to be the pivotal figure. He will be both trained and devoted to a lifetime career in teaching.

The Act of Teaching

What are the general ideas upon which a program for the proper education of a teacher might rest? The act of teaching, the essential act of a teacher—what he does in a formal, systematic, self-conscious, and responsible manner—consists of a *Classic Tetrad* which may be expressed in this form: *A*(im) *C*(ontent) *M*(ethod) *E*(valuation). The teacher provides a service (teaching) to his clients (pupils) either individually or in groups (mostly the latter) within the environment of an institution known as a school, which may be public or private; elementary, secondary, or collegiate in level. Teaching consists, when properly conceived as a professional act, of four essential elements which are, or should, always be present: Aim, Content, Method, Evaluation.

Aim—All teaching consists of an attempt on the part of the teacher to bring about desirable changes in the behavior (broadly conceived) of the pupil. Determining what changes shall be attempted is a difficult and complex task. But in every formal, responsible teaching situation the teacher needs, in so far as possible, to be explicitly aware of the changes that he is trying to effect. The teacher needs to know what is to be done for all pupils and for particular ones. He must be able to mediate between the often competing and conflicting individual and social claims that may present themselves. In a society such as ours, while the teacher must take due account of the social demands, he must be skillful, strong, and committed enough to realize that the individual welfare and dignity of each pupil (a core value of the culture) must never be sacrificed, however great special pressures may become.

Content—In attempting to bring about changes in pupils, the teacher always draws upon content, a field of knowledge, some organized part of human experience that represents the accumulated wisdom of the ages. Teachers have different assignments, especially as they work with pupils of different age levels, as to what segment of human knowledge they are mainly responsible to draw upon. But they all draw upon one or another field, and at times upon several, of the basic subject-matter disciplines. In addition to an aim, the teacher must have something to teach, a content, that will enable him to achieve his aim.

Method—The manner in which a teacher states his aim, how he communicates it to his pupils, the way in which he entices the pupil to accept the aim so that the pupil becomes highly motivated to learn, how the content is selected, arranged, and presented to the pupil so that the intended changes in the pupil may be achieved, and how the teacher assesses whether the desired changes have taken place—all of these are encompassed within *method.* That which is included here ranges from the over-all style and strategy that the teacher employs in a course for a term or a year down to the detailed techniques and tactics used in a single lesson or specific laboratory experience on one day. Properly conceived, a teacher's method is no simple collection of tricks or routine application of a few rules. Rather it is the bringing to bear, in a disciplined, skilled fashion, a method of critical inquiry to the problems that confront him. The problems of teaching each pupil and each class are not approached in a routine mechanical fashion, semester after semester, by a properly prepared teacher. The prepared teacher approaches each teaching situation as a problem to be solved. The content of his professional education, therefore, should follow closely the problems that teachers encounter as they perform their essential tasks.

*Evaluation*¾An essential part of every teaching act is evaluation, in which the teacher checks to determine the extent to which the original aim of his teaching has been achieved, and, if possible, whether the content and the method employed have been influential in effecting the change. A teacher evaluates to determine the extent and direction of the changes that have resulted from the teaching. This part of the basic tetrad of teaching is built into each of the other parts of the process. It begins with the formulation of the aim, which should be stated so clearly as to permit recognition when it is achieved. Evaluation and aim are constantly kept in mind as content is selected, organized, and presented; as records are kept; as tests are given both to measure results and to enhance learning so that data will be available to show whether or not the teaching has been successful. Whether or not the aim is realizable, or in need of modification, and whether or not the content and the method are the best that might be brought to bear- all receive attention through evaluation.

Other Roles of the Teacher

While the teaching of his pupils is the central and important task of a teacher, a qualified and responsible career teacher has other roles in which to be effective. *He must work with his colleagues,* including other teachers, supervisors, and administrators in the constant improvement of the curriculum, in enforcing high ethical standards of conduct within the profession, and in bringing about working conditions that encourage effective teaching. *He must also work with parents and the public* to interpret what the school is attempting, to secure their evaluation, cooperation, and support in developing the best possible educational program. *He also collaborates with members of other professions,* obtaining support and a proper division of labor where the services of education and those of the other professions overlap.

Essentials in Teacher Education

With the task of the teacher now broadly defined, with the picture in mind of what he must be able to do, the nature of the competence expected of him, we may now delineate the kind of persons required and the nature of their preparation.

The first question is, *Who should be admitted to teaching?* Since the quality of education provided in schools will depend more upon the quality of persons who teach than upon any other single factor, it is imperative that only superior persons be admitted. Superior in what ways? Height? Weight? Beauty? Our reply is: In all possible ways, but essentially in intellect and character. Terman's

Genetic Studies in Genius suggest the positive correlation between high intelligence and superiority in other important dimensions of human personality. Furthermore, since teaching in school is a complex activity, which has as its central aim the intellectual development of pupils, it follows that effective teaching requires persons of high intellectual capacity. Since teachers occupy a professional position of expertness in the performance of services which are vital to the client and to society over which the layman can at best exert only general control, it follows that those who are to be prepared and entrusted with such power and responsibility must be persons of highest integrity.

In considering the basic ingredients in teacher education, which is a teaching enterprise, it is necessary to understand its aim, content, method, evaluation.

Aim—The essential aim of a program of teacher education is to prepare individual practitioners (teachers) who have the knowledge, skills, and attitudes essential to the performance of their tasks as teachers (see p. 123).

*Content*¾The content of teacher education may be divided into the following categories:

1. General and Liberal Education
2. Specialized Education
3. Professional Education.

All three of these are substantial and essential ingredients in the education of a teacher. Their place in the total scheme of teacher education may be noted in the figure on page 128.

Blocks A, B, C and D represent the first phase in the education of a teacher, and concentrate upon general, liberal, and specialized education.

Block A

Block A indicates the general and liberal education that is a fundamental, substantial, and continuing part of a teacher's prepa-

A DIAGRAM FOR TEACHER EDUCATION

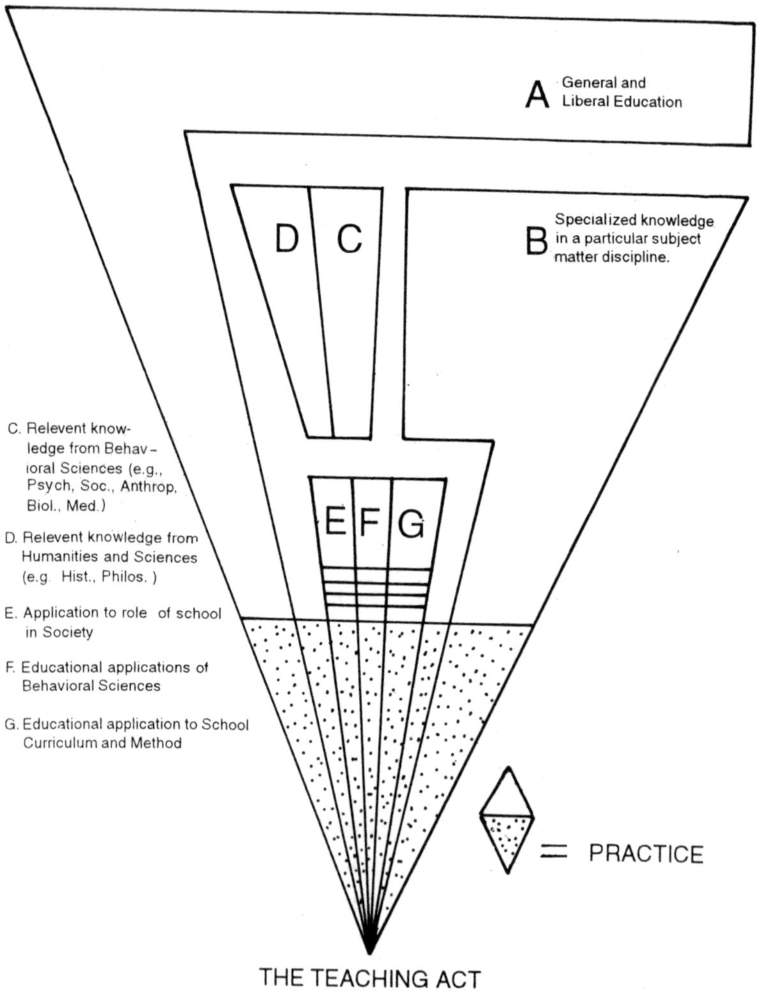

ration. While it is not the purpose here to define in detail the nature of these requirements in the proper education of a teacher, such delineation should be undertaken at some point in the formulation of a comprehensive statement on the essential ingredients in a program of teacher education. This part of a teacher's preparation begins when he first enters school, continues through high school into the undergraduate years of college, and ought to be sufficiently implanted by then so that it will continue, largely by self-study, throughout the lifetime of the teacher. The kind of teacher needed in this country will be influenced by the kind of general and liberal education that we envision as necessary for our children and youth. Hence, the nature of this general and liberal education will need to be indicated as a part of the delineation of a program for teacher educatiion. I see this as being a rigorous, continuous study, conducted by methods of critical inquiry, in all of the following basic fields of human knowledge throughout all of the years of required elementary and secondary school:

1. Mathematics
2. Languages:
   a. Domestic
   b. Foreign
3. Social Sciences
4. Natural Sciences
5. Visual and Performing Arts.
6. Practical Arts
7. Physical Education and Health.

One of the weaknesses in the preparation of teachers lies in the nature of the kind of liberal and general education with which they have been provided.

Block B

Block B together with Block A are of such fundamental importance in the proper education of a teacher that they together constitute a major portion of the education of a teacher. Mastery, both in breadth and depth, of some specialized branch of knowledge is essential for all teachers, including elementary school teachers. Subject-matter specialization is increasingly important as teachers work at higher grade levels. It is important for the prospective teacher to become versed not only in fundamental knowledge in his selected field of specialization but also for him to learn the methods of critical inquiry by which knowledge is advanced in that field. To accomplish these twin aims he should study with teachers who themselves are models of critical inquiry both in their teaching and in the study of their own fields of knowledge. The task of strengthening both A and B in our program of teacher education is as great as is that of improving the professional segment of teacher education.

In moving to Blocks C and D we begin to enter the arena where the education of a teacher becomes more clearly differentiated from that of persons who intend to enter other fields.

Block C and Block D

Block C and Block D refer to the necessity for a prospective teacher to be well versed beyond the regular college student in the behavioral science studies of psychology, sociology, anthropology, biology, and health. The material in Block C is essential to enable the teacher to understand and to influence the behavior of his pupils as they act and interact, individually and in groups. In Block D, the prospective teacher will have studied more deeply in selected parts of the humanities and the social sciences to obtain a necessary degree of sophistication in his understanding of the role of the school in society. Here is a weak portion of present programs of teacher education. It is one in which many problems exist. The chief organizational question becomes: Shall we have a pre-professional requirement to ensure coverage of this material? Many persons will, as a result of their general, liberal, and specialized education, have acquired much that is encompassed in C and D. Others will not have done so. One solution being suggested is to develop a comprehensive syllabus in areas C and D. Experts from these disciplines, together with persons who are familiar with the schools, might delineate the essential concepts that need to be understood, develop a list of readings, and a comprehensive examination that could be given individually, so that those who have acquired the essential understanding might proceed immediately without additional course requirements. Those who have not mastered this material could then be required to take essential work, not in professional education, but in the behavioral sciences, the social sciences, and the humanities where the materials are taught by the scholars in those fields in terms that are relevant to those fields and not necessarily as applied to education.

In Blocks E, F and G, we enter upon a phase in the education of teacher where the emphasis, though not exclusively, is upon his professional education. It is upon the essential nature of these blocks that our conference has concentrated. They cannot be considered isolated from all of the interrelated parts of the total program of teacher education. They need to be considered in their proper context in teacher education of which they are an essential part.

Block E

In Block E, attention focuses on developing in the prospective teacher an historical and cross-cultural perspective of the place of school and education in society. This is not knowledge exclusively possessed by the teacher; for many other educated persons in society will have such understanding. While this knowledge may be a *desirable* facet in the education of any adult, it is an *essential* ingredient for the teacher. Without it his ability to function fully would be lessened. The content in Block E is also designed to enable the teacher to understand how and why schools stand at the busy intersection of competing values in the culture and the consequences of this fact for the behavior of an effective teacher. It should help him to know why and how to modify his behavior, as well as how and why not to, so that he may be effective both in a public school in Harlem and in a private school in New England.

Block F

In Block F the teacher will draw directly upon basic knowledge of the characteristics and behavior of individuals as they interact in small and large groups and attempt to see what this means for the management of learning in schools, especially in classrooms. What does knowledge of motivation and level of aspiration in human beings mean for the teaching of arithmetic, reading, or calculus? What does knowledge of the social class origins of pupils tell about how a teacher can improve his effectiveness in teaching pupils to write better or to read more deeply and meaningfully in the best literature of the ages? What from the field of tests and measurements will enable a teacher and his pupils to assess the extent to which the aims of a particular class have been achieved? What do the findings from psychological research on the relative merits of spaced *vs*. distributed practice in the learning of a skill mean when applied to teaching typewriting in high schools? These are the kinds of questions that the content of Block F treats.

Block G

At this point the close relationship between Blocks F and G becomes apparent. In Block F, materials from the behavioral sciences are applied to general teaching situations, irrespective of grade level or field. In Block G the aim is more precise, the specific application of what is known to the problems of teaching one subject to pupils of specific age or levels of maturity. Because of the close relationships and often lack of coordination between Blocks F and G an apparent and often actual, needless duplication in professional education may occur.

Practice

Block E, F and G encompass the professional knowledge that is the *essential* foundation upon which a teacher develops his skill and his professional attitudes in teaching. It is in practice, in the shaded area, that the materials from all parts of his preparation are synthesized and brought to bear upon the development of the highest possible degree of skill in teaching. Note the lines extending down into practice to indicate that attention to theoretical foundations should continue through practice. Here is the ultimate test, the crucial place and time when all that has gone before is judged. But because this is the culmination of so much that is important in teacher education, it must not be assumed that it can stand by itself, and that what has gone before is unimportant. Here in practice the embryo teacher, under the direct and continuing supervision of experienced masters, begins to teach, to apply what he has learned. In the beginning, this practice takes place mainly under the aegis of the college and university, and under as nearly ideal conditions as possible. Gradually as the neophyte's skill becomes more established, he moves his practice out into the regular arena of school life in the community. Over a period of time the main responsibility for preparation moves from the collegiate institution to the school where the beginning practitioner is employed. Thus a third phase of the program of teacher education begins and continues as long as the teacher teaches.

Concluding Note

Two additional sections to this chapter on essentials in teacher education need development, one on Method and another on Evaluation to fill out the tetrad of teacher education, aim, content, method, and evaluation.

In method we need to consider the various possible designs for programs of teacher education that may make possible a break-through, which, it is agreed, must be achieved. Each of the institutions participating might well write its own version of this section of the report, reporting the rationale for its program.

In evaluation, we need to develop a comprehensive statement of how to test whether we are achieving what we have aimed for. This will be one of the most difficult of the essential parts of teacher education to formulate.

10

The Professional Community

The stories we tell one another about special teachers we have had or have missed out on underscore the profoundly personal and individualistic nature of teaching. At the same time, teachers are pressed to become less individualistic and more "collaborative," in part as a remedy for the supposed ills of isolation. Are these pictures at odds or in harmony? Unexplored aspects of teachers' individual identity and professional relations provide the point of departure for this essay. In the discussion that follows, I join insights derived from teachers with an emerging literature on individualism and community in American society to examine the dynamics of teachers' professional affiliation in secondary schools. My aim is to contribute to the evolving discussion and debate on the nature and consequences of teachers' individual and collective involvements in teaching their pervasive privacy and their colleagueship.

Three conditions give urgency to these explorations. First, we have witnessed repeated attempts to calibrate workplace obligations, opportunities, and rewards in ways that attract and retain capable and committed teachers. Getting the incentives right may be a matter of offering teachers sufficient scope for independent action without abrogating legitimate institutional interests in the priorities, performance, and commitment of the teacher workforce. Second, teachers now confront external circumstances and pressures that fundamentally complicate the task of teaching. Dramatic shifts in the composition of the student population, for example, make it more and more difficult for teachers to succeed by relying on their individual resources. The task of teaching is rendered more and more complex; it is arguably the case that even the most knowledgeable and enthusiastic teachers cannot credibly do the job alone. Such externalities place pressure on teachers to embrace a common set of priorities and to organize a collective response to the complexities of teaching.

Finally, questions surrounding individualism and community assume a special urgency by virtue of the very nature of teachers' work. School-teaching entails entrustment with the education of the young; it engages the teacher as a moral agent of the broader public. Ideally, teachers display a command of and enthusiasm for subject-matter knowledge, but also satisfy an "ethic of care" in relation to children and adolescents. Thus, the individualistic or collective stance of teachers toward their work matters because teaching presents, in its content and in its conduct, an intellectual, social, emotional, and moral model for children. One might argue that a special standard of collective and civic responsibility is at stake.

My thinking on these topics owes much to the accounts that teachers have offered in field studies of secondary school-teaching spanning three years. In interviews and in their interactions with one another, teachers trace the phenomenological contours of identity and community. They illuminate conceptions of "being a teacher" that distinguish teachers from members of other occupations and, within teaching itself, distinguish groups of teachers from one another. In these ways, teachers show the personal career niches that high school teaching makes possible, together with the ties among colleagues that are forged by will or by circumstance. They sketch the interplay of individual and institution, of professional identity and professional relations.

Perspectives on Independence and Community

Any discussion of professional community among teachers sits against a backdrop of teaching's pervasive and persistent privacy. Many of the proposed virtues of teacher collaboration schemes or school restructuring plans center on overcoming the individual limitations and organizational failing that result from privatized teaching and isolated teachers. The rationales that support such plans generally include a litany of problems associated with a norm of classroom privacy. Laments about privacy center on teachers' isolation from adult companionship and the support of knowledgeable peers; put this way, the problems center on the deprivations teachers experience by virtue of their solitary classroom existence. Other criticisms center on the potential losses to children and to the public at large when personal autonomy translates into freedom from scrutiny directed at classroom practice, apparent relief from defending professional judgment, and the virtual absence of collective responsibility for performance. In response, reform proposals evince a certain unquestioning optimism regarding the benefits that might be expected to follow from penetrating "the walls of privatism" and fostering more vigorous exchange among teachers.

Much of the pessimism surrounding privacy seems a reasonable response to more than two decades of case study research in schools; much of the optimism directed at close colleagueship also seems warranted. Yet these tendencies toward wholesale pessimism or optimism have helped to reinforce a narrowly constructed and compartmentalized view of teachers' work lives, obscuring the situated meanings and unanticipated consequences of privacy and colleagueship.

Recent challenges call into question the almost wholly negative or skeptical view of teachers' privacy and the relentlessly optimistic view of teachers' collaborations. These commentaries offer a more affirmative view of teachers' classroom independence, while field studies of teachers' careers suggest a more comprehensive view of the individual prerogatives that teachers exercise both in and out of the classroom. The consequence of such analyses has been to render "privacy" and "community" not as either/or conditions but as fluid, dynamic, and situationally specific norms of interaction and interpretation that give meaning to "being a teacher."

Such a perspective is implicit in the metaphor of the teacher as an independent artisan whose success comes from consistent and highly localized "tinkering" with the craft at hand. Huberman argues that the metaphor of the independent artisan is true both to the prevailing organization of teaching and to the way that teachers, over the longer term of a career, come to find satisfaction and success in their work. This model squares well with most descriptions of schools as workplaces: that is, it accords with a view that schools are organized to exert little influence on teaching practice or its improvement. The organization of time and space, combined with professional norms of autonomy and equal status, reinforce teachers' fundamental independence on matters of professional practice. In effect, Huberman leaves policymakers with the challenge of making the best use of the inevitable independence of classroom teaching.

Nonetheless, Huberman's model leaves largely unaddressed the question of civic purpose to which schools ultimately must respond. Can a pool of independent entrepreneurs, no matter how skilled, meet the aspirations for intellectual, moral, vocational, and civic education held to by the public? A partial answer to this issue may be found in a distinction between individualism and individuality. Hargreaves distinguishes between destructive forms of individualism that compromise the social good and constructive forms of individuality that give life to the relation between teachers and students. Based on his study of teachers' use of allocated preparation time in Canadian elementary schools, for example, Hargreaves elaborates two forms of individualisms that might be considered deliberate strategies for preserving and extending individual control over one's work. Each is a principled, rational response to the work of teaching as teachers experience it. Each, in specific circumstances, might be examined for its effect on classroom practice. The term "strategic individualisms" applies to the ways in which teachers buffer the complex demands of the work by limting intrusions. "Effective indivitualism" encompasses those individual prerogatives that teachers preserve in an effort to fulfill an ethic of care and responsibility toward children.

These critics join in rejecting the notion of isolation as professional pathology, though they do not dismiss its problematic aspects. Without placing naive faith in teachers' unconstrained independence in matters of professional practice, they prompt us to specify more closely both its drawbacks and its prospects. This represents a shift from a language that emphasizes privacy and isolation to a language that encompasses both the possibilities and the problems that reside in teachers' autonomous action. It proposes an expanded conception of "being a teacher" in the multiple arenas in which teachers pursue independent initiative and seek independent control of their work in the classroom, among colleagues, and in pursuit of a career.

Defenses of teachers' independence are reinforced by those who find individualism deeply embedded in the broader American society. In *Habits of the Heart,* Robert Bellah and his colleagues examine the fundamental strains of individualism in American culture and pose related problems regarding the possibility for community and commitment. "Individualism lies at the very core of American culture," according to their analysis (p. 142). At the center of this culture is "the autonomous individual, presumed to be able to choose the role he will play and the commitments he will make" (p. 47). To advocate for the open classroom door, for a more collective and less private enterprise of teaching, is not only to remain inattentive to the fundamental and persistent conditions of schoolteaching, but also to confront closely held values of western society.

Challenges to the nearly unrelievedly negative stance toward teachers' privacy thus serve to open up a wider range of conceptual and practical possibilities, and expand the arenas in which teachers are seen to exercise independent initiative and seek individual control (productively or not, for good or ill). In parallel fashion, recent commentaries dispute the overwhelmingly positive view of teachers' collaboration, and begin to specify some of the dimensions along which teachers' experience of professional community might be charted. Until very recently, analyses of teachers' collegial relations have had a characteristically optimistic cast, even when they have portrayed truly collegial work as a phenomenon achieved rarely and with difficulty. But notions of professional community are now also in flux. On one hand, opportunities for collaboration have proliferated both within the school and among wider networks of teachers who share common interests or circumstances. At the same time, the broad optimism attached to "collaborative cultures" has been tempered by critiques that center not merely on pragmatic obstacles but also on fundamental conceptual inadequacies and ideological dilemmas.

To the arguments regarding organizational impediments to collaboration among teachers have been added certain reservations based in the apparent purposes and consequences of teachers' shared work. Coining the term "contrived collegiality," Hargreaves observes that teachers are increasingly being invited to collaborate with one another and are being offered greater material resources to do so; at the same time, however, they are expected to come together in the service of agendas defined by others. The most recent reform initiatives in Canada, the United States, England, and elsewhere have all spurred initiatives in which teachers are brought together to implement curriculum policies framed at some distance from local schools and classrooms. Hargreaves and others concentrate on the nature and consequences of institutional controls over teachers' work. They take special heed of the steady escalation in formally orchestrated "collaborative" work, most commonly under the auspices of the employing district or school. Here we confront the tensions between institutional imperatives and teachers' own professional inclinations. we are made alert to the possible conflict between bureaucratic and professional (educational) concerns and to the phenomena of institutional coercion, control, and surveillance for purposes that may be quite at odds with the central purposes of teaching. Placing ourselves in teachers' shoes, we are inclined to ask, Who promotes or suppresses which forms of professional community among teachers, and for what apparent purposes? At the same time, teachers do have a record of successful overt and covert resistance to institutional initiatives (on the grounds that they violate principles of autonomy, for example). Taking the institutional perspective, and recalling that education is a crucial civic undertaking, we might ask, What do we make of a formal institution that can so little compel its members' loyalty and action by appeal to institutional obligations?

In a world and an occupation in which individualism prevails and in which individuality is treasured, what are the obligations, opportunities, and rewards of community among teachers? What bonds are formed among them, and on what basis? What kinds of claims do teachers actually make on one another? Elsewhere, in an effort to remedy "conceptually amorphous and ideologically sanguine" notions of collaboration and collegiality, I have suggested ways in which structured occasions of joint work might be examined for the degree to which they required or produced genuine interdependence among teachers and yielded demonstrable benefit for students. (We have avoided assuming, throughout our field studies, that frequent and intensive exchange among teachers necessarily reflects norms that are favorable to academic achievement and standards of equity. In Hammersley's account off "staffroom news," for example, or Woods's description of "staffroom humour," exchanges among teachers served to bolster teachers' claims to adequacy in the face of troublesome relations with students.) I still maintain that it will be fruitful to examine these overt and relatively structured professional relations in terms of their prospects for influencing individual classroom choices and consequences. Such an enterprise distinguishes both certain structural dimensions of professional relationship—interdependence, intensity, and inclusivity and the substance of belief and expertise displayed in exchanges among teachers. But I also argue here that an emphasis on structured occasions of "helping" or "sharing" or other "joint work" may blind us to the more fluid, moment-by-moment interplay of self and society in schools. In looking for community only where teachers gather in some organized forum, we are likely to miss some of the most potent features of teaching as an occupational community, and of schools as organizational cultures the way persons act or do not act in one another, and construct interpretations of one another's actions. Quite apart from the dangers that come from an ideological naivete are those that derive from an overly narrow construction of what counts as colleagueship among teachers in the first place.

By most accounts, collective orientations and involvements in secondary schools are far overshadowed by individualistic pursuits. Schools would seem to supply only the most tenuous influence on teachers' individual dispositions and practices. Yet certain between-school and within-school patterns deserve attention, showing the situationally variable ways in which teachers take one another into account in the ordinary fabric of school life. Teachers' own words and actions begin to open up the "black box" of individualisms and community.

Occupational Community and "Consciousness of Kind"

An occupational community, as defined by Van Maanen and Barley, is "a group of people who consider themselves to be engaged in the same sort of work; whose identity is drawn from the work; who share with one another a set of values, norms, and perspectives that apply to but extend beyond work-related matters; and whose work relationships meld work and leisure." At the heart of such a community is a certain "consciousness of kind" expressed in " the social dimensions used by members themselves for recognizing one another, the social limits of such bonds, and situational factors which amplify or diminish the perceived common identity." Elsewhere I have observed the relative inattention to meaningful groups within schools:

> Few studies take account of all of the ways in which groups are constituted, or the manner in which the "groupness" provides a set of lenses through which to portray a school's culture or cultures. Subgroup analyses reveal not only differences of perspective and practices, but also differences in institutional leverage.....Individual teachers may hold multiple membership in the internal groups of the school....Secondary teachers, for example, may be members of a department and members of a coaching staff; they may teach part time in two or more departments; their orientation toward their subject (and department) may be colored by the number of low-achieving or high-achieving students they teach (track assignment) or by the apparent fit between the school curriculum and "cutting edge" developments in the field.

The boundaries and meaning of group membership may be anticipated but not fully captured in the nominal labels we routinely apply. We cannot simply assume what it means to be a "teacher" or a "high school teacher" or a "math teacher," for example. beyond the distinctions made by nominal labels are the connotative dimensions that "lead some members to separate themselves from others who do denotatively similar work." In a critical treatise on the nature of community, Gusfield asks: "When do people define themselves as having important characteristics in common, and when do these become the basis for communal identity and action?"

We began our search for the meaningful boundaries of "professional community" by acknowledging the probable import of organizational subunits such as departments and by giving closer scrutiny to naturally occurring reference groups within the school (which may not coincide entirely with formal structures). Such group boundaries, and the norms of interaction and interpretation that mark them from one another, are revealed in part by the selective use of "we" (and "they") in teachers' accounts and observed interactions.

Applied to teaching, "consciousness of kind" is at root a sense of having adopted the identity of "teacher" in the first place. Nias detailed the multiple ways in which British primary teachers' sense of self was influed by "being a teacher." Yet she also found that "it is possible to teach for years, successfully and with the affirmation of one's head teacher and colleagues, without incorporating `teacher' into one's self-image." One in six of the fifty mid-career teachers interviewed by Nias did not "feel like a teacher." Judging by Cusick's inventory of the nonteaching work, family involvements, recreational interests, church or community activity, and other commitments that competed with teaching for high school teachers' time and loyalty, we might anticipate a parallel phenomenon among American secondary teachers.

Our analyses point to four aspects of high school teaching that plausibly enhance or crode teachers' sense of being a teacher and contribute to their "consciousness of kind." The *students* one teaches their present circumstances, their dispositions or talents, and their probable futures—shape the meanings attached to being a good teacher or a good colleague. *Instructional assignments* confer certain status, opportunities, and rewards that may wax and wane over time and across circumstances. Membership in particular *departments* represents direct participation in an occupational community close at hand, with varying measures of congeniality, cohesiveness, intellectual rigor, and the like. Finally, the *subject* in which one specializes supplies its own resources (or restrictions) for identity and community, both inside and outside the school. It is in their affiliations with a disciplinary tradition that teachers may find a powerful avenue to a more cosmopolitan who of relationships beyond the boundaries of school or district. (Involvement is teachers' unions, of course, is another potentially "cosmopolitan" relationship that spans the organization of schools and membership in the wider occupation.)

Although these features differentiate conditions of independence and community among teachers, groups, and schools, they do not exhaust the possibilities. They exclude, for example, the affinities that arise out of teachers' common personal circumstances or interests (say, children of the same age or common recreational interests). They do, however, permit us to trace "consciousness of kind" to commonalities in the circumstances and interactions of teaching. Each of these features may be examined for its independence-preserving and community-building aspects. Each presents resources on which teachers may rely (or obstacles with which they must contend) to forge their own sense of self and community. And each constitutes an arena of professional life that is plausibly subject to policymaking and to the exercise of leadership.

Students as a Resource for Identity and Community

The meaning of "being a teacher" is expressed as a disposition toward students. Teachers' orientations toward students vary both between and within schools. Teachers differ, for example, in the goals they express for the students they teach. They seek and achieve quite variable levels of personal attachment. In a powerful sense, teachers live a life in the classroom, whether rich or impoverished; their dealings with students may draw them further into "being a teacher" or may yield cynicism and indifference.

But the teacher-student relation, whatever form it takes and whatever level of success and satisfaction it yields, is salient for teachers in all schools. When asked "What's important for us to understand about you as a teacher here, in this school?" teachers talk often and at length about students. They speak of the school's students generally, and of the students who populate their own classes. In doing so, teachers locate themselves at the center or at the margins of the school's symbolic and material resources or rewards. At Oak Valley High School, the largest of our field sites with nearly 3000 students and more than 100 teachers, an English teacher describes a level of parental expectation, public support, and professional recognition that link a teacher's "pride" to the school's successful students: I think [Oak Valley] is a place that's pretty pride-filled, if that's appropriate. .....The kids coming in the classroom are being pushed to do well.....You have teachers who are in general enjoying their jobs and getting a reward from it. And from the outside, going to conferences and all, it's pretty thrilling to have people know I teach at Oak Valley. They'll say, "Oh, Oak Valley!" and they've heard of us. So there's a sense of pride here that, I think, affects all the different levels (I transcript 0V04301, lines 45-97).

This English teacher's sentiments are echoed consistently by other teachers in the traditional academic departments. But the "pride," to the extent that it is felt, is in fact constructed differently at "all the different levels." In this and other academically oriented comprehensive high schools, we find a pronounced difference between teachers in traditional academic departments and teachers of conventionally defined "vocational" subjects. The value placed on "college-bound" students creates the standard of worth both for students and for teachers. Teachers of industrial arts, business, consumer/family studies ("home ec"), or vocational agriculture must seek alternative grounds on which to establish their contribution or to make claims on school resources. The symbolism surrounding the phrase "college-bound" marginalizes a certain segment of students, teachers, curricula, and goals by denying them any affirmative identity (they are, emphatically, "non-college-bound"). Teacher of non-college-bound students at Oak Valley dispute the numbers of college acceptances touted by the school's administrators, and criticize what they consider to be an inappropriate concentration of resources. Nonetheless, they find it difficult to escape the lower status attached to their clientele and their curriculum. An industrial arts teacher complains: "The pride in voiced is in the people teaching it. There's limited pride, limited acknowledgement out there....They [the administrators] almost make you feel second class."

Whom teachers teach, and how those students are seen by others, is thus a major element in the identity of "teacher." Teachers are situated by their student clientele. But one's self-image as a teacher —or a "good teacher" is also bolstered or eroded by the daily ebb and flow of the classroom. Regardless of the categorical labels attached to students, a teacher's competence and confidence are tested in the moment-by-moment exchanges among individuals and in the dynamics of specific classes. In a five-period teaching day, teachers readily distinguish between the "good" classes and the "tough" ones; it is not uncommon for teachers to experience widely fluctuating levels of "efficacy" from one class to another. Indeed, the variance in measured levels of performance efficacy is nearly as great within teacher (across classes) as between teachers. The definition of "good" and "difficult" classes is not straightforward; certainly it is not summed up by students' prior academic achievement alone. In any event, one might argue that the burdens or blessings of privacy assume quite different significance in the course of the school day. So, too, do the support, indifference, or animosity of one's colleagues.

From these observations emerge two curiosities. First, we have begun to wonder how teachers' engagements with one another reinforce, alter, compensate for, or in other ways mediate the salience of "student" in shaping the success and satisfactions of teaching. What teachers require or value from a community of peers is plausibly tied to teachers' encounters with students both in and out of the classroom. Second, we have begun to trace the ways in which teachers influence (or fail to influence) the student clientele available to them. Teachers in these schools are pleased when they are assured of "good" students, though the definitions of "good" do not accord nearly or simply with records of academic achievement. But "good" students do not always appear to be within reach. Teachers at urban Valley High School, for example, decry the "creaming off" of their best students when a new school opened nearby and express a certain hopelessness over the remaining student population. Vocational teachers at Oak Valley lament a perceived increase in "dumping ground" placements; they believe themselves to be enjoying fewer and fewer of the "student" resources the school has to offer.

Instructional Assignment

The policies and practices governing the nature of the teaching assignments that teachers acquire supply the local meaning that "Math teacher" or "English teacher" or "Art teacher" comes to have in daily work. The instructional assignment assumes special importance in light of a conception of career that highlights persons' relation to work and the social identity it offers. (This is precisely the conception held out by Van Maanen and Barley's definition of the "occupational community"). Teachers attribute the success and satisfaction they find in their work to the specific assignments they acquire. In their stories of entering and staying in teaching, teachers highlight turning points that center on teaching assignments points at which they succeeded (or were thwarted) in securing a desirable school placement and a favorable configuration of courses and students.

Teachers' accounts present three levels at which "instructional assignment" is differentially subject to individual influence, the source of individual pride or embarrassment, and the basis of community. First, teachers express their consciousness of where high school teaching fits in an academic hierarchy. By the tales of "getting to high school" or "moving up to high school," many position high school reaching at the pinnacle of a status hierarchy in K-12 teaching; a few position high school teaching between work in middle schools (typically less favored) and opportunities to teach in community colleges (a source of pride for those who hold or seek them).

Second, teachers achieve (or attempt) influence over their assignments to individual schools. Their reports suggest strategies for controlling individual career pathways that could not be anticipated by reference to districts' teacher selection practices or local contract language regarding transfer rights. Teachers describe "shopping" among districts, or assessing the trade-offs between public and private school positions.

Finally, patterns of actual teaching assignment on a yearly or semester basis achieve a good or poor fit with teachers' subject preparation and preferences. Students are the first of many professional resources that may be differentially distributed within and between secondary schools. Teachers are differentially successful in negotiating preferred schedules, topics, and students. We expect that the specific patterns of distribution, and the meaning attached to them by teachers, will bear a relationship to teachers' daily performance and career commitment. It remains uncertain whether or how the configuration of assignments creates a certain de facto community through circumstance.

The Department

Subject area organization modeled on higher education creates both possibilities and limitations for teachers' professional identity and community. Despite criticisms of subject departmentalization, it remains one of the fundamental facts of life in the work of most secondary teachers. The department is perhaps the most prominent domain of potential interdependence among teachers, and one that has shown itself to be remarkably resilient in the face of repeated efforts to forge other forms of school organization. At suburban Oak Valley High School, with its 3000 students and more than 100 staff, departments are the primary frame of reference for most teachers. Yet the departments provide very different kinds of homes for the teachers who inhabit them. Here, a third-year teacher describes the "fit" he found with the English department:

> I came here [to interview] and I was really impressed right away with the teachers that were here in the English Department. They weren't the kind that were sitting back during the breaks, smoking cigarettes and complaining about kids and how they are and all that....They were really energetic and involved in what they were doing and....sharing ideas about what they were doing in class, what was working, showing students' work, you know...(Transcript 0V07701, lines 43-61).

In this instance, a teacher's sense of confident autonomy in the classroom rests in part on the place he finds within a like-minded community within the department. Yet there are limits to the like-mindedness. This teacher, like most others in the department, lists members of other departments among his closest associates. He also points to systematic differences within the department with regard to classroom practice. By his description, echoed closely by others, this is a department that takes pride in being an intellectual center without expecting or achieving consensus with regard to the subject or the methods by which it is best taught. Its members display and discuss their course outlines, lesson plans, and student assignments, and show one another samples of student work, but they also accord one another a wide degree of latitude with regard to classroom pedagogy. Individuals gain the respect of their colleagues by satisfying criteria that combine classroom prowess with other kinds of professional activity. Some, though not all, publish fiction and poetry, are active in professional associations, and lead writing workshops for teachers from other districts. a picture of the group is prominently displayed in the department office, and the office swirls with activity throughout the day. Teachers dignify one another's individuality, but also expect one another to be both productive and sociable members of the group.

Other departments provide very different grounds for individual teachers' work. A science department generates competition among its members by its practices of teacher assignment and the allocation of classrooms, laboratory space, and equipment. The psychic rewards that secure the commitment and enthusiasm of new teachers in this department are jeopardized when senior members of the department hold hostage the most favored teaching assignments. Members of a social studies department hold competing views of what Ball and Lacey have labelled "subject paradigm" and "subject pedagogy." Unlike the members of the Oak Valley English department, these teachers are polarized by their differences.

Although their salience may vary within and across schools, departments represent a naturally occurring ground for teachers' interactions. In future analyses, three aspects of departmental life will command special attention: the department as a meaningful reference group for teachers with regard to curricular and instructional priorities; the department as a source of professional expertise and a model of professional commitment; and the department as a resource for influence within the school, specifically with regard to control over human and material resources.

Subject Specialization

Persistent stereotypes paint high school teachers as resolutely "subject-centered." Until very recently, however, there have been few efforts to penetrate that stereotype to discover the meaning of subject specialization for teachers' conceptions of task, their actual work in schools, and their commitment to teaching. The few exceptions suggest some of the possibilities that await a more extensive probe. A comparative study of secondary art and science teachers in England reveals differences across subjects in teachers' orientation toward the discipline and toward the reward system and career possibilities of teaching. Meaningful differences within subject disciplines are expressed in part as differences in individuals' "subject paradigm" and "subject pedagogy." Such differences serve both to bond departments and to divide them. On of the four English departments studied by Ball and Lacey formed a cohesive subculture with shared views of the subject and the way it should be taught. A second department found itself in agreement on pedagogy despite differences over subject paradigm. Both these departments, in which all members were English specialists with full-time assignments to the department, were positioned to operate as relatively powerful instruments of curriculum policy. The remaining two departments, by contrast, were divided by substantive issues (disagreements over paradigm and pedagogy).

To what extent and in what manner does the subject constitute a form of affiliation among teachers? One plausible answer is that secondary teaching closely approximates a world of entrepreneurial individualism in which teachers and students alike pursue self-interested activity in a "shopping mall high school." By this view, individual teachers draw upon the resources of subject specialization to construct a personal niche to which they bring idiosyncratic preferences for content priorities, pedagogical style, and favored instructional assignments. Community at the level of the school, in so far as there is one, resides in a set of tacit agreements that preserve the widest possible latitude for independent action. At the level of the occupation, "consciousness of kind" might amount to no more than diffuse participation in an abstract community of scholars within a disciplinary tradition. Surveys of nearly 700 teachers suggest that attendance at subject-related conferences is a common (nearly universal) form of participation in a professional community. But conference attendance alone communicates little about the nature and extent of one's links to a subject discipline or one's affiliations with others who teach it. Further, this form of participation in "community" is affected by fluctuations in local resources, board policies governing released time, and the like.

It is perhaps less important to know the frequency or scale of teachers' participation than to grasp the meaning of such involvements for the teachers who pursue them, and to understand the way in which district policies and practices promote or inhibit those involvements. We know little of these out-of-school involvements and the extent to which they supply teachers with intellectual stimulation, emotional satisfaction, personal recognition, or status in the broader occupation. The permeability of the school walls is of special interest for secondary teachers, given the demands placed on "staying current in one's field."

We might productively distinguish between the school or district (the employing organization) and the wider occupation of teaching as meaningful domains of action and affiliation. Membership in subject-matter associations, networks, and other informal collaborative enterprises is a unexplored and potentially consequential element in teacher's professional identity and career satisfaction. A small supplemental study of participants in two Urban Mathematics Collaborative projects has enabled us to trace the way in which subject affiliations and departmental ties are maintained or attenuated by relatioships in the larger occupation or community.

In sum, a school's prevailing stance toward its students, its formal (typically departmental) design, and the demands and opportunities of daily work (instructional assignment) appear to constitute the principal organizational ground on which secondary teachers construct identity and community. In addition, subject specialization provides a source of identity and collegial relationship that reaches to the teaching occupation more widely and to connections in higher education, industry, the arts, and other arenas. Although these are not the only contributors to one's "sense of self" or "consciousness of kind," they are prominent in teachers' talk. They provide windows into the intersection of teachers' independent action and their participation in a professional community both inside and outside the school.

The Claims Teachers Make on One Another: Mutual Obligation and Mutual Support

More often than not, secondary teachers have been portrayed as going their own way within an institution in which school-level goal consensus is (for many reasons) difficult to achieve and in which the linkage between institutional goals and individual practice is insubstantial. Efforts to detect "community" among high school teachers have not been fruitful. Cusick concluded that there were no meaningful "professional networks" among the staffs of two midwestern high schools he observed; rather, teachers engaged in a form of competitive entrepreneurialism to control course offerings and content, student enrollment, discretionary time, and the like. Their work lives were a mosaic of personal and professional commitments that included second jobs and other out-of-school involvements, chosen and sustained quite independent of institutional interests. Departments were administrative conveniences rather than intellectual homes or instruments of curriculum policy.

Whole-school studies (especially those of elementary schools) tend to emphasize community as "goal consensus." In some secondary schools, most commonly independent schools, small size coincides with singularity of purpose in much the same way. More often, however, secondary schools appear to be generally absent any powerful mechanisms by which institutional and occupational obligations come to hold sway over personal prerogative. Rather, teachers' affiliations approximate "community as a voluntary gathering of autonomous individuals." Professional community defined in this way would seem to have only the most insubstantial hold on teachers. Comprehensive high schools stand in dramatic contrast, for example, to religious or utopian communities in which there are both symbolic and structural mechanisms that subordinate personal to communal interests. The broadly permissive character of such professional relations is underscored by those unusual cases in education in which teachers' individualism is substantially constrained by public and powerful expressions of mutual obligation, and in which personal prerogative is expressed fully by institutional goals. In the "total world" of Bethany Baptist Academy, teachers describe institutional obligations and collective responsibilities that stand in startling contrast to those present in Cusick's comprehensive high schools. Bethany's teachers (all themselves born-again Christians) submit not only their work but also their lives to the scrutiny and the pragmatic control of the larger institution. They attend Wednesday and Sunday services, participate in evening meetings, make home visitations, and in other ways blur the boundaries between professional and personal time, space, and activity. Teachers both witness and participate in rituals that secure and sustain commitment and that define the patterns of obligation that keep commitment alive.

Taken together, Cusick's observations of the self-interest reigning in "typical" comprehensive high schools and Peshkin's observations of the rituals and rhetoric required to sustain Bethany Baptist's level of collective commitment underscore the utilitarian individualism of the wider society and the generally permissive collegiality of schools. Bellah et al. (1985) frame the dilemma this way:

> [I]f the entire social world is made up of individuals, each endowed with the right to be free of others' demands, it becomes hard to forge bonds of attachment to, or cooperation with, other people, since such bonds would imply obligations that necessarily impinge on one's freedom.

A major question, then, is the extent to which a "consciousness of kind" is manifest in a pattern of mutual obligation and mutual support. Again, descriptions of the broader American culture have their echoes in teachers' views. Personal freedom, in the society at large "...turns out to mean being left alone by others, not having other people's values, ideas, or styles of life forced upon one, being free of arbitrary authority in work, family, and political life." This is strikingly reminiscent of (in accord with) teachers' views of autonomy: freedom from scrutiny, the right to make professional judgments that fit personal preference, and the implicit obligation to solve one's own problems. Autonomy may be expressed as the limits of departmental constraint on course content, pedagogy, and treatment of students.

Where do we find autonomy tempered by obligation to the group? For example, is "sharing the load" part of a definition of colleagueship and for whom? Here, teachers' independent interests and preferences may be in conflict with principles of service to students. The past chair of Oak Valley's English department describes the group's stance toward teaching assignments in a way that expresses collective obligations to teach remedial classes:

> So I think the school is pretty much philosophically doing what it says it should do and that's provide the college-bound track to most of the students. I know that we in the English Department feel very strongly that our objective is to get the kid out of that remedial track and get him into the regular track and I know that that's, it's we talk

about it all the time...Our "remedial, non-college-bound," we rotate. ...And everybody in the department will be involved in those courses and that's the way it goes (Transcript 0V04301, lines 451-462, 534-535).

The same department expects its members to "add to the wealth" and to subordinate personal curriculum preferences to a principle of departmental curriculum coherence:

We started something a couple of years ago where every teacher is, not forced, but encouraged to pick up a new prep every other year. And the ideal behind that one is so that courses didn't become so specialized to teachers that if a teacher were to leave the department and all of a sudden the course, you know somebody's stuck teaching it and doesn't really know how it's supposed to go and all that, and tried to remove the idea of special interest classes and say, "Look, if it's in our department then it's worth being taught and so let's have people who can teach it." (Transcript 0V04301, lines 569-587).

Where independence is in tension with collective obligations, membership in a professional community appears to take on the form of elective and sporadic "involvements." Americans' penchant for "getting involved," according to Bellah et al., Signals a distinctive and peculiar relationship between self and society. Getting involved is a way of both pursuing and protecting one's personal interests; it is therefore both possible and legitimate to remain uninvolved. This argument has its direct echoes in teachers' insistence that voluntary staff development is preferable to mandated participation. Examples proliferate in our chronicles of secondary teachers' work. Teachers active in the urban mathematics networks report quite varied success in securing the "involvement" of their departments in activities of the network. In most instances, involvement was secured by displays of personal enthusiasm and by appeals to self-interest or anticipated personal benefit. Although the teachers who participate display a consistent and intense concern for "reaching the kids," there are few instances in which their initial involvement could be explained by appeals to the collective obligation that is part of being a "math teacher." "Given such assumptions about the [self-interested] purposes of involvement," say Bellah and his colleagues, "what kind of vision can one have of the public good?"

These examples suggest that the nature and extent of community might be traced through situationally specific rights and obligations on matters of professional practice both within the school and in the larger occupational domain. In doing so, we discover empirically the kinds of claims that teachers can and do place on one another. Community emerges in the form of multiple ties with differential significance to individuals and to the institution, and with differential capacity to engage a teacher's loyalty and action.

Conclusion

In this essay, I have examined the ties between teachers' individual interests or inclinations and their membership in a broader professional community. The consequence of "opening up" our conceptions of independence and collegiality is to render them at once more conceptually robust and more empirically sensitive. It becomes apparent that "privacy" of teachers can be grasped only in the context of the organization and occupation of teaching, and that the character of professional independence is closely linked to the nature of professional community. "Being a teacher is not a single identity grounded only in classroom life, nor is professional community a seamless fabric, a single unity to which one is committed or not.

Recent debates and discussions both in regard to schools and in commentary on modern society provide us with the set of lenses and conceptual dimensions by which we might move beyond the "conceptually amorphous and ideologically sanguine" stance toward independence and collegiality in teachers' professional work. This analysis introduces dimensions of colleagueship that have gone largely unattended in a research literature that to date has achieved only a modest level of conceptual discrimination. In reexamining the distinctions between a norm of privacy and a norm of collegiality, it begins to distinguish strong from weak ties among teachers, and the way in which the norm of privacy is itself a form of collegial relation. To an emphasis on the forms and processes of collegial exchange, it adds a focus on the knowledge and beliefs that teachers express to one another either directly or indirectly. It extends colleagueship beyond the school walls and thereby renders problematic the critically unexamined link to value consensus. It acknowledges the multiplicity of locally meaningful reference groups. From a policy standpoint, this pursuit enables us to grasp the forces that contribute to teachers' performance and commitment and the specific ways in which those forces are linked to the contexts of the school and the occupation of teaching.

Acknowledgments

The research that informs this paper was supported by the Center for Research on the Context of Secondary School Teaching (Stanford University) with funds from the Office of Educational Research and Improvement, U.S. Department of Education; by the National Center for Research on Vocational Education (University of California, Berkeley) with funds from the Office of Vocational and Adult Education, U.S. Department of Education; and by the Educational Development Center, Inc., with funds from the Ford Foundation.

11

Teaching to Learn

A friend recently noticed that I was reading a copy of *Learning to Teach* by Richard Arends and commented that I was too close to retirement to learn how to do it correctly now. At the time I laughed, but in reflection I know that it is never too late to learn to teach. That is the basis for the excitement, strength, and motivation of the Puget Sound Professional Development Center renewal program. We at the middle level can learn better methods and strategies whether we are student teachers or veterans of twenty-five years.

Nanna S. Brantigan, 1991

The middle school teacher quoted above fulfills multiple roles in her daily life. She teaches language arts to seventh graders, serves as the school librarian, presents at conferences nationwide on team-teaching and cooperative learning, engages in action research, and participates actively in the restructuring of her own school. In addition, she has served as both the on-site supervisor for student teachers and as the Teaching Associate for the core seminar in a pilot middle school teacher education program offered through the Puget Sound Professional Development Center. Her story illustrates the core contention of this chapter that engagement in the preparation of the next generation of teachers provides rich opportunities for teacher learning.

When we speak of teacher learning, we are speaking of many things. Buchmann, for example, defines teacher learning as both "developing specific skills, dispositions, and understandings for enabling youngsters to learn worthwhile things in school" and "bringing one's education, experiences, and knowledge of people to bear on one's work over time." Within the first definition, teacher learning can consist of improvement of pedagogical skills, changes in attitudes or beliefs regarding teaching, or the acquisition of particular knowledge. Each of these goals for teacher learning suggests differing approaches to learning, as we do not acquire a skill in the same manner in which we change a belief. The second definition highlights the relationship between new learning and changes in classroom practice, a particular variety of learning from experience. In this conception of teacher learning, the everyday work of teachers becomes the crucible for teacher learning, as they transform their practice to reflect what they have come to know and believe over time. The most "authentic assessment" of teacher learning within this definition resides in teachers' actual classroom practices, for on can come to know something within the first definition without being able to bring it to bear upon one's practice.

Research on teacher learning comes from many sources. Some research has looked at teachers' acquisition of generic pedagogical skills, while other research has looked at the development of beliefs and perspectives about teaching. Recent work on teachers' subject-matter knowledge has explored the ways in which teachers acquire knowledge and construct new understandings about the subject-matter they teach, and the relationship between subject-matter knowledge and teaching. Research on staff development provides yet another resource for research on teacher learning. Each body of research illuminates a different facet of teacher learning. The nature of teacher learning in each of these research tradition, however, has been implicit rather than explicit. While several of these lines of research take a developmental perspective on what teachers know and are able to do, the processes of teacher learning have not been the central focus of these investigations.

For too long a curious dichotomy existed between conceptions of student learning and conceptions of teacher learning. While research in cognitive psychology and anthropology demonstrated the complexity of student learning and the persistence of students' prior conceptions, staff developers and teacher educators continued to act as if teacher learning were relatively unproblematic—one could simply tell teachers that telling students is insufficient. Recent research suggests that assumptions regarding student learning hold for teachers as well. Teachers must also be able to situate their new knowledge and understanding within the context of their actual classrooms. When teachers acquire new knowledge outside the contexts of teaching, they may find it difficult to bring this knowledge to bear upon actual classroom practices. As ampe argues, teachers' attempts to bring their new research-derived understandings about the nature of children's thinking into their teaching lead to unforeseen practical dilemmas. In order for learning within Buchmann's second definition to occur, teachers must both see the connections between their learning and their everyday work as teachers and resolve the tensions between abstract principles and the complexity of classroom practice.

Contexts which Support Teacher Learning

In discussing the processes involved in learning to teach, Feiman-Nemser argues that "formal arrangements for teaching teachers and helping them to improve do not fit with what we know about how teachers learn to teach and get better at teaching over time." She identifies two perspectives on the professional development of teachers, one which focuses on the individual teacher as the agent for change, and a second which focuses upon the school itself as the context in which teacher learning does, or does not, occur. Shulman argues that schools as they currently exist are not structured to support the capability of teachers to learn from experience; in order for learning to occur, teachers must have the opportunity to get feedback on what they are actually doing as they teach and to understand fully the consequences of their actions. Because the limits of individual rationality post obstacles to accomplishing these tasks, Shulman argues for the importance of collegiality in learning from experience, a contention supported by the work of Little. Through observing one another's teaching, colleagues can help each other see more accurately and completely what each teacher is doing and the consequences of those actions. Collegiality, then, is an important feature of contexts which support teacher learning.

What contributes to the development of norms of collegiality and collaboration? Little argues that "nonroutine tasks tend to drive the formation of collaborative relations." According to this analysis, opportunities for teachers to engage in new tasks, including developing curricula at the school or district levels, mentoring beginning teachers, participating in school-based management, or engaging in the work of a professional development school, support the development of collegiality, which in turn contributes to a context which supports teacher learning.

Schools that provide a supportive context for teacher learning must also define teachers' engagement in these novel tasks as contributing to their own professional growth, either as classroom teachers or as members of a larger professional community. By expanding their conception of teachers' work beyond the classroom walls, administrators, as well as teachers, can value learning that does not provide specific ideas for classroom teaching, but may provide new ways of thinking about teaching more generally or new skills for fulfilling their expanded roles on site councils, interdisciplinary teams, or in teacher education programs.

Finally, contexts that support teacher learning create specific structures to promote reflection and experimentation with teaching. The nature of these structures may vary widely, but their presence reminds us that opportunities for learning can be structured into organizations; without explicit structures, learning from teaching is left largely to chance.

The second wave of reform has provided a number of novel tasks for teachers, including participation in school-based management, work as mentor teachers, and involvement in teacher education through professional development schools. In this chapter I examine the specific example of a professional development center as a changing context for teaching which offers both opportunities and constraints for teacher learning.

Opportunities for Teacher Learning through Engagement in Teacher Education

The professional preparation of beginning teachers and the education of students form the entwined raison d'etre of a professional development school. Professional development schools assume that these responsibilities will be shared by educators at the school site and university facult. Explicit in the concept of a professional development school is the assumption that all teachers are learners who are engaged in ongoing inquiry into their practice. Less explicit in discussions of professional development schools are the processes through which participants will come to see themselves as a community of inquirers into teaching and into the nature of the learning that can result from inquiry.

In the Puget Sound Professional Development Centre, a team composed of a university faculty member, a middle school principal, a middle school teacher, and a student teacher proposed the skeleton for a pilot middle school teacher preparation program to be run through our professional development centre. Our program, now in its second year of implementation, brings together university faculty, teachers, principals, and counselors to share in the responsibility for both the field experience and a core seminar for preservice teachers. Middle school teachers can participate directly in the preparation of preservice teachers through three distinct roles: cooperating teacher (often defined as a team of teachers responsible for one or two student teachers); site supervisors, responsible for supervision and evaluation of student teachers at their school site; and teaching associate, responsible for team-teaching the core seminar along with university faculty members. Each of these roles provides distinct opportunities for professional development; each role also contains its own constraints to the realization of these opportunities for teacher learning.

The Core Seminar

At the centre of this preservice program lies a core seminar for all students. The course is team-taught by a middle school teacher and three or four university professors with different areas of expertise. This core seminar collapses four required courses in the general teacher education program—general methods of teaching, educational measurement and evaluation, multicultural perspectives, and crucial issues in education—and incorporates content related to middle school philosophy and curriculum and to early adolescence. Throughout the seminar, issues and strategies related to special education are woven into the fabric of the course. Curriculum deliberations involve not only the seminar instructors, but site supervisors and cooperating teachers as well. Instruction of the seminar is shared by all team members, and middle school teachers from our professional development schools come to class occasionally to teach specific topics.

The core seminar has several purposes. One of its central purposes is to connect the two major components of the teacher education curriculum—the curriculum of the university and the curriculum of the field experience. Assignments for the seminar are often carried out at the school site, as students are engaged in writing case studies based upon data collected at the school site. For example, students write a case study of an exceptional student in one of the classes they are observing. For this assignment, they shadow the student throughout the day, collect other information regarding the student's individual educational plan, analyze the data, and write a case study which synthesizes their observations with their readings and discussions from the seminar.

The concept of reflective practice provides one leitmotif for the course. Students are expected to provide reasons for their pedagogical decisions and to scrutinize their decisions from the perspective of the readings and class discussion, as well as from the perspective of their observations in schools. The team of instructors attempts to model reflective practice by making our own teaching transparent to students. We provide a running commentary on our teaching dilemmas, our own reasons for various pedagogical decisions, and the class critiques the decisions on the basis of their own experience. The seminar becomes a common case of teaching in which we all participate and which is therefore available for analysis and reflection.

The seminar also strives to create a perspective on the joint construction of knowledge and the problematic nature of teaching. Because we have created a course that crosses the boundaries of academic disciplines, as well as the worlds of school and university, we have created a curriculum in which none of us is expert; we all have much to learn from each other. The multiple perspectives regarding teaching are represented in the very construction of the teaching team. As our class discussions represent, vividly at times, reasonable people disagree about many aspects of teaching. This planned disagreement helps represent to students the fundamental complexity of teaching and the lack of unambiguous answers in education.

The intent of this core seminar, then, is to create the hub of the wheel around which other experiences in teacher education are organized. Students learn to question what they see and hear from us as well as from their experiences in schools. They learn that knowledge can be constructed rather than transmitted and that colleagues can disagree and still respect each other. These expectations for students help shape the nature of their field experiences, as students carry these perspectives with them to their school sites

The Cooperating Teacher

The role of cooperating teacher is most familiar to the teachers in our program. A number of the middle school teachers have served as cooperating teachers in the past, sometimes for more than one university program. While theoretically the role of cooperating teacher offers a rich context for teacher reflection and renewal, the very familiarity of the role and the meanings traditionally associated with it may also work against teachers' use of this role as a route to personal professional development.

Serving as a cooperating teacher can provide opportunities for reflection both about one's own practice and about teaching more generally. Trying to explain what they do, and the reasons for those actions, to a novice may help experienced teachers make more explicit their tacit knowledge regarding students, classrooms, curriculum, and instruction. As Karen McElliott, a cooperating teacher in our program, commented, "This has made me more explicit about what I do. You can't keep your mouth shut and hope they'll figure our what's going on. You need to explain, elaborate, ask." Observing student teachers may also contribute to reflection by experienced teachers, as the beginner's mistakes can reacquaint teachers with skills that have become routinized over time. In helping student teachers analyze their practice, cooperating teachers may clarify their own craft knowledge and their understandings of the relationships between, for instance, classroom management and curriculum.

Both explanations and observations can also serve to stimulate cooperating teachers' reflections on classroom practice, which in turn may stimulate new learning. Cooperating teachers often commented that having a student teacher in their classroom "forced" them to verbalize the reasons for their actions; the very process of verbalization may require cooperating teachers to reexamine both their actions and their reasoning. Teachers may rethink their actions subsequent to a discussion with a novice teacher or may come to understand more clearly the connections, or lack of connections, between their goals and their actions. Having a beginner in one's classroom provides at least the opportunity to stop and reflect. Many of the cooperating teachers in our program used the words "forced to reflect" as they considered the benefits of being a cooperating teacher. As Karen McElliott commented, "The experience forces you to be reflective. You have to ask yourself *why* am I doing this and *should* I be doing this?"

Serving as a cooperating teacher also holds the possibility for acquiring new knowledge about teaching, including new methods of instruction, alternative approaches to curriculum, or different perspectives on classroom management. Fresh from their university classes, student teachers bring word of these new ideas and are eager to try them out in actual classrooms. In theory, this partnership with student teachers can serve as a source of new knowledge. As McElliott remarked, "Student teachers share ideas from their methods courses...mention books. I test what I know against what they're learning." Other cooperating teachers in our project talked about the feeling of being on "the cutting edge" of new knowledge through their association with the project and gave examples of new ideas and perspectives they had encountered through their student teachers.

Finally, the role of cooperating teacher within our professional development center holds the potential to open the classroom door to new relationships with colleagues at both the school and university and to forget a broader professional identity as a teacher educator. To take the role of cooperating teacher seriously is to expand one's definition of one's task from educating children to educating the next generation of teachers. This new role offers the opportunity to learn more about adult learning, about teacher education, about the wored of educational policy and research in teacher education. In talking about what the had learned as a cooperating teacher, McElliott mentioned her realization that "teachers really do have a responsibility to the profession. That's part of what we need to do. Find the best student teachers we can to replace us and....fight for better working conditions for these future teachers."

To suggest that serving as a cooperating teacher in our professional development center holds the potential for teacher learning these areas is not to claim that such learning inevitably occurs. A number of factors, both historical and structural, work against the realization of the learning the role theoretically could promote.

The very familiarity of the role of the traditional cooperating teacher poses formidable obstacles to recasting the role as an opportunity for teacher learning. As a number of our teachers have told us, in the past being a cooperating teacher has been seen as a reward for past performance. Rather than an incentive for further professional growth, taking on a student teacher has been seen as an "on-site sabbatical," a chance to retreat from the demands of the classroom, as the student teacher assumed increasing responsibility for teaching. No specialized knowledge was seen as necessary to fulfill the role, nor did the role require a new relationship to the university. Becoming a cooperating teacher in the past has not meant rethinking one's own practice or expanding one's professional identity. While many cooperating teachers have assumed these responsibilities on their own initiative, no explicit structures existed to support teachers' growth in this role.

Being cast as the "expert" in relationship to the student teacher may also provide obstacles to teacher learning. When student teachers bring in new ideas regarding curriculum, instruction, or classroom management, areas in which experienced teachers may have regarded themselves as expert, cooperating teachers may become defensive about their practices, rather than open to rethinking what they do. One cooperating teacher commented on the desire to "play it safe" when other adults are in the room. Defining cooperating teachers as "experts" may work against the very experimentation with teaching techniques that student teachers need to see modelled, as the connotations of expertise may preclude the possibility of necessary failures. In their determination to model exemplary practice, cooperating teachers may come to see less than perfect practice as a failure, rather than as an opportunity to think out loud with the student teacher about the dilemmas of classroom practice and the difficulties inherent in experimenting with new approaches to teaching and to teach student teachers how to learn from mistakes.

The division between experts and novices may also work against cooperating teachers taking advantage of the new knowledge and ideas brought by student teachers. While our cooperating teachers have mentioned instances of becoming aware of new methods or approaches from student teachers, relatively few talked about working to integrate these new ideas into their own classroom practice. New approaches may threaten the delicately balanced routines that manifest the teachers' expertise in the first place. Student teachers, then do not have the opportunity to see experienced teachers struggle to implement a different approach to teaching, nor do cooperating teachers take advantage of the opportunity to try out new methods or approaches in their classroom.

The reasons underlying the constraints to teacher learning do not necessarily lie with the individual cooperating teacher, but with the lack of explicit structures to promote learning in the sense of bringing new knowledge to bear upon classroom practice. Changing one's teaching is difficult in the best of circumstances, and changing any one aspect of teaching may cause new, unanticipated dilemmas to arise. Change is all the more difficult in the presence of an audience. If we expect that cooperating teachers' new knowledge or understanding will affect classroom practice, together we will need to create more explicit structures that build experimentation with teaching into the very hole of the cooperating teacher. We also need to create structures in which cooperating teachers can meet together to reflect on their teaching and on the dilemmas involved in balancing their responsibilities to student teachers with responsibilities to students. Our first attempt to create such a structure through an ongoing workshop for cooperating teachers was met with great enthusiasm. Cooperating teachers appreciated the time set aside to reflect on the nature of their roles and broader issues related to teaching and learning to teach. This structure, however, still stops short of supporting actual changes in classroom practice.

The Site Supervisor

A less familiar role in the preparation of new teachers in our model is that of the site supervisor. Rather than using university-based personnel to supervise and evaluate student teachers' field experiences, we have delegated these responsibilities to experienced teachers at our professional development center sites. The supervisors meet weekly with the student teachers throughout the year, orient them to the school site and key personnel, and observe and evaluate the student teachers using the university's evaluation system. In addition, the supervisors meet monthly with members of the teaching team from the core seminar. The preservice teachers consistently identify the site supervisors as one of the strongest features of our model. They appreciate the ready access to a supervisor who is knowledgeable about the particular contexts of both the school and district and who is committed to their development as beginning teachers. While the benefits to the preservice teachers seem clear, there are also potential benefits for the experienced teachers who fulfill this role.

One opportunity for learning is similar to that available to cooperating teachers. Through both observing novices and engaging in discussions with them about teaching, supervisors are challenged to make their own understanding of teaching more explicit. The need to provide feedback to student teachers has challenged supervisors to find a more precise vocabulary with which to communicate about teaching. While in disagreement with some aspects of the university evaluation system, the supervisors appreciate the access it provides to a common technical vocabulary for observing and discussing aspects of classroom instruction. In addition to making explicit their more intuitive knowledge, supervisors have commented on the stimulus provided by the observation for reflection on their own teaching. As two of our supervisors discovered, evaluating the lack of closure in student teacher's lesson prompted them to reexamine their own problems in closing lessons. As one of the site supervisors, Karen Gosney, commented, "Whatever I see in them, I try to analyze in my own teaching." She talked about her discussions with one student teacher who planned marvelous activities but found it difficult to connect the activities with what he wanted students to learn. This discussion stimulated her to "go back and ask, `Why am I doing this? What do I want students to learn?" This supervisor saw her role in teacher education as a "wonderful chance for me to grow in my own teaching."

Site supervisors also see their new roles as a redefinition of their relationship to teaching. They see themselves as active contributors to the preparation of the next generation of teachers, extending their influence beyond the sphere of their own classrooms. As Gosney commented, "Perhaps being part of the `big picture' of teaching is what I really like the most. I don't feel isolated in the classroom. I have experience that makes me feel valued, respected, a contributor." One important feature of the role of site supervisor is that teachers do not need to leave teaching to expand their role. As Gosney remarked, "being valued in a mentoring capacity makes me happy to be in the classroom." Little argues that "as they mature personally and professionally, teachers also seek involvement and influence beyond the classroom." Through participation in preservice education, teachers can expand their influence without abdicating their primary responsibility to classroom teaching.

By virtue of their responsibilities, site supervisors are thrown into novel relationships with their peers. When relationships between student teachers and cooperating teachers create conflict, the site supervisor is the first person to know and often the first person to act. Supervisors have served as mediators in these situations, a role that can cause both discomfort and professional growth. While talking with peers about aspects of their teaching that trouble student teachers does not come easily to site supervisors, in the process they may acquire new skills in communicating with colleagues about difficult topics related to practice. When one cooperating teacher argued that the classroom techniques advocated by the student teacher would simply not work in his school, the site supervisor mentioned that other colleagues at the school were using these same approaches. These conversations challenge the norms of nonintrusiveness and isolation among teachers, as the practices of cooperating teachers become the concern of the site supervisor. The role itself creates new negotiated relationships at the school site, since the university supervisor must mediate between collegial responsibilities to the cooperating teacher and responsibilities for the supervision of student teachers.

We have created a few explicit structures that provide some of the conditions necessary for learning. In monthly meetings with all the supervisors and several of the instructors from the core seminar, supervisors have the chance to share their emerging knowledge of supervision and the difficulties associated with their job. While they learn that they are not alone in their dilemmas, they also acquire new approaches to supervising and mediating between teachers and student teachers.

These monthly meetings also provide information about the university's intentions and goals and a chance for supervisors to contribute to curriculum deliberations. Supervisors bring student teachers' concerns to the attention of the seminar instructors and together we discuss dilemmas and tensions in educating new teachers. These meetings provide supervisors with a "behind the scenes" look at the role of university coursework in preparing new teachers and the challenges of articulating coursework and field experiences. For example, supervisors and seminar instructors discussed what beginning teachers needed to learn about lesson planning and the disjunction between what they heard in class and what they saw at the school site. With a fuller understanding of the university's reasons for requiring lesson plans for beginners, supervisors were better equipped to help student teachers work on planning. Supervisors also gained an awareness of the ways in which they inadvertently contributed to "mislearning" on the part of students with regard to lesson planning. When bemoaning one student's failure to write a lesson plan for a lesson she had evaluated, one supervisor wondered how the student could have thought that she did not need a lesson plan. During the course of the discussion, the supervisor remembered that when the student teacher had asked her about lesson planning, she had commented that she no longer wrote elaborate lesson plans; in the context of our discussion, she suddenly realized that the student may have "learned" that good teachers do not write lesson plans, a lesson the supervisor had not intended to teach. These discussions help surface the ways in which the university and school site can work at cross-purposes in the preparation of teachers.

A second structure consists of a cross-site supervisor who works with supervisors and student teachers at all four sites of our professional development center. The site supervisor and cross-site supervisor do at least one common observation of a student teacher and share their perceptions with each other. This structure provides opportunities for supervisors to get feedback on their observations. Areas of disagreement between the two supervisors can also provoke reflection.

These newly acquired skills serve on-site supervisors in good stead as teacher leaders, while their role challenges prevailing norms of teaching. The divided loyalties inherent in the role of on-site supervisor—between school site and university, between student teachers and school colleagues—can be a potential deterrent to, as well as a stimulus for, professional growth and learning.

The first obstacle to learning, not surprisingly, is the lack of time available to supervisors not only to fulfill teaching and supervisory responsibilities but to reflect on what they are learning in the process of supervision. The role of the supervisors provides access to a number of other classrooms and opportunities to see a variety of teaching approaches. While supervisors have many opportunities to acquire new ideas for teaching, they may find it difficult to spend the time changing their own practices in light of the other demands on their time. A second obstacle involves the lack of feedback on one's own teaching. Unlike cooperating teachers, supervisors do not have another adult in their own classrooms to provide feedback as they question their own practices or experiment with new approaches.

The Teaching Associate

The final role in which classroom teachers participate in the preparation of preservice teachers is the role of teaching associate. The teaching associate is part of the team that plans and teaches the core seminar for the student teachers in our program. The teaching associate is expected to contribute to curriculum development for this innovative course as well as share responsibilities for instruction.

The role of teaching associate requires the teacher to reconsider what beginning teachers need to know and how they can best acquire that knowledge. Again, the role requires teachers to make their craft knowledge explicit in curriculum deliberations with the teaching team. As Nanna Brantigan, the current teaching associate, commented:

> One of my contributions to the seminar should be that of a practitioner's craft level of knowledge about middle school education, and I do feel that I have substantial knowledge in this area. However, this knowledge now needs to be documented and validated as part of a body of knowledge that is important for student teachers to have. I have read and reread much of my middle school

literature in addition to the assigned course materials in order to more thoroughly integrate the seminar goals with the reality of life in a middle level school.

During curriculum planning sessions, practitioners' and researchers' assumptions about middle school education may be challenged by other team members. As Brantigan implied, claiming the importance of a particular aspect of the curriculum also requires providing support for those claims, a requirement that may be more familiar to professors, used to citing sources at the drop of a hat, than to teachers. In these curriculum deliberations, teaching associates may begin to look more critically at the existing literature and deepen their own understanding of how middle school philosophy and curriculum fit into a broader theoretical framework about teaching and learning.

By virtue of literally being in two places at once, in both a field site and in university coursework, teaching associates have the potential of developing a broad understanding of teacher education with its inherent tensions and dilemmas. They are in the best position to see the fit, or lack of fit, between the instructional, curricular, or assessment approaches advocated by the university seminar and the practices students are likely to encounter at the school site. These potential disjunctions again provide opportunities for reflection, as well as for the acquisition of new knowledge and approaches to teaching. The teaching associates have described encountering for the first time the language of instructional scaffolding or of concept attainment and concept formation and the theories of learning that underlie these approaches. Already familiar with methods that draw upon these assumptions, teaching associates are able to build upon their existing craft knowledge and acquire a language that enables them to talk to both university and school-site colleagues as well as a better understanding of the theoretical assumptions underlying particular methods. As representatives from the field, teaching associates are often called upon by students to explain the disjunction between images of practice offered in university courses and practices encountered at school sites, which again provides an opportunity for reflection and the potential impetus for action.

These opportunities for learning are constrained, however, by the ways in which the role is currently structured. In commuting between the two worlds of school site and university classroom, the teaching associate may feel lost by the roadside. With not enough time at either site, they may feel disconnected from changes occurring at their own schools. Brantigan writes of her frustration with her inability to attend meetings at her own school because of the seminar: "Rather than being a bridge between the building and the university this year, I sometimes feel estranged from my school program." Responsibilities to the university may conflict with responsibilities to the school site. This estrangement may also make it difficult to bring new knowledge and insights gained through participation in the seminar to bear upon either school or classroom practices.

While each of these roles in teacher education contains its own unique opportunities and obstacles for teacher learning and renewal, common to all roles is the need to balance the demands of teaching students, teaching prospective teachers, learning for oneself, and bringing one's new knowledge and understanding to bear upon teaching. The very complexity of these demands suggests the need for a community response, rather than leaving it to the individual to manage the dilemmas inherent in these sometimes conflicting roles.

Communities for Learning to Teach and Teaching to Learn

The promise of professional development schools lies in the potential to create communities of learning about teaching. All of us must balance the roles of practitioner and learner, with the inherent assumptions of expertise and uncertainty. We all have much to learn from each other; we must all abdicate the authority for knowing the answer to every question raised by student teachers. But in creating such centers for teacher learning, we must also grapple with questions concerning the necessary conditions for a school in which all participants are indeed learners. How can we exploit and support opportunities for learning inherent in new roles for teachers and faculty?

Changing contexts for teaching can create rich opportunities for teacher learning. Emerging evidence from professional development schools and from restructured schools suggests that by fulfilling new roles within these sites, teachers can acquire new knowledge and understanding about teaching and broaden their sense of professional responsibility to include school governance and decision making or the preparation of tomorrow's teachers. Less evident is whether or not teachers draw upon their new knowledge to change existing school or classroom practices. Numerous obstacles ¾structural, historical, practical, individual¾ exist to forestall changes within classrooms. As we engage in the rethinking of schools, we need a clearer understanding of both the nature of these obstacles to teacher learning and how we can overcome them.

Just as research on children's learning has led to understanding the social context of cognition, research on teacher learning must look toward interactive theoretical models that look at both the individual and the social organization of schooling to understand teachers' learning. Creating opportunities for teacher learning by creating new roles will not suffice, in the absence of a better conceptual understanding of the nature of teacher learning and of explicit structures within schools that support teacher learning over time.

This chapter provides initial speculations about the ways in which teachers can learn about teaching through engagement in new roles and tasks associated with the changing contexts of schooling. As we engage in the effort to change the contexts in which teachers work, we also need research that will help us understand more clearly the various forms of teacher learning and the features of contexts that support them. We too have much to learn, if we are to realize the potential of professional development schools as learning communities, in which learning to teach and teaching to learn become part of the everyday landscape of teaching.

12

Teacher Leadership in a Teacher-Run School

Across the country there is despair over the flagging quality of public education. Everywhere people are looking for classrooms from which students emerge able to participate in and contribute to contemporary society. Everyone is searching for teachers who can lead our schools to new practices which can be responsive to changing student needs. That search is manifested in a variety of ways: weekly newspaper articles on exceptional teachers; a spate of books about the odds teachers face (*Among School Children Small Victories, Walking Trees*); state by state legislation which promotes teacher leadership and school change; and television specials ("Schools That Work" and "Solving the Education Crisis"). Underlying all these examples is a kind of unspoken hope that teachers can lead our students to more productive lives and salvage our hopes for public education.

Several years ago, in order to better understand teacher leadership and its potential to improve schooling. I studied a small group of experimenting teachers who were in positions of leadership. I knew that teachers had been taking leadership roles in districts for years and I believed that those teachers might contribute greater depth to the growing conversation about the potential of such leadership positions for improving educational experiences for students.

I learned that current roles tell a great deal both about the possibilities that teacher-leader positions bring to the improvement of educational practices and about the problems that arise as a result of these roles. In theory all the positions I studied were created to bring about changes in faculty practices on behalf of better student learning. Whether or not teacher leaders could actually match these theoretical intentions seemed to depend on a number of conditions. Teacher leaders were successful if (a) they worked with willing colleagues and had time to collaborate; (b) there was shared agreement on the need for change; (c) they were not diverted to administrative work, such as scheduling assemblies and organizing volunteer teas; (d) the instructional focus of their work supported changing practices rather than reinforcing current common practices; (e) their role had been created and implemented by those who were supposed to change as a result of the teacher leader's work;(f) that role was flexible enough to provide different kinds of collaborative relationships for a faculty with diverse needs.

When most or at least some of these conditions were in place the possibilities for improved practice were compelling. I visited classrooms where teacher leaders were working with students who were engaged in rigorous work, functioning as historians, journalists, film makers, archivists, environmentalists social activists. Youngsters worked at problem solving, simulating think tanks in which experts struggle with confounding problems that face our nation and others. Students shared the fruits of their intellectual labors and were articulate about the gains they had made. They pointed out the connections among disciplines and the advantages of the technology they were using. Perhaps, most important, their classrooms were places that the students, their teachers and I found interesting. They were at once casual, intense, varied in pace depending on the activity, sometimes noisy, sometimes quiet, sometimes conflicted, but always places where students, were doing the learning were engaged, and had left passivity in the hall or in front of their televisions sets at home.

In addition to illustrating the problems and the possibilities for teacher leadership, that study proffered two confounding paradoxes. By their very nature teacher leadership roles suggest that shared leadership is possible in the midst of hierarchical systems. Principals and department heads must share their authority and responsibility if teachers in leadership positions are to have a legitimate opportunity to bring about change. District offices must be willing to expand the leadership team in a school if the roles are to be authentic. Given the years of hierarchical practices in schools, traditional norms are challenged when teachers have leadership responsibilities.

At the same time, if teacher leadership positions are to be effective, teachers must be willing to learn from their colleagues. Teachers have spent years going outside their schools for new ideas and for growth opportunities. In addition, because of salary structures, most teachers have equal status, differentiated only by the number of years in the district. Frequently there is an inherent mistrust of anyone who rises above the rest, an immediate relegation of teacher leaders to the ranks of administrators, even if the teacher leader spends part time in the classroom. Another common attitude is often reflected in such statements as "Any teacher who has taught next door to me for years can't know more than I do! We've been in the same faculty meetings for years, struggled with the same students. We've even taken a couple of the same courses in the summer. I like him (or her) a lot, but we teach different subjects.

Despite these two unresolved paradoxes, interest in teacher leadership continues grow and expand.Shortly after I finished this study, I was invited to Aguilar Elementary School. It is a K-6 elementary school serving 700 students in a small urban center in the high southwestern desert. Eighty percent of the students are Hispanic, 15 percent are Anglo and the rest are Native American, Afro-American and Asian. In its seventh year, Aguilar had 50+staff members. Aguilar recently joined "Re:Learning'' but had been working for a number of years to find better ways to support their students. (Re:Learning- is a partnership between the Education Commission of the State a number of states the Coalition of Essential Schools at Brown University, and some 100 member schools across the country. The objective of the partnership is to create educational systems which support schools as they redesign their practices to help students learn to use their minds well.) Aguilar was also experimenting with multi-aged grouping in a program called Winter Exploration (WE). They had begun an early intervention program that had a number of components. A year before, the principal had taken a new position, and the teachers undertook the management of the school in order to protect the changes they had begun to make. They believed they were pioneering in the field of teacher leadership, and invited me to help them think about their work. In this chapter I report on Aguilar's rather remarkable, story, using numerous quotations taken from taped records of my group sessions with the faculty. Then I reexamine teacher leadership through the lens of Aguilar; its case offers fresh insights on the problems and possibilities for educational change.

Aguilar Elementary School

As the yellow school buses roll into the school, yard, the morning sun illuminates a big school. Students swarm around, playing, while teachers usher them this way and that. The atmospheres is lively. Several languages zing through the air; the intonations are cheerful and energetic.

Students and teachers move into the building and into the classrooms, ready for the day to begin. While it is a warm, caring place, Aguilar reflects a number of the pressing challenges a majority of our schools face. A minority of its students come from two-parent homes. A majority of the parents work and as a result have little time to tend to their children's academic progress. Few students are gaining the essential skills they need in order to participate in our complex society. The surrounding community is very poor. Many students come to school hungry; many are disconnected from the purposes of schooling.

Like many schools across the country the staff at Aguilar has rallied to address these challenges. Rather than railing over changing conditions while clinging to traditional practices, these teachers have determined that they must find better ways to serve their students.The changes they wish to make are difficult because they require that everyone involved teachers, parents, administrators—question familiar, comfortable, practices, which no longer seem to be effective. They have mustered the courage and the flexibility to suggest alternatives. Then, toughest of all they have begun to experiment. All this takes extra time and new reserves of energy. Everyone knows that both these resources must come from a professional commitment to students, for there is no money to compensate teachers for extra time and effort.

Changing Leadership In a Changing School

Aguilar Elementary School is a young school in a growing district. For seven years. Al Stevensen was the principal. A twenty-six year veteran in the district came with him to open the school. She described Mr.Stevensen as follows:

> He was an easy, laid back kind of guy, and I think he purposely hired very strong people who had a very deep philosophy about what they were doing, people who were not afraid to stand up and express opinions. He was very child, oriented, always reinforcing the idea that everything we did should be based on what is good for children. He let the teachers and the staff know that we were the professionals: "You know what you're doing.I trust you. Go to it." He involved us a great deal in the decisions as we developed and built this school. It is no accident that this school has turned out the way it has.

In the summer of the school's seventh year Mr. Stevensen sent a letter to the staff to announce his retirement. Although it was not common practice at the time, two of the teachers were invited by the central office to sit on the committee for selecting a new principal. Tim Senoza, a teacher who had been at the school for two years, was selected. The veteran teacher described him:

> He shared Al's philosophy, but was more of a pusher, a mover, and a shaker. He said to us, "Come on. We can do all kinds of wonderful things. There is lots that can be done for these kids that we're not doing now." He brought us together socially. We did a

lot of eating together, and we celebrated everything. We got involved with a foundation which supported us in thinking about restructuring. They brought lots of speakers in who told us about different possibilities. Tim kept telling us, "This is our chance. what do we want to do?"

Another teacher commented:

For two years, the staff worked together to develop a mission statement and goals. We started our early intervention program which has a lot of pieces to it¾peer tutoring, adult tutoring, summer school. We stopped pulling some kids out for remedial help.

And the veteran teacher again:

We just started doing all of this stuff. No one told us to. We talked a lot about who we were, what our kids were, what our philosophy is, and then more ideas came up to the top. We all felt that we wanted multi-aged grouping and we wanted a more experience-oriented curriculum. And we wanted our kids to feel comfortable in a large school. We wanted them to know more adults than just their teacher and more kids so they wouldn't feel lost. And so we started our Winter Exploration (WE) program, which is still evolving.

Then, in the summer of 1989, the staff received a letter from the principal saying that he had taken another job. Members of the staff described their reactions to the principal's leaving.

We were happy for him, but it sent us into a panic. We thought "What's going on here? We've got all these programs going. We're the biggest elementary school in the district. How are we going to...?" I mean this is not an easy task. So several of us got together and camp up with a plan for a team of teachers to run the school.

Another teacher put it this way:

It wasn't a statement against principals. In fact, our principals had really helped us to get to the point where we were ready to take more responsibility. It's just that we knew that if someone came who didn't like what we had started.....

Other teachers added their concerns about what happens to innovative programs in schools when leaders leave: "Who'd want to deal with a staff like us?" "I've worked in several schools. Each new principal has different ideas about what should be done." "Or how things should be run." "Remember that library program we started at Watervale Elementary? That died after our principal left".

The dilemma is a common one. Educational leaders change jobs frequently. The reasons for this are quite simple: it is necessary in order to move up the very limited career ladder. Department heads become assistant principals. Principals in small elementary schools move to larger elementary scnools before moving to secondary schools or to the central office. Teacher leaders become staff development or curriculum specialists working out of the central office, or they move to assistant principalships. Everyone on the staff at Aguilar had experience with changes in leadership. At this particular time the staff was fearful, based on previous experiences that they might lose momentum during the transition to a new principal, or worse,that the work they had begun might be dismissed as unimportant while the new administrator set to work on a more personally compelling agenda.

Planning for Teacher-Managed School

After learning that Mr.Senoza was leaving a self-selected committee of eight teachers quickly gathered to discuss their options. The committee was aware that a number of the elementary principals would likely be interested in transferring to Aguilar. They also knew that there was no one on the staff who expressed any interest in moving into administration. In addition, the staff was in the midst of several experimental programs that were important to them. They were about to begin the third year of the WE program—an experiment in interdisciplinary instruction with multi-age grouping of students. Their continuing hope was that as they became more comfortable with the very different teaching practices involved in WE, they would redesign the regular school program to include multi-age grouping and team teaching. They had just completed their third year of the early intervention program with its multiple foci. Several staff members had submitted a proposal for additional funding the U.S. Department of Education. They received a grant of $101,000—no small feat for a group of teachers. That award would strengthen and sustain their early intervention program for a year, and they were in the midst of determining best uses for the money.

Energy was high on the staff. Everyone felt that they were building a more powerful, more caring and progressive place for students. They had been innovating and experimenting for a couple of years and their efforts had taught them that they need not be bound by traditional structures or practices. Moreover, they had watched two principals run themselves ragged in their large elementary school. A senior teacher observed.

Currently, no matter how large the elementary school is there is only one principal. Period. It doesn't make any difference if the school is bigger than a junior high or a middle school, both of which have assistant principals. The elementary schools are perceived to need only one administrator. We've watched firsthand. It's too big a job for any one person. So we thought about how we might improve that situation.

The planning group generated a plan to establish a management-team approach to running the school and went to the superintendent with their plan. His response was:

I think it's great. Why don't you try for it, but you have to do a couple of things. You'll need to get waivers from the State Department of Education. You'll need to prepare job descriptions for each of the team members and describe how the team will work. You'll need to make a presentation to the board, and you'll need to get the agreement of the entire staff.

The planning group conceived of a management team of four people—a "facilitator" and three coordinators. Each would have special responsibilities but all would work together to coordinate their efforts in running the school. All members of the team would receive a stipend in addition to their regular salaries. The total amount available for stipends would be determined by subtracting a veteran teacher's salary from the principal's salary. The difference would be divided among the team members according to their responsibilities. The facilitator, to be selected by the planning group and approved by the staff, would be released entirely from teaching and would receive a stipend of $3,000. The three coordinators would be selected by the staff. Each coordinator would teach full time and would receive a stipend of $1,500.

The special responsibilities envisioned for each member of the team were as follows:

The facilitator. The facilitator would have responsibility for the day-to-day running of the school, would attend all district-—level administrative meetings, and would be the liaison between the central office and the school staff. Other responsibilities would include: doing all the paperwork required by the district and the state, evaluating teachers who were up for comprehensive evaluation (required every third year); making employment recommendations to the superintendent; carrying out board policies; maintaining student records and personnel records. coordination community relations; overseeing building and grounds; overseeing instructional matters.

The coordinator for staff evaluations. The staff evaluations coordinator would supervise the peer evaluation program, including assuming responsibility for appropriate documentation, contact the assistant superintendent on all evaluations that required growth plans; chair the peer evaluation committee and communicate its work to the rest of the faculty.

The coordinator for building and grounds. The coordinator for building and grounds would be responsible for maintaining a safe environment; for coordinating the work of the custodial staff; for ordering supplies and materials, including textbooks for dealing with all maintenance issues; for coordinating bus schedules; and for maintaining the inventory of the school's equipment.

The coordinator for academics. The academics coordinator

would be responsible for the instructional program in the school. This responsibility would include working with staff assignments, keeping track of students' cumulative folders, organizing plans for professional development and curriculum development participating in committees dealing with curriculum and instruction.

The planning group wrote up this plan and approached the State Department of Education. An official of the department described its position as very supportive— "sort of like the Wizard of OZ giving the Tin Man a heart when he had a heart all along. We conferred upon them the right to do what they already had the right to do". There were no policies in place that prevented a team from running a school.

The planning group then brought the staff together during the summer. They explained what they were proposing and why and held a staff vote—everyone from custodial staff to teachers. A woman who had some administrative training and had been in the district a long time was suggested by the planning team for the facilitator's position. A member of the planning team, she had already agreed to take the facilitator's role if the staff were supportive. The rest of the management team would be selected by the staff once the board approved the plan. The vote was 35 to 2 in support of the plan for a management team. Comments like the following describe how the staff felt about the plan:

One of the things about this staff is that we don't think of all the worst possible scenarios to figure out why something won't work. We just think, "Hey, that sounds really near Let's try it.''

We like the ownership of our own work. We thought if we vote to do this we will really be in charge of our own program. We wanted it to work.Then we took the proposal to our parent group. It was summer and so we had a small percentage (of parents present) but the really interested active parents came and we presented it and they voted to support it, too.

The planning group and the facilitator then approached the board with the plan. After a grueling and very difficult session the board approved the plan by a 4 to 1 vote. The board viewed the proposition as both interesting and problematic. As one teacher noted, "they were reticent to pay elementary teachers a stipend even though high school teachers receive stipends all the time." The board also perceived that the management team approach would create tension with the existing principals' group. At the same time the board enjoyed a reputation for innovation and were convinced by the superintendent that new ideas should gain a hearing. Like the teachers, board members had attended a number of sessions sponsored by a foundation on the need for change. They approved the experimental team on a year-to-year basis.

The assistant superintendent in charge of principals stated that she would supervise the facilitator in the same way principals are supervised. The rest of the management team would be supervised by the facilitator. The staff then proceeded to recruit people to fill the other three positions on the management team.

When the 1989-90 school year began, the management team was in place.

We knew it was going to be chaotic that first year. We were pioneers and none of us really knew what to expect. So we just dug in and worked hard to define roles and figure out who was going to do what. The first year was hard but we made it, and we had lots of ideas about how to improve things for the second year.

Over the summer months, the board unanimously approved the management team for another year.

A Teacher-Rum School in Action

At the time of my visit in October, 1990, the staff had made a few revisions in their original plans for the management team. One of the management team members stepped down because the additional responsibility took too much time away from her students. A replacement team member was just learning the ropes. The staff had conducted a session to clarify who makes what decisions, and was operating under those new understandings. Parents talked about the schools as an exceptional place, and indicated that they were happy to support the teachers. Parents' Night attendance was way up. Two of the seven board members believed that they represented the board's opinion that, at least for this second year, the school was well managed.

Protecting Changes being Made

The major purpose for establishing the management team was to protect the changes the staff was in the midst of making when the principal left. A brief look at their most ambitious projects will illustrate how their work was proceeding.

The early intervention program was established to give children who are likely to fail a series of boosts to make their academic success more possible. The program had several components ranging from the conduct of workshops for parents to a six-week summer school for a multi-aged group of thirty children who ended the school year the farthest behind. Each of the early intervention programs was managed by a committee, and each committee was in the process of putting in place the previous year's recommendations gathered from parents, students, and staff members.

The WE program, in its third year, consisted of interdisciplinary courses offered to multi-aged groups of students by self-selected teams of teachers. As the WE committee was planning for the 1991 program, they were rethinking a number of their previous practices. Teachers were in the process of building new teams with a stronger interdisciplinary focus, and they hoped to experiment more with the nine Common Principles of the Coalition of Essential Schools—student as worker, teacher as coach among others—because these were new to the staff.

Other changes in their school program had occurred since they began to manage the school. The special education teacher mainstreamed her students and began working with them in the regular classroom. The school improvement committee—a committee begun under Mr. Senoza—continued to work in issues related to site-based management and professional development. A committee was in its second year of dealing with Aguilar's participation in Re:Learning. All told, there were some fifteen working committees each designed to address changes the staff wished to make in the school.

In addition to continuing the programs begun earlier the management team approach gave those programs a new thrust. During the 1989-90 school year, a peer evaluation committee established a process for annual review. Their belief was that in a teacher-run building they should share responsibility for the quality of instruction. A second objective of the peer review program was to break down the isolation in which teachers traditionally work so that they might begin to learn from one another. The staff talked animatedly about the peer evaluation program. Some of the comments were:

Last year, we all wanted this to work well so we were very — well, kind. I feel a transition in this now. I feel like we're going to get a little tougher with each other; we want to really talk about things we see.

This was pretty exciting. I've taught here all these years and have never seen the people teach who are next door to me. Now I am able to see how they deliver curriculum, how they handle discipline problems, how they manage the flow of things in the classroom.

And to have another person from your level, an experienced person, come in and observe you and then dialogue with you is just a tremendous learning experience.

But it was tough. A lot of us nervous about it. Some said, "Wait a minute. That's not what I signed up to teach for I'm not an administrator. I don't want go in there finding fault with people."

We were all nervous. And we learned a lot about our differences.

I asked about the differences in instruction they were seeing. They agreed that some people used more cooperative learning techniques but that the majority of the staff used pretty traditional methods and resources. I asked whether they believed they would eventually take a stand in favor of one type of instruction over another. A lively debate ensued. Several noted that all teachers need a variety of instructional methods, and that the old should not be discarded altogether. Others claimed that they need more staff development in order to know more about different methods. Others noted that they were going to have to face it—some teachers would never change, and that they were going to have to say something. A teacher in his second year at the school said, " What is remarkable here is the overall climate. Forcing methods of instruction could undermine what the staff has begun. They need to evolve." As the complexities of the conversation opened up, the volume went up and emotions rose. One of the veterans said," Whoa! Hold it. We're starting only our second year of peer observations. Each year we'll move forward. We have to keep track of the benefits we're gaining as well as think of how to make these observations more powerful. Lighten up!" The rest of the group laughed and then admitted that they were not a particularly light group.

Teacher Management: Comments by Teachers

In their discussions with me the staff expressed the view that managing the school had provided important benefits, had brought some unanticipated challenges, and had taught them a few good lessons as well.

Benefits

The benefits were important to sustain their drive to keep going. For instance, outsiders were interested in what they were doing, which had a double benefit. The staff at Aguilar clarified their purposes for visitors but also learned from hearing what other schools were doing.

A veteran teacher said, "We are helping each other more. I have gotten to know my colleagues better, so we talk things out together, which reduces the stress teachers feel. I help Tanya, who takes everything very seriously, to be less—well, serious." Nodding emphatically, Tanya responded, "We've become better friends. It makes the pressure of change easier to manage."

A newcomer in the school said:

One thing I've noticed being here is that children and their needs are being discussed everywhere. In the lounge. In the bathroom. I think the reason why people feel good and successful here is that the focus is on the children. It is very intense here, much more caring of students. And, the management team approach encourages everyone to be a leader where they feel they can effect positive change. That is one of the best aspects of this school.

There was a good deal of discussion about stress, which was also perceived to have beneficial effects, as the following comments suggest:

The thing is, that it's different kind of stress than fighting with the principal, fighting with the system, always being told you have to do something when you know philosophically it is wrong.

There's big difference between the stress you create for yourself and stress that's created outside of you. I have control over the stress I create. I can say to myself, "I'm overdoing it, and I'm going to put this committee or responsibility aside right now." When outside forces create stress, I have no control.

All this has been important to me. Mr. Senoza was a good principal, and I liked working with him. Still I have had run-ins with other principals. Those experiences tended to make me want to work alone in my own room. I wanted to do this in order to have some say in the running of the school. I am normally an introvert, but my colleagues asked me to get involved and so I have. It has been very positive for me personally.

The other thing is that we've been able to hire people to come into the school who want to work in a school like this. Let's face it. We all work more hours in order to get our lessons done, to plan WE with our team members, to conduct observation and dialogues, and we're all on a million committees. Our new teacher is an example.

When we interviewed him, we really grilled him. In fact, I think we did more talking than he did because we really wanted him to know what he was getting into.

The newcomer responded to this last comment:

Truth of the matter is that I thought it was probably more psycho-babble rhetoric!. They said they were running the school by a team of teachers.... It was intriguing enough for me to be willing to drive 150 miles per day. And you know they—we—are running the school and it has been a great experience for me. One thing that surprises me is, really considering all the things they've done here and they new appropriation of responsibility I don't see any more problems or difficulties doing this than arise in the other places I've worked. I've encountered few difficulties here, and plenty of help.

Challenges

The staff talked openly about the challenges they faced. At the beginning of their second year of managing the school, they identified a number of unresolved issues.

Stress. The stress level among staff was very high. Everyone talked about it. "I eat, sleep and dream this place!' "In a school like this, we expect more of ourselves. We place more demands on ourselves and we all give a lot more time." They knew that they must find ways to preserve energy if they wanted to maintain staff and their efforts. No answers seemed readily available although people were trying a variety of strategies.

Communication. Communication among staff, the fifteen committees, and the management team posed a major challenge. Several teachers spoke to the problem.

We opened the door for people to participate and they started believing in it when they saw that their opinions; now they want to do it all the time and on every issue. Everyone wants to be heard.

The more programs we run, the less time we have to communicate. I spend a lot of time trying to contact teachers I need to communicate with, and I am frequently unable to get to them when I need to.

The facilitator also spoke of her concerns about communication:

> I often have to share decisions made by various committees. The most frequent response I hear is, 'Why wasn't I told about this?" The problem is that we have so many committees going and we try to put the minutes of the meetings in people's mailboxes, but people don't have time to read it all. So they feel left out of the communications loop.

In addition the management team was having difficulty communicating among themselves. Early in their second year they had not had a single meeting to coordinate their efforts. Several members of the team noted that they seldom met in the first year, that it was difficult for them to get together as they had not been given a ny released time to work together, and that their individual responsibilities and other committee meetings took place after school.

Decision making. Decision making constituted another major challenge. In the faculty meeting where the staff were told by the evaluation committee when and how the evaluation observations would be done for the 1990-1991 school year there was a great deal of tension in the room. The evaluations coordinator believed that the committee had taken the feedback the whole staff had given and had incorporated their suggestions and that the staff had vested the committee with the right to make decisions. She made it perfectly clear that the committee would not be flexible as they had been the previous year with scheduling evaluations and that people needed to follow the schedule. The plan was presented with little time for discussion. It appeared that the committee did not believe that discussion was necessary. Some of the staff were disgruntled. Time ran out at the meeting and a number of staff left feeling that several issues were unresolved. The committee felt some frustration as well.

The facilitator talked about the difficulties they faced with decision making:

We have so many committees the no one can attend all the meetings they'd like to so everyone ends up being left out of some decisions, which makes people unhappy. I am stumped as to what to do. We make all the meetings open so that anyone who wants to can participate. And sometimes people complain about decisions made even when they could have attended but chose not to. That's when I really want to tear my hair out! I don't know what to do with those people.

Staff who felt left out of decisions agreed that meetings were open, and also agreed that it was impossible to attend all the meetings they were interested in. They noted, however, that there were times when they had to forego participation in order to help students. Recognizing the dilemmas, they were not willing to concede that all avenues for legitimate participations had been explored.

A number of staff members talked about the obscurity which clouded decision making in general. The staff recognized a need to clarify who has the authority to make what decisions. After a lengthy meeting a list of agreements was distributed—which decisions would be made by management team members, by committee members or by the whole staff—but it was clear that many staff still felt that the issue of decision making was murky. In addition most decisions were made by majority vote, and they all felt the tension which resulted when there was significant division.

Role clarification. Another challenge was role clarification. The facilitator's role was the most confounding. The teachers in the school and personnel in the state department clearly believed that the school was run by a team of teachers, while board members and central office administrators described the school as run by a kind of principal. The facilitator was caught between the role as perceived by those higher up on the hierarchical ladder, and by her own colleagues with whom she worked daily—many of whom were fiercely committed to establishing the legitimacy of a teacher-run school. There was a kind of unspoken tension caused by the disjunction between these perceptions.

The teachers were proud of the extra responsibility they had all undertaken, and wanted recognition for their shared responsibility. They were also supportive of the risk that the facilitator had agreed to take on their behalf and believed that she, like everyone else, was trying hard to make things work. Several staff felt that the role was not open for discussion. There was some distrust over the fact that this position had not been selected by the whole staff, but appointed by the planning team. The staff recognized that the management team and the planning group did not feel that the district in general would support the management team approach if they felt that the staff disagreed about how it should be done. As a result, the staff which generally did not hesitate to open controversial discussions, remained quiet about the facilitator's role in order to secure the legitimacy of the management team first. There was no indication that anyone wanted to do away with the facilitator's role or replace the person serving as facilitator; they simply wanted to have the opportunity to talk about how it was working and to suggest possible revisions in much the same way they were critiquing other innovations. Given the tenuousness of the management team, the topic seemed particularly sensitive.

Paradoxically, the staff also found it difficult to make the shift from a principal to a management team. Individual management team members noted that everyone tended to go first to the facilitator for everything. The janitors went to the facilitator instead of to the building and grounds coordinator. Individual staff members ran their ideas for professional development by the facilitator instead of by the academic coordinator. Everyone had to be reminded to go to the appropriate person.

In addition, there were unanticipated problems which again raised questions about role clarification. Earlier in the year the staff noticed that several staff members were coming late. They asked, whose responsibility is a problem like that? The facilitator did not believe that she could facilitate for the staff and function as the disciplinarian as well, not did she want to watch people's comings and goings. She felt that the disciplinary role was traditionally the principal's role, but she was not a principal, and that there should be alternatices. any of the teachers wanted her to take that responsibility, believing that was why she had been released full time from teaching and given the largest stipend. One staff member suggested that it might be the responsibility of the peer observers. It was an issue on which they were still working.

Other role clarification issues surfaced as the management team members noted that their duties were much larger and more complicated than had been anticipated. The academic coordinator, the building and grounds coordinator, and the evaluations coordinator all taught full time and like everyone else, worked on several committees. Each of them was struggling to find ways of involving the staff in decisions rather than establishing policies in an authoritarian manner. They felt the separation from the rest of the staff that their new roles created, and they noted that they would like more time to meet together to form a stronger support group and a better team.

Time. Everyone on the staff talked about the lack of time. They needed time to work together in order to build stronger programs for students. A person who had been on the management team the first year quit because she believed that her outside responsibilities took time away from her students and that this directly contradicted her purposes in assuming management responsibility for the school. Full-time teachers on the management team noted that it was difficult for them to take full responsibility for their assigned duties because they were in class. There was no released time available for them to work together, and no support for occasional release when needed. All staff noted that because of so many meetings they could do little else during the regular school day than teach and attend meetings. Individual planning and preparation had to be done at home. Heightened involvement between specialists and regular teachers meant more meetings, as did increased parental involvement. Teachers were eager for more time to work together to plan their curriculum and to share instructional techniques, but they described the days as absolutely jampacked and meteoric in tempo.

New staff. Introduction of new staff proved another challenge. The staff seemed clear that this school was not for everyone and noted that several people had already left for more traditional settings. They believed that this was a positive thing. Furthermore, they were aware that this innovation—a teacher-run building—had been undertaken because the staff was uniquely willing to "give it a shot." The challenge lay in how to bring new people into a staff that shared common goals and a spirit of innovation so that the newcomers felt equal partnership. During their first year of managing the building, the staff noted that some newcomers felt left out of the decision making. When included, they often lacked the valuable historical background which helped to shape certain decisions. New-comers to the WE program and to the summer school program did not know about the philosophy upon which these programs had been built. The school had never had an explicit means of inducting new staff members into the school. Not until the beginning of the second, year,when several second-year returnees voiced their concerns, did it occur to the veteran staff that they needed a system for inducting newcomers. They were just beginning to discuss the kinds of possibilities—a buddy system, a mentoring partnership, or some sort of seminar for newcomers, with which they might experiment.

Coherence. The staff agreed that it was difficult to keep track of everything they were doing and to make sure that it all fit together. There were some fifteen committees in operation. The staff was not at all sure that there wasn't some overlap between committees or whether all fifteen were completely necessary. "Whenever we think of something that needs to be done, we form a committee. I'm not sure that we ask what existing committee might undertake a new task. I'm also not sure that we ever examine old committees to see whether we still need them".

Legitimate participation. The last challenge dealt with legitimate participation in the new management system. A number of staff worried that there were teachers who were silent partners, who didn't say much about what they thought should happen. Staff worried that these people felt left out or that they disagreed with the directions the school was taking, but were too intimidated by the more vocal staff members to speak up. Others mentioned that thee was a small group of dissenters, who complained no matter what and dragged the potential of the entire staff down with them. Everyone wondered how best to provide them with a voice without allowing them to undermine what the majority wanted to do. In another vein, four people suggested that the management team and the original planning group did not allow open conflict, that they kept the time for discussion too short in meetings, and used meetings to announce decisions made rather than to offer possible decisions and allow the staff the opportunity to have input. These staff members were worried that, while these actions revealed sincere hopes to protect the team concept, the management team was not allowing others to voice their legitimate concerns and as a result was undermining the potential of the very thing they were trying to create.

Lessons

The staff agreed that in their year of managing the school while attempting to carry on the changes they had begun they had learned several important lessons—some old, some new.

We learned about the importance of documenting decisions that are made in meetings, to have a historical record.

Yes, all of us have experienced selective memory. Things get so confusing sometimes that it is hard to keep track of exactly what we said we were going to do. Time and again we've had arguments because different people heard different things. So, we've learned to review decisions made at the end of each meeting for clarification and to commit those to the minutes. It helps to avoid more conflict later on.

We've learned that we have to work on alternative structures for meetings so that we can involve everyone. The funny part is that some of us were taking cooperative learning classes, but didn't think to apply it to the work the adults do until we wanted to review everything we'd been working on last year.

We put everyone in small groups and had them summarize

what they thought should be changed in all the areas where we had been working. It was a great meeting and everyone participated. I don't know why we don't do that more often.

We learned this summer that we really have to plan ahead. We were so busy during the school year with all the aspects of the early intervention program that we left the planning for the summer school until the summer. There we were with sex weeks of programs to run and not enough time to plan it as thoroughly as we would like.

The big problem was that we believed that we had planned it adequately because we had run it the summer before. What we didn't plan for were the changes in staff and the need to coordinate the curriculum. While the parents and kids loved what was offered, we knew that we could have done a better job.

I think we've learned to get things out in the open. I personally hate conflict, but I know that we can't work together unless we know who's thinking what. We're still not very skilled at it.

I don't think we know the best ways to air conflict yet. Doing it in an open forum, asking people to say what they think, necessarily becomes very personal at times. We need to get the issues out in a way that is less personal, less painful.

We have learned that there is more to be done. We'd like to find more ways to involve parents—those who work and can't get here during the day.

We want to look at alternative assessment. We haven't even begun to think about that.

We'd like to figure out how to measure the effects of the early intervention program by tracking some of the kids through high school.

Some of us want to team like we do for WE permanently, but WE has been a whole staff project and so we need to discuss that with everybody else.

We need a professional library. We go to workshops and

discover that people are reading things that would really help us—but the materials are hard for us to get. We should have them right here for all of us to share. We might be able to use part of our grant for that.

We need to do more work on our curriculum to make sure that the kids are getting everything they need.

The changes we've made at Aguilar are changes that we felt were important here for these children—the children we have here. It's not like a recipe. It's not like saying, "Okay, everything we've done here is terrific and you ought to try it in your school." So many of the reports we've read suggest that we adopt the ideas of another place. Or a new principal comes in and says, "We did this at my other school. I think we should do it here, too." We looked at our population. We tried to identify needs as we saw them as the children presented them to us and tried to devise something that will fit our students' needs. It's not a blueprint. I think, instead, we have learned to look within and ask, " What does our population of kids need?"

We've learned another thing. You can start a new program and you can change, but the change never stops. One change makes you change something else which makes you change something else. Like the WE program—we had to build an all-day kindergarten program if we wanted kindergarten kids to participate. Now some teachers want to do WE all the time. See what I mean? ''Once you start,it's hard to stop.''

As the staff developed this list of lessons they felt they had learned, each individual seemed to drew energy from the ideas of others. They generated enough projects and directions to last well into the next century. The room was full of energy, full of a feeling of challenge and potential—like the energy one feels among team members at the beginning of a race or a game. There was no flagging, no sense of exhaustion here.

A New Web of Questions

Teacher leadership at Aguilar is impressive¾the staff development a climate of experimentation, an innovative new management structure, and vested confidence in one another. However, as is to be expected with any new role, the Aguilar approach to teacher leadership spins its own web, and raises new questions. Each of the questions forces a more thorough examination and understanding of the most important issues related to teacher leadership.

Does Aguilar have a teacher-run school? Or are the perceptions of the board and the central office correct? For example, is the facilitator really a principal with a different title and some collegial support? If the facilitator is really a pseudo-principal, what gains have been made? If this is not the case and the role is legitimate, what is the difference and what are the costs and the benefits to students and adults? What are the advantages of a teacher-run school? Is the fact that the staff feels empowered to run their own school enough of a rationale? Should other school faculties be encouraged to run their own school? What does this say about the role of the principal? Does it suggest that the principal's role is in need of changing just as classroom practices are in need or revision?

Do the project which the staff has designed affect the quality of experience that students have in the classroom? The underlying purpose for the creation of the management team was to protect the changes the faculty had begun to make in projects such as WE, early intervention, and peer evaluation, each of which was designed to respond to the needs of students. To date, the Aguilar teachers have only their collective observations about WE to help them determine whether it is making a difference for their students. Because it was an extra program, they were not formally assessing student performance, but agreed that students seemed more motivated during WE than they did during the regular school day. Their assessment of the summer program was really focused on whether students and parents were satisfied with the program, or what changes they would, recommend, rather than on an investigation of whether the program led to a difference in achievement. Furthermore, while all these projects were aimed at helping students, none of them specifically addressed changing practices. Teachers described much of the pedagogy in the building as traditional—many teachers used texts, had reading groups, seated children, in rows, expected students to recite information gained. Even in their exploration of multi-age grouping and interdisciplinary work, teachers indicated that they were using fairly traditional methods. Each teacher was preparing his or her speciality while colleagues provided management support. My observation here is not designed to judge these methods but to consider a critical component of the purposes of their projects and of teacher leadership in general. If the projects are designed to improve the quality of students' learning, will doing more of the same really make a difference?

Will the management of the school influence the kind of instructional techniques and methods used? Perhaps the most essential question is whether undertaking the management of the school makes it more likely that teachers will provide students with better educational experiences. Will teachers eventually provide students more opportunities to think critically and to solve problems when they themselves have those opportunities or will students continue to find themselves filling in blanks and looking for teacher-approved answers? Turning the question a bit, is the net gain of participation in management of the school worth the time that teachers must take away from curriculum, instruction, and student assessment? This dilemma extends beyond those involved in the management team to the whole staff. The members of the management team indicated that they worked to include others in the decision making that falls under their respective responsibilities. Does staff participation in decision making and in peer evaluation, among other things, make them better able to provide students with powerful learning experiences? Or does the time they spend on management issues decrease the energy available to examine instructional practices?

Where does the coherence of the school's efforts come from? Aguilar is a large school. With a staff of more than fifty teachers and some fifteen committees, some confusion and overlap of effort is inevitable. One of the teachers pointed out that the greatest advantage of the school was that all teachers had the opportunity to contribute leadership where they felt most comfortable or most interested. This suggests a king of leadership density model designed to foster greater investment and creativity in a larger number of the people on the staff. While this is clearly desirable, it is equally desirable to consider the coherence of the entire effort. Surely someone or some group should be assessing the quality of each project and committee in light of the overall goals of the school. It is entirely possible that one committee might be engaged in work which contradicts or undermines the efforts of another. I was not sure whether this problem already exists in the case of two separate committees on school improvement. If the management team never meets, who is taking responsibility to make sure that the school, its committees, and its projects are headed in a direction which will improve schooling rather, than rearranging responsibilities for traditional school experiences? Who works to ensure that each new effort fits into the overall goals of the school so that the school can move forward in significant way rather than simply diffusing its efforts?

What effect does a tramsition in leadership have on the work of change and on teacher leadership in general? At Aguilar, teachers were fulfilling leadership roles long before Mr. Senoza left. They established the management team in order to protect the work they had begun. Teachers, principals, and superintendents change jobs frequently in order to move up the rrlatively limited career ladder and it is not uncommon for new leaders to arrive with their own agenda and to overlook or devalue the work already underway. Several of the Aguilar teachers shared previous experiences they had had where their efforts had been dismantled because of a change in leadership. This common occurrence contributes to the cynicism teachers feel when confronted with a new initiative to improve schools. The action taken by Aguilar's staff indicates that this is an issue worth investigating more thoroughly. If the teachers established the management team in order to further their efforts to change, and if running the school detracts from efforts to change, an earlier question bears repeating: What gains are made?

In broader terms, if we hope that teacher leadership positions will enable the larger faculty to improve the quality of education, do these positions not require some constancy? If teachers in leadership positions move too frequently, the potential for serious change is diminished. Unfortunately, Aguilar provided an example here. Each year the management team had to go to the board to get approval to run the school for the next school year. As I write, the superintendent who supported them has left, and three board members are up for re-election. The teachers face a great deal of uncertainty, and everyone is fearful of what will happen if the team, approach is not approved again. Several staff members who have invested heavily in the experiment claim they will leave taching should it not be approved.

Teacher Leadership Reexamined

Teacher leadership became the focus of national attention as traditional practices in schools worked for fewer and fewer students each year. As the urgency for better schools grows, more and more people are convinced that in order to engage students, to help them learn to use their minds well, to keep them in school, we must change the kinds of interactions that take place in classrooms. The hope is that teacher leadership positions will facilitate, promote, and direct that kind of change. Earlier findings reinforced the idea that the primary focus of any teacher leadership position should be to change the nature of the interactions between students and their teachers.

Given the dedication, the willingness, and the professional commitment I see in the teachers at Aguilar, and in other teacher leaders around the country, I am hopeful about teacher leadership and its potential to improve schooling in the country. The staff at Aguilar and their colleagues in the school district indicate that traditional hierarchical structures are more flexible than many might imagine. They also demonstrate that given the opportunity to create their own forms of teacher leadership, teachers can and do learn from their colleagues. Teachers at Aguilar point out several additional considerations important to any discussion of teacher leadership. If teacher leadership positions are created to support and facilitate change, their efforts should fit into a coherent whole. Transitions in leadership both at the teacher level and at other levels should be anticipated in order to guarantee as much constancy to a particular change effort as possible. Furthermore, teachers do not work in a vacuum, but in a system. They work in partnership with school board members, central office administrators, principals, parents, and community leaders on behalf of the children they serve. Teachers cannot assume important leadership roles without the support of these partners, nor can that make necessary changes if they do not have the support of these partners over time. Most important, everyone in this partnership must be resolute that the central purpose of any of the changes they wish to make, of any work they hope to do, is to more powerfully engage the minds of the young people they serve.

13

Proper Education

I, Thou, and It

(1967)

I want to talk about children's understanding in the context of a proper education, more specifically of a good school. My topic, therefore, is the relationship between the teacher and the child and a third thing in the picture which has to be there and which completes the triangle of my title.

This is a relationship that has been much talked about, but truncated too often. People have made analogies between the teacher-child relationship and many other sorts of relationships. For example, in olden times people said, "What this child needs is good hard work and discipline," and that sounds rather like a parent-child relationship, doesn't it? Or they said, more recently, "The child needs love." That also sounds rather like a parent-child relationship. I'm sure that neither of these statements is completely false, but it seems to me they're both very unsatisfactory and that the relationship between the teacher and the child is something quite unique that isn't exactly paralleled by any other kind of human relationship. It's interesting to explore what is involved in it.

I know one rather good teacher who says he doesn't like children. He says this. I'm sure, with a rather special meaning of the word "like." He doesn't like children to be bewildered, at loose ends, not learning, and therefore he tries to get them over this as soon as possible. I mention him because I think the attitude of love, which is the parental attitude, isn't really the appropriate one. Perhaps the word "respect" might be more appropriate. I don't want to deny a very important element of affection for children in the make-up of good teachers, but the essence of the relationship is not that. It is a personal relationship, but it's not that kind of personal relationship. I want to talk about this in the context of the kind of thing we've been investigating in recent years, in the context of the kind of schooling we are interested in exploring further, marked by the more frequent and more abundant use of concrete materials by children in schools, and by their greater freedom of choice within this enriched world. I'd like to talk about how the third corner of the triangle affects the relations between the other two corners, how the "It" enters into the pattern of mutual interest and exchange between the teacher and the child. Being an incurable academic philosopher, I'd like to start on a very large scale and talk about human beings—of which children are presumably rather typical examples.

There's a tradition in philosophy which always comes to my mind when I'm thinking about this kind of question and which seems to be a more significant tradition than some others. It's a tradition which is expressed by saying, in one way or another, that people don't amount to very much except in terms of their involvement in what is outside and beyond them. A human being is a localized physical body, but you can't see him as a *person* unless you see him in his working relationships with the world around him. The more you cut off these working relationships, the more you put him in a box, figuratively or literally, the more you diminish him. Finally, when you've narrowed him down to nothing more than the surface of the skin and what's inside, without allowing him any kind of relationship with the world around him, you don't have very much left.

The ancient Hindu philosophers expressed this definition of human nature by using the metaphor of the mirror. In the *Baghavad Gita,* the Hindu scripture, there is a marvelous image of the soul which is said to be "the reflection of the rose in a glass." Like most religious philosophy, this one is concerned with the problems of death and consolation. The theory of immortality in this philosophy is expressed by saying that when death occurs, you take away the mirror—but the rose is still there. This image seems to me a very powerful one. It's not the same as the Christian idea of the soul, of course, but it emphasizes the thing I want to talk about, which is that you can't dissociate the person from the world he lives and functions in and that you can somehow measure the person by the degree of his involvement in that world. The soul is not contained *within* the body but outside, in the theatre of its commitments.

The most precise expression of this idea that I know of in our literature is by a famous English poet. I want to quote it because it says something rather nicely about the relationship of two human beings, and the great It, the world. This is in *Troilus and Cressida,* where *It* is a famous hellenic enterprise. There was a time when Achilles was having some difficulties about the siege of Troy and people were trying to buck him up. At one point Ulysses comes on. It's part of the play where nothing much is going to happen for a few minutes. Sometimes in Shakespeare when nothing is going to happen, you have an exchange of bawdy jokes for the boys in the pit and sometimes you have a bit of relevant philosophizing. In the play this bit of philosophizing is relevant to Ulysses' effort to goad Achilles into action; but it has a universal relevance as well:

Ulysses A strange fellow here

Writes me that man — how dearly ever parted,
How much in having, or without or in—
Cannot make boast to have that which he hath,
Nor feels not what he owes, but by reflection;
As when his virtues shining upon others
Heat them, and they retort that heat again
To the first giver.

Achilles This is not strange, Ulysses.

The beauty that is borne here in the face
The bearer knows not, but commends itself

To others' eyes; not doth the eye itself—
That most pure spirit of sense—behold itself,
Not going from itself; but eye to eye opposed
Salutes each other with each other's form;
For speculation turns not to itself
Till it hath travell'd and is mirror'd there
Where it may see itself. This is not strange at all.

Ulysses I do not strain at the position—
It is familiar-but at the author's drift;
Who, in his circumstance, expressly proves
That no man is the lord of anything,—
Though in and of him there be much consisting—
Till he communicate his parts to others.
Nor doth he of himself know them for aught
Till he behold them formed in th'applause
Where th'are extended: who, like an arch, reverb'rate
The voice again or, like a gate of steel
Fronting the sun, receives and renders back
His figure and his heat.

(*Tudor Text, Player's Edition, Collins.*)

No Ajax, no Achilles even, can be the lord of anything, much less his own worth, save through resonance with others engrossed in those same matters. No child, I wish to say, can gain competence and knowledge, or know himself as competent and as a knower, save through communication with others involved with him in his enterprises. Without a Thou, there is no I evolving. Without an It there is no content for the context, no figure and no heat, but only an affair of mirrors confronting each other.

Children are members of the same species as adults, but they are also quite a distinct subspecies and we want to be careful about not exaggerating the differences and not forgetting them, either. It seems clear to me that there are many complicated, difficult things they learn or can learn, and such learning occurs in an environment where there are other human beings who serve, so to speak, as a part of the learning process: Long before there were such things as schools, which are rather recent institutions in the history of our kind, there were teachers. There were adults who lived in the village and who responded to the signals that children know very well how to emit in order to get attention from adults. These adults managed, quite spontaneously and without benefit of the theory of instruction, to be teachers.

I really need a kind of electronic analogy here for what goes on in a child's mind. Think of circuits that have to be completed. Signals go out along one bundle of channels, something happens, and signals come back along another bundle of channels; and there's some sort of feedback involved. Children are not always able to sort out all of this feedback for themselves. The adult's function, in the child's learning, is to provide a kind of external loop, to provide a selective feedback from the child's own choice and action. The child's involvement gets some response from an adult and this in turn is made available to the child. The child is learning about himself through his joint effects on the non-human and the human world around him.

The function of the teacher, then, is to respond diagnostically and helpfully to a child's behavior, to make what he considers to be an appropriate response, a response which the child needs to complete the process he's engaged in at a given moment. Now, this function of the teacher isn't going to go on forever: it's going to terminate at some time in the future. What we can say, I think, and what we clearly ought to provide for, is that the child should learn how to internalize the function which the adult has been providing. So, in a sense, you become educated when you become your own teacher. If being educated meant no longer needing a teacher—a definition I would recommend—it would mean that you had been presented with models of teaching, or people playing this external role, and that you have learned how the role was played and how to play it for yourself. At that point you would declare your independence of instruction as such and you would be your own teacher.

What we all hope, of course, is that as the formal, institutional part of education is finished, its most conspicuous and valuable product will be seen to be the child's ability to educate himself. If this doesn't happen, it doesn't make sense to say that the processes we try to initiate in school are going to be carried on when people leave school.

The image I want, then, is really the image Shakespeare is working with. You grow as a human being by the incorporation of conjoint information from the natural world *and* of things which only other human beings are able to provide for in your education.

I sometimes think that working in the style we like to work in—which is much farther along in English primary schools, I'm sorry to say, than in American schools—we forget the unique importance of the human role. We tend to say "Oh well, if children just have a good rich, manipulable and responsive environment, then everything will take care of itself." When you visit a class which is operating in this way, with a teacher who has a good bag of tricks, you're often impressed that the teacher doesn't seem to be very necessary. He can leave the room and nobody notices it. If *you* don't have that bag of tricks, you always rather marvel at what goes into it. After everything is accomplished it all looks as though it's very spontaneous. But, of course, that's a dangerous illusion. It's true only in those periods—in good schools frequent periods—when children don't need the external loop. When they do need it and there's no one around to contribute the adult resonance, then they're not always able to carry on the process of investigation, of inquiry and exploration, of learning, because they need help over a hump that they can't surmount through their own resources. If help isn't available, the inquiry will taper off, and that particular episode, at least, will have failed to accomplish what it otherwise might have.

Now, I'm speaking as one very much in favor of richness and diversity in the environment, and of teaching which allows a group of children to diversify their activities and which—far more than we usually think proper keeps out of their hair. What seems very clear to me and I think this is a descriptive, factual statement, not praising or blaming is that if you operate a school, as we in America almost entirely do, in such a style that the children are rather passively sitting in neat rows and columns and manipulating you into believing that they're being attentive because they're not making any trouble, then you won't get very much information about them. Not getting much information about them, you won't be a very good diagnostician of what they need. Not being a good diagnostician, you will be a poor teacher. The child's overt involvement in a rather self-directed way, using the big muscles and not just the small ones, is most important to the teacher in providing an input of information wide in range and variety. It is input which potentially has much more heft than what you can possibly get from the merely verbal or written responses of a child to questions put to him or tasks set for him. When we fail in this diagnostic role we begin to worry about "assessment."

I think this is fairly obvious. It doesn't say that you *will* but that you *can* get more significant diagnostic information about children, and can refine your behavior as a teacher far beyond the point of what's possible when every child is being made to perform in a rather uniform pattern. But of course you will not get the information, or will not use it, if you are just sweetly permissive and limp, if you don't provide the external feedback loop when you think it is needed. We know children never do behave uniformly even when they're supposed to. When it appears thay are, it's just because they've learned the trick of pleasing you—or displeasing you if they're all on strike! —and then you aren't able to make the needed discrimination.

But I think the real importance of teacher-intervention comes out in situations where a child is not involved in very many things, is not responsive to anything you provide. That child may be a problem; that child who doesn't give you much information, who is tight and constrained, often called "good." But you get little suggestions or inklings of interest and involvement, you get hunches about what might prove absorbing to him. If you have enough of these hunches and enough persistence you find *something* that works and when you do you have laid the basis for a new relationship between yourself and that child, and this is the thing that is really important.

The rest is good and important and not too hard to describe: when children are being diverse in what they're doing, selective in what they're doing; when you're giving them genuine alternatives— then you are bound to get much more knowledge of them from reading the language of their behavior. Of course, you certainly aren't going to succeed all the time with every child in this diagnostic and planning process. There are going to be several misses for every hit, but you just say, "Well, let's keep on missing and the more we miss the more we'll hit." The importance of this in the "I-Thou" relationship between the teacher and the child is that the child learns something about the adult which we can describe with words like "confidence," "trust" and "respect." You have done something for the child which he could not do for himself, and he knows it. He's become involved in something new which has proved engrossing to him. If he thus learns that he has a competence he didn't know he had, then you have been a very crucial figure in his life. You have provided that external loop, that external feedback, which he couldn't provide for himself. He then values the provisioner with the provision.

What is the feeling you have toward a person who does this for you? It needn't be what we call love, but it certainly is what we call respect. You value another person because he is uniquely useful to you in helping you on with your own life. "Love" is, perhaps, a perfectly good word, too, but it has a great variety of meanings and has been vulgarised, not least by psychological theory.

The relationship that develops with different children will be different just because they are different children. When *you* give a child a range from which to make choices, the choices *he* makes in turn give you the basis for deciding what should be done next, what the provisioning should be for him. That is *your* decision, it's dependent on *your* goals, it's something *you* are responsible for—not in an authoritarian way but you do have to make a decision and it's your decision, not the child's. If it's a decision to let him alone you are just as responsible for it as if it's a decision to intervene.

The investment in the child's life that is made in this way by the adult, the teacher in this case, is something that adds to and in a way transforms the interest the child develops spontaneously. If, as sometimes happens, a child gets particularly interested in a variation on a soap bubble theme that you've already given him, you can just happen to put nearby some other things that might not at first seem related to soap bubbles—some geometrical wire cubes, tetrahedra, helices, and wire with a soldering iron. The resulting soap films are almost bound to catch the fancy of many human beings, including children. What have they got? Well, they've got a certain formal geometrical elegance, they've got color; when you look at the films in the right kind of light you see all those marvelous interference colors. Such a trap is bristling with invitations and questions. Some children will sample it and walk on; but some will be hooked by it, will get very involved with it. Now, this kind of involvement is terribly important, I think. It's aesthetic, or it's mathematical, or it's scientific. It's all of these potentially, and none of them exclusively. The teacher has made possible this relation between the child and "It," even if this is just by having "It" in the room; and for the child even this brings the teacher as a person, a "Thou," into the picture. For the child this is not merely something which is fun to play with, which is exciting and colorful and has associations with many other sorts of things in his experience: it's also a basis for communication with the teacher on a new level, and with a new dignity.

Until the child is going on his own the teacher can't treat him as a person who is going on his own, cannot let him be mirrored there, where he may see himself as investigator or craftsman. Until he is an autonomous human being who is thinking his own thoughts and making his own unique, individual kinds of self-expression out of them, there isn't anything for the teacher to respect, except a potentiality. So the first act in teaching, it seems to me, the first goal, necessary to all others, is to encourage this kind of engrossment. Then the child comes alive for the teacher as well as the teacher for the child. They have a common theme for discussion, they are involved together in the world.

I had always been awkward in certain kinds of situations with young children. I didn't know them very well and I'd sort of forgotten that I'd once been one, as we mostly do. I remember being very impressed by the way some people, in an encounter with a young child, would seem automatically to gain acceptance while other people, in apparently very friendly encounters with the same child, would produce real withdrawal and, if they persisted, fear and even terror. Such was the well-meaning adult who wanted to befriend the child—I and Thou—in a vacuum. It's traumatic, and I think we all know what it feels like. I came to realize (I learned with a good teacher) that one of the very important factors in this kind of situation is that there be some third thing which is of interest to the child *and* to the adult, in which they can join in outward projection. Only this creates a possible stable bond of communication, of shared concern.

My most self-conscious experience of this kind of thing was when a few years ago I found myself with two very small tykes who had gone with me and my wife to the hospital to get their mother, who had just had a third baby. The father was ill and there was already some anxiety. With Frances Hawkins they were fine; indeed it was she who had earlier been my teacher in this art. They were perfectly happy with us two but they had never been with me alone. Suddenly the nurse announced in a firm voice that children could not go beyond this point, so my wife had to go in and we three had to stay. It was one of those moments when you could have had a fairly lively scene on your hands. Not being an adept, I thought quite consciously of the triangular principle. There had to be some third thing that wasn't "I" and the two children, otherwise we were all going to be laid waste. And there wasn't anything! I looked around and there was a bare hospital corridor. But on one wall there was a collection of photographs of some recent banquet that had been given for a donor, so in desperation I just picked them up, rushed over to it, and said, "Look!" That's a sort of confession, because I'm sure many of you would know how to handle this kind of situation: for me it was a great triumph and it was a demonstration, if an oddly mechanical one, of a consciously held principle. And it worked.

It seems to me that this kind of episode, which is in itself trivial and superficial, can symbolize a lot that is important in terms of the teacher-child relationship; namely, the common interest, the common involvement in subject-matter. Now of course, you never really deceive a child in important matters, so this interest can't long be feigned, as it was in my story. If you don't find something interesting, and try to feign an interest you don't have, the investment won't last. But if there is that common interest it may last and may evolve. You need to be capable of noticing what the child's eyes notice and capable of interpreting the words and acts by which he tries to communicate with you. It may not be in adult English, so the reception of these signals requires experience and close attention.

Visualize a king transparent corked plastic tube with water and other things in it, as fancy may dictate. Many years ago I would have thought that this was rather trivial, rather silly, and would have said, "What's there to be learned from that?" To tell you the truth, I honestly still don't know, there is so much! We can use a lot of words in physics that have something to do with it; or we can talk about color and motion and other things of some aesthetic importance. By now I've seen enough children involved in this particular curious apparatus to be quite convinced that there's a great deal in it and I don't mean just this particular tube but many similar artifacts, as well as samples of the natural world. Such things can serve as an extraordinary kind of bond. The child is in some sense functioning to incorporate the world; he's trying to assimilate his environment. This includes his social environment, of course, but it also includes the inanimate environment; it also includes the resources of the daily world around him, which he's capable of seeing for the most part with far fresher eyes than ours. The richer this adult-provided contact, therefore, the more firm is the bond that is established between the human beings who are involved.

Finally, I'd like to mention something which is perhaps of special interest and which takes me into psychological theory. It has to do with how human beings come to attain the sense of objectivity, the sense of reality, with how they come to get a stable, reliable vision of the world around them and how, without losing their capacity for fantasy, they are able to make clear discriminations between what they know, what they have learned, what they merely believe, what they imagine, and so on. It has to do with how they are able to get straight the orders and kinds of belief and credibility. This is one of the most important accomplishments of a human being.

It seems to me that for some children and not for others this capacity for fitting things together into a coherent whole, into a coherent pattern, comes first mostly in terms of their relations with the human world, while for other children it comes first mostly in their relations with the inanimate world.

The capacity for synthesis, for building a stable framework within which many episodes of experience can be put together coherently, comes with the transition from autistic behavior to exploratory behavior. The first is guided by a schedule which is surely inborn, and is connected with satisfaction of definite infant needs. the second has a different style, and is not purposive in the same way, not aimed at a predetermined end-state. Its satisfaction, its reinforcement as a way of functioning, comes along the way and not at the end; in competence acquired, not in satiation. Both modes of behavior are elaborated through experience, but exploratory behavior is not bound and limited by a schedule of needs—needs which must, to begin with, have the highest priority. A child's first major synthetic achievements in exploratory learning may come in relation to the human world, but they may come equally, and perhaps more readily, in his exploration of the things of his surrounding physical environment, and of their responsiveness to his testing and trying. In either case, or so it seems to me, the exploratory motivation, and its reinforcement, is of a different kind from the libidinous, aimed as the latter is at incorporation and possession. And the child's development will be limited and distorted if it does not, by turns, explore *both* the personal and the non-personal aspects of his environment; but explore them, not exploit them for a known end. Most psychologists, in my reading and my more extensive arguing with them, tend to say that the roots of human motivation are interpersonal. They say that the fundamental dynamics of the child's relation to the rest of the world as he grows up stem from his relation to his mother, his relation to other close figures around him, and that these will be the impelling forces in his life. It is, of course, in such terms that Freud built up his whole systematic theory and although perhaps there aren't many very orthodox Freudians around now-a-days this key feature of the theory persists, I think—the feeling that the only important formative things in life are other human beings. And if people pay attention to the non-human world—it may include animals and plants as well as the physical environment, enriched to contain bubble tubes and soap film—one tend to trace this to some desire to exploit the human world: for example, the child does something because he thinks it pleases you or because he thinks it displeases you, or because he's escaping you—but never because he wants wholeheartedly to do what he's doing. In other words, there's been a systematic tendency to devalue children's thing oriented interests as against their person-oriented interests. It is assumed that the latter are basic, the former derivative. All I would like to say is that I think the interest in *things* is a perfectly real, perfectly independent and autonomous interest which is there in young children just as genuinely as the interest in persons is there. And some children are *only* able to develop humanly by first coming to grips in an exploratory and involved way with the inanimate world.

We've certainly seen examples of children who very early have got on to the tricks which I suppose in some sense babies are born with but which infants can elaborate as they grow older, tricks for getting what they want from persons by planning how they shall behave. It's exploiting, and some very young children are already skillful at it. If you know such children as a teacher you'll know they're smarter than you are because they've put a lot more investment into this kind of thing than you have. You have to be very shrewd to cope with them.

One thing such a child cannot do is to get wholeheartedly involved in anything else; he has to be watching all the time to see what the adults and the other children think about it. But if you can set enough traps for him, if you can keep exposing him to temptations, if he sees other children involved and not paying any attention to the teacher, he's left out in the cold. So the temptations of bubbles or clay or sand or whatever it is are reinforced by the fact that other children aren't playing his kind of game. If such a child once forgets his game, because he *does* get involved in shaping some inanimate raw material, in something that's just there to be explored, played with, investigated, tried out, then he has had an experience which is liberating, that can free him from the kind of game-playing which he's got so expert at. He comes, after-all, from a species that is called *homo faber*. If he doesn't get free of manipulating persons somewhere in his life, that life is going to be a sad one. In the extreme case perhaps it will even be a psychotic one. Children of this extreme sort are a special case, but being extreme, in a way they tell us a lot about what is involved in the three-cornered relationship of my title. They seek to get and to keep, but cannot yet even begin to give. For the verb *to give* has two objects and only the indirect one is personal. The direct object must be something treasured which is not I, and not Thou.

One final remark. It seems to me that many of us, whether our background was in science or not, have learned something about ourselves from working with children in this way that we've begun to explore. We've begun to see the things of the physical and biological world through children's eyes rather more than we were able to before, and have discovered and enjoyed a lot that is there that we were not aware of before. We don't any longer feel satisfied with the kind of adult grasp that we had of the very subject-matter that we've been teaching; we find it more problematic, more full of surprises, and less and less a matter of the textbook order.

One of the nicest of this kind that I know comes from a young physicist friend who was very learned. He had just got his Ph.D. and of course he understood everything. (The Ph.D. has been called "the certificate of omniscience.") My wife was asking him to explain something to her about two coupled pendulums. He said, "Well, now, you can see that there's a conservation of...Well, there's really a conservation of angle here." She looked at him. "Well, you see, in the transfer of energy from one pendulum to the other there is..." and so on and so on. And she said, "No, I don't mean that. I want you to notice this and tell me what's happening."

Finally, he looked at the pendulums and he saw what she was asking. He looked at *it*, and he looked at *her*, and he grinned and said, "Well, I know the right words but I don't understand it either." This confession, wrung from a potential teacher, I've always valued very much. It proves that we're all in it together in it together.

14

The Bird in the Window (1969)

The reason we made our way to England this year is that we had come, over a period of time, to believe that in England we could find more schools of the sort we wanted to look at, and more people to talk to who were involved in these schools, than anywhere else in the world. I think that is probably true. Since we've been here, since the autumn of 1968, we have, of course, had a chance to get over any romantic illusions we might have had about the trouble-free schools of your country, but on the whole, as far as we are concerned, the romance holds up pretty well.

I want to talk about a topic that I know is vexing many people nowadays. It vexes you because you have probably got the matter coming up soon and it vexes us because we are trying to start some battles in the United States. I think you will find yourself in a more defensive position, because you have done some things in primary schools which we've been trying, rather unsuccessfully, to get started in the United States. We're more on the offensive because so far we haven't made much of a dent, in terms of changing some of the rudimentary patterns of traditional school life, patterns which you are very familiar with from your own past. It's an interesting historical business. There has been some interchange over a long period between the United States and England, particularly with respect to primary education. I think there was a time about three or four decades ago when the slogans of progressive education were probably more resonant in the United States than in England, although in England there have been for a long time the traditions of progressive education, going back to the early influence of Froebel and others. Of course, we have had the same influences. We've produced some fraction of the materials, some of the components of infant school work of the kind that would be familiar to those of you who are infant teachers. You have produced a larger fraction of them, and some fractions have come from other sources. There's been a kind of international pooling of work-a-day ideas about the organization and the equipment of infant classes.

When we first walked into an infant class in Leicestershire my wife, who has been a kindergarten teacher for many years, sniffed the air, and said, "This is familiar, but I haven't seen it in the United States for a long time." What is now the tradition of a majority of your infant schools was the tradition in the United States of only one year of school, called kindergarten, which was as you probably know the year that was put in under the first grade of our schools, starting at age six. This five-to-six-year-old group was not introduced universally in the United States but did come about in many states as a result of this same progressive education movement which managed to get in under the establishment, so to speak. It created a new year of school which had a pattern quite radically different from the pattern which we call primary, a term which in the United States means the ages six to seven, seven to eight, and eight to nine. The kindergarten was almost without influence on the later years of school. In a typical American school of the 1930's you would see a kindergarten which you infant teachers would recognize as very familiar in style. Then you would go into a first grade which was very formal and almost completely lacking in concrete equipment of any kind, which was dominated by primers and pencil and paper, and which had the children sitting in neat rows and columns. The most extensive influence I know of from the kindergarten in the United States was that there was a great burst of progressivism which resulted in the unbolting of the desks from the floor. But that didn't mean they were ever moved! It was a symbolic achievement. Children were free to move but in fact they were not allowed to.

One of the things which we contributed to this movement was a rather good philosopher, John Dewey. Nobody *reads* Dewey very much but everybody knows how to say some things about him. I think actually John Dewey is very well worth reading, but not unless you're prepared to dig in and not unless you're prepared to argue with him to try to recover the context in which he was talking, and to talk with your friends about it. Dewey is responsible for some good and very careful thinking which is almost totally unknown in most educational circles. When I was an undergraduate, students in education were usually required to read a book by Dewey called *How We Think,* which is a neat little thing he did for pedagogical purposes at some point. It classified thinking into stages and talks about the transition form one stage to another. It's dull, and the important ideas in the book are developed elsewhere much better, with much more sense of qualification and realism and with much more vitality. But there was at least a period in which Dewey was widely known in the United States and in which many people in colleges of education were devoted to him, at least in theory. But these people had very little influence on the schools. So neither the influence of the kindergarten nor the influence of the colleges of education was enough to make any real dent in the American public school system. This system isn't overtly authoritarian: it doesn't keep you out the way that schools in some continental countries might tend to do; it's just very resistant, it has lots of built-in feedback mechanisms for avoiding change. You can get in and you can do something and things will sail along very nicely but two years later you won't find much residue of effect.

Dewey was not only a very good, very thoughtful, very deep philosopher in many ways, but he was also a man who had personal acquaintance with children and with schools. As you probably know, he was for a time involved in the operation of a school which was called "The Experimental School" at the University of Chicago. The record of that school is quite an interesting one. The pattern of what was generally identified as progressive education was dominant throughout the primary or elementary years. Dewey was a theorist, however, who didn't savor the practical details. He knew them, he learned: there's quality in much of his writing which couldn't be there unless he was familiar with teachers and schools. But he loved to take off into realms of theory and polemic. He hardly ever illustrates what he is saying with any of the concrete stuff that would make a teachers say, "Ah,yes, I really know what he's talking about." So, he is a difficult person in his own way. Well, because of the battle we may have to fight—or the battle we would like to fight—I think that this level of concern and of theory, of getting our ideas straight and getting them into a form which we can verbalize clearly and which will hold up against neutral or even hostile criticism necessary, this is an important thing.

I for one have found that since I've become practically involved in work connected with the early years I've acquired a great distaste for theorizing in the old style. I don't like to talk about general questions having to do with learning and teaching in the abstract, because I am so aware that when you do this you talk past people all the time. If they don't already know what you're talking about, if they're not already tuned to your wave-length, you can say things and then when they say them back to you don't recognize what's happened. This is a very real difficulty, and it isn't a difficulty that has to do with the degree of academic training people have had: I think it's a difficulty in principle. Another way of putting this is to say that I think teachers—not all teachers but those who have a genuinely professional feeling about their work and who have learned and grown in their profession over a long period of time—do know more about things than is codified in any book. I think they know more about the psychology of learning than is written in the books. The psychologists, unfortunately—and I might be forced to name a few exceptions but I don't think there would be many—are unacquainted with this level of operation. They don't know children. They don't observe children. They don't know teachers except as people they teach. They don't regard teachers as their instructors in psychology. To do so would turn upside down some sort of social pecking order and that would be almost unthinkable. But it may need to be done. More is known and understood on the practical level by people who work effectively and successfully with children than is codified in any of the books. And it's doubtful whether the codification which is in the books is for the most part particularly relevant to this level of knowledge and understanding. When you try to formulate ideas about learning and about education you have to get into the psychologists' league and play that kind of game one way or another. You have to try to make explicit, to find ways of verbalizing, things which you'd much rather just know in your bones and in your practice. Teachers are craftsmen, artisans artists, whatever you want to call them,not theoreticians. And just as the good craftsmen of the Renaissance expressed themselves through the work they did and not through writing books about it (or research monographs) so teachers express themselves through the work that they do, through the human beings who have been their pupils, and not by writing little papers.

On the other hand, in the academic world the thing is geared the other way and the end-all be-all of existence is that you write a little paper. Those of us who are in the academic world are very much torn. If we get involved in school work at a practical level we come to realize how empty a lot of the theoretical discussion is compared to the practice. We either struggle to express it—some of us are foolish enough to keep on trying to do this—or we acquire a distaste for our own academic ways of functioning. And I know that I myself am very much torn as the result of this. I want on the one had to do battle with the psychologists and a good many of the American educationists, but that requires that I get into their league and read their papers and books and so on. But then I'm very dissatisfied because they're not talking about things I think are important, and I don't myself quite know how to talk about those things that seem to me to be important. So I'm in trouble. Everybody in this business is in one kind of trouble or another. Other people who haven't been in the academic world feel, often incorrectly, I think, that they don't have the means to express themselves, to develop theoretical ideas. In fact, I think they more nearly have the means than do the rest of us, because they have the raw experience, or rather, the experience they have culled and analyzed over and over again to guide their practical work. What we want to do is somehow to get those ideas not only into practice but into the marketplace where they can be argued.

I want to try, with just one or two ideas that seem to me to be crucial to talk about learning and teaching. It is said, and I think sometimes with justice, that the traditionalists in education have a more cogent rationale for the things they believe in than do the progressives, with whom I would identify myself. We are people who talk in vague generalities and don't really have any consistent theory at all. When we are called on to discuss something we tend to point to particular concrete examples rather than to develop tight,consistent logical positions. I think this is often true. But it has also been true in the past in other places, and the places I know best are in the history of science. I think it's always true in principle that when new ideas are in the process of development those who are devoted to them and who are trying to bring them to definition have a very hard time expressing themselves, whereas those who represent some established order have very easy time because the language patterns which have been worked out fit their ideas, against which the innovators are reacting. And the language the innovators have to use is, therefore, the language of their opponents, so to speak. You can find many examples of this in the history of science. For example, consider the very slow acceptance of something like the germ theory of disease. People who advocated this point of view were simply laughed out of court because the way they had to talk was in a framework of ideas which made the notion of little, invisible micro-organisms something that just had no reality at all. There weren't yet words for the things which are now part of the established pattern in, say, medical education. You had to coin words, and you had to use words in a new meaning, words that meant something else to other people.

This, I think, is very much our situation now. So, for example, I have said on various occasions that it seems to me a fundamental aim of education to organize schools, classrooms and our own performance as teachers in order to help children acquire the capacity for significant choice, and that learning is really a process of choice. If children, are deprived of significant choice in their daily activities in school, if all their choices are made for them, then the most important thing that education is concerned with is simply being bypassed. Children have to be encouraged, supported in self-directed activity. And that means that you give children certain kinds of freedom. But now you're talking a language which has a lot of emotional loading. So, if you believe in giving children a lot of freedom this means, in terms of the emotional loading, that you are withdrawing discipline. To say the child is free is to say you are not coercing him and if you think of discipline as coercive then you are not imposing a discipline on the life of the child in school and that means you are not imposing a discipline on the life of the child in school and that means you are turning him loose to do whatever he wants to, and now we're on the merry-go-round of the old, familiar argument.

It's very clear, isn't it, that in traditional ways of thinking the opposition between freedom and discipline is of this kind. Discipline is an externally imposed mode of acting under the influence of something called "authority" and authority is something externally imposed and coercive. Look the word up in the Oxford English Dictionary if you don't believe me. There is no other primary meaning of "authority" except that of constituted authority, legally constituted authority or the authority of a person who has power because he has status or because he has special knowledge or something of the sort. Now, if that's what authority means and if discipline is something which is imposed by authority, than freedom in the usual sense is simply negative, and that means you're getting rid of authority. So the stereotype of progressive education is, "Turn the children loose and let them do whatever they want to." If you don't do that then it means you are imposing structure, order, discipline, and so you have this dichotomy between two things which are inalterably opposed: that's the way our common, everyday marketplace language works. Whenever you get into a futile, frustrating argument with somebody about education, you recognize that this is the pattern you have allowed yourself to fall into. The interesting thing is that you get annoyed at the other person for pulling this trick on you, but you also get annoyed at yourself because you've let yourself get trapped in it. You don't want to say something, but he's made you say it, and you've had to assent because that's the way the ordinary language works. What is sometimes called "ordinary language philosophy" has sometimes been used, illegitimately. to support such arguments. One just rings the changes on the ordinary stereotypes of English speech and forces you into a corner. He doesn't force you very hard and you may not be much impressed but he thinks he's forcing you. If you take *his* meanings of the words then everything is pretty clear and cut and dried and people who talk the language of progressivism are mushy and unaware of the logic of their own language.

So I think we are in a difficult position because we're trying to say something that's rather genuinely new, and I don't think that our ordinary modes of expression allow us to do this without falling into traps. We have to think very carefully about what we're saying, how we're saying it, and what kinds of illustrations we use to pin down our meanings. It's a difficult task to argue and to reason cogently at a level which corresponds to the understanding of many practicing teachers. "Authority" is a particularly interesting case. If you look at the practice of the best primary schools (I'll reserve to myself the privilege of saying which ones they are but I think you'd probably agree with me) one of the important roles of the teacher in those, schools is something that could be described by the word "authority." I think it is a different meaning of the word, and one which isn't in the Oxford English Dictionary, or if it is, it's buried in some special context. Authority is a way in which human beings are related to each other and it is connected with the word "respect." If someone plays a role as an authority in your life this means that you respect him. His activities or contribution to your existence you value because it has proved itself to *be* valuable. If you respect and trust someone you may follow his suggestions or his style, knowing that you are getting something that you will come to value even though you don't yet know enough to develop it for yourself.

In other words, authority is one of the primary sources of learning . To be an authority in this sense, to be a teacher whom children honestly respect because you give them something which helps them on the way and which they know they couldn't get for themselves, is to be a teacher. If you are not that kind of authority, you are not a good teacher, you're not functioning properly as a teacher. Therefore the word "authority " is very important, but if we let it get captured by that kind of opposition which is arguing against the primary importance of encouraging children's autonomous, self-directed learning, then we don't have any way to talk about this important part of teaching.

There's another way you can look at this which is very familiar. The polarity that is in the ordinary language reasserts itself between two stereotypes of the classroom, and I think many of us are guilty of these stereotypes ourselves. There's the old, authoritarian classroom—notice the word "authority" again in the same sense; an authoritarian is one who advocates or who imposes, who believes in the propriety of imposing discipline by authority, and that means by coercion. The word has a disparaging tone. So there's the authoritarian classroom and in opposition to it there is the permissive, *laissez-faire* classroom. Get a lot of good, stimulating environment for children and turn them loose in it and seven years later they'll come up with the requisite education. Or at least they will have been expressing themselves, they will have been creative—and all the other "sloppy" words that the philosophers object to. So, again, we're in this trap. How do you devise ways of calling to people's attention that there is such a trap? You can say to an opponent in an argument. "Look" I don't want to accept this dichotomy, this is not what I'm talking about." But then you have to have some general ways of describing what you are doing. You can give illustrations, but your opponent will say "Yes, that's very nice, but you can't build a whole school on that basis." Or he'll say, "Yes, but that's an unusually good teacher and after-all we must be prepared for the ordinary sort of teacher who can't do that." These arguments are all so stale, so repeated, so rehearsed that you can hardly mention them in any audience without getting a lot of people smiling because it's in the experience of all of us. Well let's try.

One scheme that I've tried is to say, here is the authoritarian classroom, the stereotype: children are doing things in unison, they're told to open the spelling book at page 23 and do the following and when they're busy doing that the teacher goes and gives some similar busywork to other children or perhaps has all the children doing the same thing at the same time. I won't develop that, we all know what it is;it's a conventional stereotype of a classroom. Many classrooms have approximated it and still do. Then there is the permissive classroom in which children are running wild and running out of stem, which they will inevitably do if they're given a good environment and then not given any kind of reinforcement and help; they'll try all the things that are tryable by them at that stage, they'll exhaust the possibilities and then the possibilities will get narrower and narrower. Finally they won't have any choices left and they'll get into the same kinds of troubles that children get into who live in the authoritarian classroom because both of them are now bored. Children who are bored exhibit similar symptoms no matter what the cause of the boredom is. You have behavior problems and all that sort of thing.

So, how can you break out of this contrast? Well, one way of doing it is to think of a triangle. The authoritarian classroom is at one corner, the permissive classroom is at another and at the third is a classroom which isn't either of them. It's as far off that axis as you can be. Because you have that contrast of teacher direction *versus* child freedom sometimes you look at this classroom from one point of view and it will look authoritarian and other times you will look at it from the other point of view and it will look permissive. In fact it isn't either of them and it's a distortion of the classroom to describe it in this language at all. So, how will you describe this third alternative? Well, one thing I certainly don't want to do is invent a label for it. God help us, I think we ought to get along without labels for things that are really important. Maybe that's mistake, maybe you have to have a label but I, at any rate, don't intend to invent one. It's a classroom in which there are two kinds of choices being made, one kind of children, the other kind by the teacher. So it isn't either the teacher making all the choices or the children making all the choices. It's a more complex situation, and we all know that it is. We're trying consciously to break out of the stereotype.

Sometimes children are making decisions because the classroom, the atmosphere of the school, the behaviour of the teacher are such that they're encouraged to make choices and they have alternatives before them that ate meaningful to them: you can properly say they are making choices. The teacher is observing what they are doing,following what they are doing and interpreting what they are doing, diagnosing their state, their level, their special problems and thinking of ways of making provision for them in that situation. This is now the choice, the freedom, of the teacher. What a teacher does in this way is just as genuinely a matter of choice as anything the children do. So it's absurd to say that this is a classroom which is permissive. A teacher may in such a classroom make a choice, sometimes quite properly, which involves a very firm use of the adult role. "Why do you make me do this?'' "Because I'm bigger than you are and let's not argue about it." If that was the only kind of choice the teacher was making it would be pretty bad, but it's quite another thing to say that no good teacher ever makes choices of that sort, because this is patently false. There are times when coercion in particular is a very salutary thing. There are times when it's the only *educational* thing that you can do.

We know a young man who told us in great detail that the first time in his life he thought he might be a normal human being was when a teacher whom he had struck caused him to be arrested and put in jail. This was a vital component of his education. To say that you could have had the same effect with sweet reasonableness is just plain false. He'd had sweet reasonableness all his life and that in fact was the chief malady he was suffering from. On the other hand, a teacher may at other stages be consciously withdrawing, consciously be non-interventionist, may give the child complete freedom with a perhaps anxious calculation that the only way in which that child is going to get over a particular hump is to be entirely on his own in confronting it. These are contrasting kinds of decisions made by the same teacher under different circumstances for different children. So the whole range of choices is there. Some are very like the authoritarian model and some are very like the permissive model, but they are quite different in character because this is now a teacher operating, dealing with human beings and using observation, interpretation, wit, strategy, to play the role in reinforcing the self-directed learning of children. It can't be put more simply than that because it isn't any simpler. It seems to me that such a description has to be made and it has to become familiar. I probably don't do it right. I'm only making a rough cut at it, there are lots of qualifications, lots of filling in of detail, lots of discussion about how you know when to do this and that and the other thing. It's a very complex matter. But these are questions that can be solved in practice to some good approximation, otherwise we wouldn't have good teacher. There may not be an elegant theoretical formulation about it but it's still possible to describe the range of considerations that are involved in a teacher's making intelligent choices.

Once you are committed to the belief in the primacy, the priority, of children's choice-making capacities as the main thing that education is after, then there are many things that follow which likewise run afoul of the traditional stereotypes. Once you accept this basic aim of education you discover some other things that come along with it that are vital to the process. For example, if a teacher has children doing things, or ostensibly doing things, that are pretty much according to a pattern which he has laid down, then the opportunity for significantly observing the child's behavior is very much diminished. If you tell a child to do a set task and there are many ways of failing and one way of succeeding—solving a particular kind of set problem that has a unique right answer, for example—then essentially the only thing you can observe is the success or failure of the child in doing that particular task. This will divide children into categories, but no more. There may be some incidental observations you make along the way—some children grown when set the task; others try to act cheerful about it and so on. But you don't really learn much from the success or the failure of the children in a situation where you are requiring uniformity of behavior from every child. Whereas, if you encourage diversity, which you're bound to do if you encourage choice, then you will observe that much-too-large number of human beings doing different things. The range of choices they make is very wide and therefore the amount of information you get about them is much greater. It is just common observation that if you watch a child working with a particular kind of material quite successfully and voiding everything else, you're learning something about that child which is a much more important guide to your behavior as a teacher than his success or failure in particular set tasks. If you give a child a choice, for example, and he does nothing but work with paints and acquires a certain status in the class because he does have something of a flair in painting that other children don't have, but he's a total failure in everything else—he simply avoids everything else, he doesn't read, he doesn't write, and so on—then you know a great deal about the child that is relevant to you as a teacher. What strategies you will use now will be very much determined by your knowledge of the way this child has homed in on one activity and avoided a lot of others.

I still have very limited personal experience in teaching primary school children, so I speak only as an amateur. My experience has been with college students. I do believe they're not really so different under the skin, but there are some differences. Mainly, college students have learned very well how to avoid giving you important kinds of diagnostic information. They know how to look bright, alert and to pretend they've turned you on when in fact they've turned you off fifteen minutes before. Nine-year-olds don't know how to do this or at least don't care to do it, in my experience. So I learned much more about myself as a teacher as soon as I went to that age. And even more when I first, with fear and trembling, got involved with four- and five-year-olds. One of the things that became very clear to me was that when children were engaged in a considerable diversity of activities. I had no trouble at all remembering what they were doing and no trouble recalling information about their behaviour and what it probably signified. Whereas when they were all doing the same set piece I'd have to go around and make records all the time in order to keep up with them. In fact I think the familiar phenomenon called "The Test" is largely a crutch to replace the good means of evaluation we have when we don't suppress children's capacity for choice. Children simply distinguish themselves individually when they're working at different tasks in different ways, You get so much more information you don't have trouble remembering.

Many teachers in the United States who've become involved

with us and are somewhat interested in the things we are doing and think may be they will try some of them bring up this question: "Yes, but how will we test them, because they'll all be doing different things?" And again, that's part of that stereotyped pattern. How can you test? If people are not doing the same thing you can't compare them. And you say, "Yes, that's true, isn't it." But that's terribly unsatisfactory, because there's that hole left there, that demand for evaluation. Of course you're evaluating much more effectively, in another meaning of the word. But you've got to say what that meaning is, because it isn't the business of putting people on a liner scale. It's a much richer scale you're putting them on, with many dimensions to it. You're saying, "This child is best at telling stories, this child is best at numbers and this child is best at catching frogs!" These are three dimensions and each of them gives a different permutation of the children. That's the way human beings really are. It is not the way the traditional demands of education have seen them and therefore we have real problems in meeting the traditional demands: that is, in meeting the people who make the traditional demands with the kind of information we want to give them. So there is a very close and important relation between children's actual level of choice-making in the classroom, or in the field if they're in the field, and our own ability to interpret and diagnose, but it's not the kind of thing that will yield information on a paper and pencil test of any kind that anybody I know has ever devised. And I doubt in principle whether it can be devised because the paper and pencil test imposes a set of criteria which are preconceived by the tester and this reduces not necessarily just to one but to not very many dimensions of comparison. The teacher who is skillful at this kind of observation can tell you a great deal that's quite important about a child but will not give you numbers on scales because the nature of the thing being measured is not a lot of little points along a line: it's a lot of points that are in different directions defined by completely different qualities and attributes. Many of these are not in any catalog. They are too numerous to catalog.

The demand fro testing is bound to be one we have to confront, to think through. I'm not making any recommendations for how to cope with this on the practical level. I'm just saying that I don't think the demand for this sort of thing on the practical level should confuse us about our basic thinking, as I'm afraid it sometimes does. We say, " I would like to think that way but it isn't practical." Nonsense! In thinking the only important question is whether it's true or not, not whether it's practical. When you're making decisions about how you're going to behave, you may have to make compromises, but for heaven's sake, let's not start shading our beliefs in order to make an uncomfortable situation more comfortable to live in, because that doesn't make it more comfortable.

Another thing that comes up here has to do with the business of curriculum. There was a time, I think, when the word "curriculum"didn't mean what it means now. I'm not sure what it means in England. In the United States a curriculum is apt to mean the whole works—curriculum, syllabus, timetable—because in the United States many groups of people who have been involved in curriculum development have in fact spelled everything out at a level of detail that amounts almost to giving daily instructions to the teacher about what to do next. This means that the choices are not available to the children: the choices are not even available to the teacher unless the teacher is bold enough to disregard the curriculum guide. The choice are mate "up there" by somebody. The word "curriculum" used to mean a general outline of subject-matter and areas of competence that children were supposed to be systematically exposed to. You wanted them to understand arithmetic, for example. You didn't list 25 number facts for the first three months. That wasn't curriculum. That was something that some teacher might do, but it was no concern of the adult community, because the curriculum was primarily a set of decisions by the adult community about what children ought to be learning and how the general aims of education could be made more specific in terms of areas of competence and skill, subject matter and so on.

Dewey, for example, is very strong in asserting that The Experimental School, which he ran for a time, had a definite curriculum and there was no freedom to depart from this curriculum. This was imposed: it was a pattern which could be argued about, it wasn't sacrosanct, but at any given time there was a curriculum and everybody understood what it was. Within this framework, teachers were *enormously* free to pursue these general subject-matter situations in any way they wanted to. It was quite clear also, to many of them at least, that an important group involved in making those decisions was the children themselves. I don't know how romanticized they are—it's hard to tell at this distance in time—but if you read some of the accounts of what some teachers and some children in that school did you can see that they were having a great good time making their way through some aspect of the curriculum but diverging all over the place. They were diverging into other areas which were also on the curriculum. Nobody regarded it as a waste of time, therefore, if in the process of studying some primitive society they got heavily involved in the craft of pottery, because that also was part of the curriculum. So there was great freedom within a general framework that was rather clearly that was rather clearly spelled out. I think today we would find this framework to be a bit special and narrow and would perhaps accuse Dewey of being a bit of a traditionalist about some of it. But it was very interesting for me to discover that Dewey in no sense subscribed to the *laissez-faire* belief that the curriculum was up to the children, so to speak. These were decisions made in the patterning, the organization of the school itself, and in the provisioning of the school. Well, we all make such provisions, don't we? We can't dodge the responsibility for the things we put in classrooms. These are not put there at the request of children—they may be added to at the request of children, they may be subtracted from because children don't use some of them, but that represents our learning and not the direct decision of the children.

The other problem that we face, however, is that as soon as we talk about self-directed learning this implies—correctly, I think—that we cannot lay out in advance a track that children are going to follow, because we don't yet know the things we will learn by observing them that will cause us to make decisions we haven't yet thought of. Therefore, there is an essential lack of predictability about what's going to happen in a good classroom, not because there is no control, but precisely because there is control, of the right kind; precisely because the teacher is basing his decisions on observation of the actual children in their actual situation, their actual problems, their actual interests and the accidental things that happen along the way that nobody can anticipate. A power shovel moves in next door to the school; this throws all your plans for studying batteries and bulbs into a cocked hat—or it should! But, you say there are many aspects to science and this is also part of the curriculum. You can't anticipate those things. Everyone knows that the best times in teaching have always been the consequences of some little accident that happened to direct attention in some new way, to revitalize an old interest which has died out or to create a brand new interest that you hadn't had any notion about how to introduce. Suddenly, there it is. The bird flies in the window and that's the miracle you needed. Somebody once said about great discoveries in science, "Accidents happen to those that deserve them." If the bird coming in the window is just a nuisance you don't deserve it and in fact it never happens. If you deserve it, the bird *will* fly in the window or there 'll be a door that opens into the jungle. There will be some romance around the corner that will be there to be captured. This is again something very different from the stereotype of the permissive classroom because what's involved all along is a teacher who is making educational capital out of the interests and choices of children and out of the accidents that happen along the way, as well as out of his own cleverly designed scheme for getting something new into focus. He fails part of the time but sometimes he succeeds. When the school year is over, you say-or at least I used to say in my college teaching—the best times were when we got off onto something that had no relation whatever to the timetable, something that wasn't envisioned but that turned out to have a lot of relevance to what the course was really about. I just had never had the wit before to see this ; it came up accidentally or it came up because of some question or some argument with a student and we got off on a new track, and that's when things really came to life. We all know that this doesn't happen successfully all the time or even very often, but we all also know, I think that when it does succeed it's worth a great deal because in fact far more is learned under those conditions than under conditions of routine presentation of subject-matter.

One of the other things one has to fight against is the belief that because the central priority is self-directed learning there is never any value in instruction or didactic teaching. There are times when a group of children is very ready to be instructed about something, or to engage in a set task which might even be rote learning under certain circumstances. Their readiness to do this means that it has become for them a significant choice, and it is there fore by no means violating the principle of choice to say there is room, and sometimes a significant amount of room, for quite formal instruction.

I think the people who advocate formal instruction greatly exaggerate its relative importance in terms of the learning of subject- matter. For example, in mathematics as far as I can see, the set pattern of the text, whether it be old mathematics or new mathematics, makes very little difference. Some people really believe that the set pattern of the text is *the* way mathematics is to be learned. Or they might grudgingly admit that there are three or four alternatives, but all of them would be carefully sequenced. outlined series of steps. They say, "But you can't *possibly* understand multiplication before you understand addition." You *can* of course double or triple a collection of pennies; *we* see this as a special case of adding, but a child doesn't have to know the general case first. That's the logical order and you expect children to come to it; but it's not always where they start or should start.

Addition and subtraction are a more obvious case. How can you subtract if you can't add? Well subtraction I would suspect, is the more primitive of the two operations. It's easier to think of taking something away from a collection than it is to think of putting two collections together, which is a rather artificial activity that we don't often engage in, whereas we've very often taken candy out of a box—we're depleting a collection by taking things away, There is a logical objection here too—you have to stop when the box is empty. whereas you can always go on adding. "The set of natural numbers is closed under addition, but not under subtraction." A reasonable child might object that you have to stop when the box is *full,* as well as when it is *empty* Whose logic are we consulting here? The child's logic may be limited but it will guide him; our logic is more adequate but can easily confuse him. When his logic leads him into trouble, *then* is the time to help him expand his logical framework.

We all know that learning doesn't have any very close or intimate connection with adult logical organization. The order in which children come to understand such a logical pattern is not by following it from the beginning. They don't have it yet so they can't follow it. You can lead them by the nose, but that also means they can't follow it. We all agree there is some body of connected ideas and propositions that we can call mathematics. Nobody has ever written it all down but it's there; all the logical connections that exist among all the ideas in the area which we agree to call mathematics. There isn't any linear order among them. They're connected in a very complex sort of network and you can make your way through them along thousands of different paths, depending on your momentary readiness. your understanding, your fund of analogies and your interests. You can get into it in many different ways. The obvious thing from the point of view of teaching is to say. well we want to find that way which is optimal for a particular child at a particular time. This will be in terms of all of the things which characterize him as an individual. We don't know how to do this, we're not omniscient, but one of the very practical ways of getting on with it is to give the child himself some choice. This doesn't mean that he will always, unerringly, choose the way that is best for him but it means that you will get evidence from his choices that will help *you* to define a pattern for him that will probably be much more effective than a standard pattern for him that will probably be much more effective than a standard pattern that is distilled out of mass instruction of the past.

Just as a personal comment about mathematics, I feel very strongly that there are two things the word refers to. One is mathematics and the other is the pedagogical tradition, and they don't necessarily have a very close relation to each other. Mathematics is what mathematicians do and it's what people do when they're being like mathematicians, solving problems of various kinds, bringing certain kinds of understanding to bear on these problems. I don't want to try to define mathematics. But the pedagogical tradition is something not very closely related to that, because the pedagogical tradition is one particular slice, one particular pathway through this network of ideas, or through part of it. "Through it" is the wrong phrase to use because you never get through it, you get into it. You don't cover it. You get into it by many paths, and some of these have been standardized because they have a certain average level of effectiveness, I suppose, and because they happen to appeal to the taste of people who have been engaged in the teaching process under certain kinds of conditions. But I think many people in education think that mathematics *is* what is in that syllabus. Therefore they talk about going through it because you get to the last page in the syllabus and you're through it. But this isn't the nature of mathematics. Mathematics is infinite and it has this kind of structure and complexity, which means you can't reduce it to the linear order of words in a book. There are just too many cross references. You can't put it on a computer, which can cross-index a lot more than a book can—the organization is too rich for that. People are forever discovering new paths in very old mathematics. Only four or five years ago a very able mathematician found a new method of proving that there are infinitely many prime numbers. He just went back and looked at this old problem from a fresh point of view. That's not very important,but it is the nature of mathematics that it should be this way. The thing that is really important is the capacity to function as a human being in this domain. You acquire this capacity for functioning by functioning. Along the way there are many disciplinary elements which you may decide to accept or which you may have imposed on you and completely reject—and which of course we know that most children, in terms of the habits of the disciplinary pattern, have in fact rejected.Or they have they cleverly invented a way of accepting these elements only as far as necessary to get through something called an examination, being careful to protect their minds from contamination in the process.

So, the disciplinary argument is really a very weak one. It implies that we progressives are just cutting loose, not giving children the strict order and discipline that is really necessary to become competent in mathematics, when in fact, the practices of the past have created almost universal failure. It isn't very hard to beat the past record. We shouldn't pat ourselves on the back very much just because children are doing a little better on the eleven-plus as a result of some new mathematics program. That's a cheerful thing, but it's almost unimaginable that they would do worse, not given three months, but given five or six or seven years of work in the style I think we could recognize as that of present-day progressive tendencies (which we can certainly vastly improve on). But given the opportunity to get children repeatedly exposed to the development of mathematical interests and give lots of material which does in fact embody a lot of the things which we regard as basic to mathematical understanding they won't do worse. It's almost unimaginable. If yet set children to memorizing the multiplication table on day one, then on day thirty they will do better on a test than will children who have not been memorizing the multiplication table. That's perfectly obvious, if the test is a test on multiplication tables. But we're not interested in one-month results; we're interested in, let's say, seven years. And here—and partly I'm safe in saying this because the seven-year test hasn't been made yet—it does seem to me almost unimaginable that people could point and say, "See? It's disastrous failure; they don't know mathematics the way they used to."

If children will not know mathematics the way they used to it will be because they know it differently, and better. I and many others have had many —indeed most—freshmen coming into college with two or three years of secondary school mathematics who are non-functional with respect to any interesting use of it, applied either to practical activity, to science or to itself. They were not inducted into the art of using mathematics to develop more mathematics.

I have chosen school mathematics for my illustration because of all the curricular subjects it is the most "disciplinary." If we can demonstrate that this discipline, better understood, gives us a wider range of choice and context to match different children's experience and power. then the whole argument about discipline will be turned around, which is the way it should be.

I have tried to pick a few central terms in educational theory and to suggest ways in which we can start to "turn around" some of the traditional issues, can begin to say what is important without falling into traditional traps. *Freedom* is related to opportunities for significant choice in the optimization of learning. *Discipline* is related to the very nature of subject-matter; it is accepted and prized as it is seen to extend the power of the learner, to increase his range of significant choice. Freedom and discipline together imply an environment which is rich in the opportunities for their exercise. A curriculum becomes functional in proportion as it is reflected in the material provisioning of that environment and as teachers grow in the art of matching those provisions to children's own changing valences and capacities.